The Essential Gu
to Managing Sm...
Business Growth

The Essential Guide to Managing Small Business Growth

Peter Wilson and Sue Bates

WILEY

Copyright © 2003   John Wiley & Sons Ltd, The Atrium, Southern Gate, Chichester,
West Sussex PO19 8SQ, England

Telephone (+44) 1243 779777

Email (for orders and customer service enquiries): cs-books@wiley.co.uk
Visit our Home Page on www.wileyeurope.com or www.wiley.com

This publication is designed to provide accurate and authoritative information in regard to the subject
matter covered. It is sold on the understanding that the Publisher is not engaged in rendering
professional services. If professional advice or other expert assistance is required, the services of a
competent professional should be sought.

Other Wiley Editorial Offices

John Wiley & Sons Inc., 111 River Street, Hoboken, NJ 07030, USA

Jossey-Bass, 989 Market Street, San Francisco, CA 94103-1741, USA

Wiley-VCH Verlag GmbH, Boschstr. 12, D-69469 Weinheim, Germany

John Wiley & Sons Australia Ltd, 33 Park Road, Milton, Queensland 4064, Australia

John Wiley & Sons (Asia) Pte Ltd, 2 Clementi Loop #02-01, Jin Xing Distripark, Singapore 129809

John Wiley & Sons Canada Ltd, 22 Worcester Road, Etobicoke, Ontario, Canada M9W 1L1

Wiley also publishes its books in a variety of electronic formats. Some content that appears
in print may not be available in electronic books.

British Library Cataloguing in Publication Data

A catalogue record for this book is available from the British Library

ISBN 0-470-85051-5

Typeset in 10.5/12pt Garamond by Laserwords Private Limited, Chennai, India
Printed and bound in Great Britain by Biddles Ltd, Guildford and King's Lynn
This book is printed on acid-free paper responsibly manufactured from sustainable forestry
in which at least two trees are planted for each one used for paper production.

Contents

Foreword

It is estimated that there are currently 3.7 million active businesses in the UK. Of these firms, a massive 99.8 per cent are classified as either small (fewer than 50 employees) or medium-sized (50–249 employees); in fact, approximately 2.6 million of these businesses comprise only a self-employed owner-manager. Together, these companies employ more than half (55 per cent) of UK plc's non-government workforce and account for 45 per cent of its turnover – contributing significantly to the UK's GDP and to employment.

It is clear that, despite the lion's share of media publicity and credit going to big business where the UK economy is concerned, small and medium-sized companies are at least as important as their FTSE peers.

However, one-third of businesses fail within three years of start-up. That is a stark statistic, but not one by which aspiring and current entrepreneurs should feel enslaved. Business is a tough game, piled high with challenges, obstacles, problems and, of course, rewards. Owner-managers and founding directors face major dilemmas throughout both the start-up and growth phases of their businesses, such as how to write an effective business plan that allows initial finance to be raised; constructing a business and marketing strategy to drive business growth; how to find, hire and retain the best talent on the market; and how to manage a business's finances effectively and aid its survival and growth beyond the initial two years of trading.

Many entrepreneurs may not have the entire requisite reservoir of skills and experience to meet these challenges; as a rule, few people do. The key to avoid becoming another statistic or being another failed business is to augment your skills – to be smarter. Taking appropriate, relevant and practical advice is therefore a keystone in achieving commercial success.

That is why I am delighted that this book has been written specifically for growth-stage business owners and their key managers who are striving to build a successful business. The book aims to help entrepreneurs achieve business success through providing fundamental skills and knowledge – enhancing the ability of business people to overcome obstacles and make the most of the opportunities that present themselves. It contains the lessons that Peter Wilson and Sue Bates of The Enterprise Partnership have learned from working with businesses at this stage of development over the years. It is a great manual for the time-pressed owner-manager and I am sure you will find it valuable.

Once you have read the book, you may wish to receive a more personalized and in-depth level of advice that cannot be imparted by the written word alone. For those who wish to take this step, there are numerous options on the market.

Among these is the Business Link network,[1] which is run by the government's Small Business Service, the agency within government that champions business.

At Business Link for London, we work with a huge network of partners[2] to make sure that business owners can access a range of impartial and affordable business services, giving you the choice to work with the right support provider for your organization. Whomever you choose to work with, you can be assured that they will have your business's best interests at heart.

However, the first step on the path to business success is to read this book and try to implement as many practical tips as possible to aid your business's growth, profitability and success.

Together with Peter Wilson and Sue Bates, with whom I have worked for over ten years, we at Business Link for London hope that the information contained within this book, linked to additional business advice where desired and appropriate, will help you to realize your business dreams.

Judith Rutherford
Chief Executive, Business Link for London

Notes

1 The Business Link network can be contacted at www.businesslink.org or on 0845 600 9006.
2 The London Business Support Network can be accessed via Business Link for London at www.businesslink4london.com or on 0845 6000 787.

Preface

This book is about the essentials of managing a growing small business. How do we define 'small' and 'growing'? 'Small' means not big in scale or part of a larger business, not quoted on a public stock market, and owned and managed by the founders, or their progeny. The founders (or their progeny) continue to work in the business and depend on it for their livelihood, since it has survived the start-up stage – the first five or so years. In these early years, teething troubles in production, delivery and operations have been successfully resolved (a large proportion of small businesses fail in their early years: figures from the UK Department of Trade and Industry[1] show that 65 per cent do not survive beyond three years and research by Barclays Bank[2] puts average survival rates at 34 per cent five years from start-up). The business is now producing a quality product or service for its loyal customers, most of whom have been retained since the very first sale was closed. The business has satisfied customer needs to an acceptable standard all this time. Most of the first people recruited by the founder are still there, though many new faces abound. The founder and the management team have a modicum of management skills between them and these bare essentials give rise to some optimism that the firm can, if internal and external conditions are propitious, grow from small to medium-sized.

So we come to growth. By 'growth' we mean a business that demonstrates (or shows visible signs of) a propensity to expand operations significantly, because it satisfies a number of important growth criteria. These criteria include: there is continuing excellent service to customers (generating repeat orders, customer retention, referrals from satisfied customers and sustainable gross margins); the founders demonstrate their ability to manage internal operations effectively and efficiently (resulting in control of unit costs and satisfactory net margins); the business has a track record of sustained profitability (even though that may not be abnormally high); and the founders have sufficient credibility to raise the necessary finance externally, although, because of rising profitability, the business can finance a proportion of fixed and working capital from internally generated funds. The growth business we have in mind typically exhibits some or all of these characteristics, though usually erratically. The main reasons are that management resources are volatile and also that there are few, if any, systems in place to support sustained, profitable and orderly growth.

Finally (and some would say critically), successful growth is achievable because the founders have an empathy with people. They have well-developed interpersonal and communication skills and they know instinctively what motivates people to give of their best – this in spite of being considered mavericks or 'black sheep' themselves. Although they might lack 'professional' general management skills, they probably have expertise in at least one key functional area, i.e. sales, production or operations. The founders are typically good examples of hard-working, diligent and effective contributors to the business and they manage to engender similar responses in their key people. They lead from the front.

The fact is that there are few people like this running growth businesses successfully. Many dream of transforming their small business from an informal 'lifestyle' activity into a medium-sized fast grower, lured by the challenge of managing rapid growth or by the prospect of large earnings and selling out at a fabulous price. Many of these business owners have written a business plan, which is usually gathering dust in a filing cabinet, setting out a growth strategy, and a smaller number have tried unsuccessfully to put the plan into action. However, most business founders prefer a simple and sedate existence, which is achieved by working long hours at relatively low rates of pay. They typically don't want the bother of recruiting and managing staff; the product or service *is* the business for these people and they often excel at making and delivering it. They play an important economic role as generators of wealth and social progress, but they aren't interested in running a growth business.

We have aimed this book at the many business founders who aspire to be among the few, at key managers working alongside the many, and at others who work with or need to understand the nature of the management task that faces founders of growth businesses.

Why should you read this book? It has some serious themes; it also has a hidden agenda – how to run your growing business and stay sane, to succeed on your own terms while simultaneously tuning in to the demands of customers and staff. The book came to be written because, having worked with small, sometimes rapidly growing businesses for many years, we believe that our experiences of how clients strive to manage business growth and the lessons that can be drawn from their endeavours are worth recounting. We know how difficult it can be for busy entrepreneurs immersed in day-to-day operations to get away from the office or factory floor and stand back to consider how they can move forward rapidly and profitably, and not collapse under the weight of their own success. A short, practical book on the main management issues facing growth businesses could help. There are modest advantages to reading above other learning media, and many entrepreneurs have a preference for learning in small, bite-sized chunks, which is what a short book can readily provide. For one thing, it is possible to telescope the most important issues into a very small space and make it portable. A book is cheap and disposable – if you don't like it, just throw it away! It can't come back. It's hard to get rid of an expensive business consultant quite so quickly. And a book requires no explanation. You can leave it lying around and it won't complain, it won't phone you up and remind you how useful it can be (some assumption!). And you can pass on the book without any implied insult to colleagues and key managers.

This book is full of fundamental insights into how growing businesses should be managed. You might be doing very well managing the business with consummate professional ease; but then you might read this book and get just one good idea from it. That single idea could be worth tens or even hundreds of thousands of pounds. Or it could give you an unparalleled opportunity to get away more, do more strategic thinking and, who knows, improve your golf handicap or spend more time with your long-suffering family. Wouldn't it be worth it?

Notes

1 Department of Trade and Industry, VAT deregistration statistics, www.sbs.gov.uk.
2 Barclays Bank, Barclays Small Business Survey Q3 2002, www.business.barclays.co.uk.

Managing Business Growth

'You see things; and you say "Why?" But I dream things that never were; and I say "Why not?"'

George Bernard Shaw

Key issues dealt with in this chapter are:

- Management issues in the transition from small to medium-sized.
- Factors limiting the relevance of management theory to small organizations.
- Reconciling personal, family and business goals with the needs of the business.
- The meaning of effectiveness and efficiency.
- Synopsis of the book.

Making the transition

So you are contemplating growing your business? Perhaps it has been growing rapidly in recent years and has now come to a crossroads; or perhaps you have been focusing on internal efficiency and feel that, with a solid platform firmly in place, the time is ripe to step up the pace and go for growth. In either case, one thing is certain – growth from small, informal and simply organized to medium-sized, formal and more complex does not come easily without undergoing difficult changes to the organization's fabric: to its structure, people, processes and systems, and to its very core, the distinctive competences that set it apart from its competitors and make it successful at the moment.

The responsibility for making a successful transition from small to medium-sized falls on the founders, directors and key managers. No outsider can possibly tell you what to do. Although the ultimate goal might imply a revolution in the way you currently conduct your business, you have to strike a balance between stable evolutionary change and the rollercoaster ride of rapid growth. While your long-term goal might require a fundamental upheaval in your organization, the key to sustained profitability and positive cash flow should be incremental, systematic change led by disciplined, thinking managers.

Consider for a moment a business organization in its formative years (it could be yours). The early years are usually characterized by a sharp focus on the needs of a small number of customers, a lack of formal structures, processes and systems, and extreme informality of management style. Satisfying these customers with the highest possible level of service is usually of paramount importance. Sales are generated by the founders forging close relationships with a few key customers. The founders understand the fragility of competitiveness and are prepared to bend over backwards to provide high and rising levels of service. For them, nothing is too much trouble; they see the creative possibilities in any commercial situation; and it is their vision and drive that turn the germ of an idea into pulsating business reality.

Customer retention is usually particularly high in the early stages of growth, even when standards slip a little and prices veer out of line with those of competitors. The psychological and emotional resilience of the relationship between the founder and the customer is one factor; it is quite another that the customer's access to the chief decision maker (the founder) makes it easier to secure a prompt response when things go awry. The customer's unrestricted access to this vital resource is a major criterion of success in the early years, though few founders explicitly recognize this as a key strength or plan for its perpetuation. Not being able to 'clone' the rare *customer-satisfying* qualities of the founder as the business grows is a potential barrier to rapid growth, because it requires a high level of customer retention and continuing development of key accounts.

Another major advantage in the early years is rapid transmission of vital information, the outcome of short lines of communication. This is usually the result of a) the absence of a reporting hierarchy; b) the physical proximity of most staff to each other and to the boss; and c) a culture of consideration, of sharing things and a willingness to 'muck in'. Understanding the role of information and how it oils the inner workings of the organization is necessary to ensure that the smooth flow of information is actively nurtured in business development plans. The founders are invariably the repository of all important information – they are closest to markets, customers, bank managers, suppliers and employees – and to ensure that ever-increasing quantities of information flow smoothly to key decision makers *other than to the founders* (a requirement of effective delegation), the fact that it might not has to be recognized and a solution found and implemented.

In the early years, systems and processes do not have to be formal. With the founder in control and at the centre of the organizational 'spider's web' (explained in Chapter 4), and with all staff within easy proximity and on first-name terms, informality is an advantage. Formality makes life more difficult because it imposes costs and disrupts people's normal relationships and working habits.

Where do the founders go from here? There are distinct advantages in remaining a small, 'lifestyle' business, that is with a total complement of, say, 10 to 12 staff. Research has established that a small group finds it easier to function as an efficient, coherent unit and that eight people constitute the 'natural' span of control for a single boss. However, a small, 'lifestyle' business will not be a satisfactory achievement for those entrepreneurs who relish the challenge of managing growth.

Success in the formative years can establish a solid platform for development and, combined with further market opportunities and the drive and management skills of the founders, can soon lead to a complete transformation of the business as growth takes its course. Customer focus remains one of the keys to making a successful transition from small and informal to medium-sized and complex. Conflicts arise because the need to create and build new functions becomes paramount and can be at variance with the concurrent need to remain strongly customer oriented. Non-operational functions, e.g. accounts, finance and personnel, become disproportionately important. The success of the business in negotiating this transitional phase is dependent on the founders recognizing that the old ways of doing things are no longer good enough. The area of greatest growth is in staff numbers and the diversity of operational tasks, and all too soon the strains begin to tell – they start typically with customer complaints and defections, breakdown in internal communications, a collapse in morale in parts of the business, growing staff disaffection and high staff turnover. The founders might ignore these problems, believing them to be temporary and leaving people to cope as best they can; or they might attempt to deal with the *symptoms* without having the relevant skills and knowledge to understand the *root causes* – essentially, problem solving and decision making have entered a new plain outside their sphere of experience. Their response might also be to avoid formality and to 'muddle' their way through busy periods, preferring to cope with stress rather than investing time and money in diagnosing the real causes and setting up new ways of doing things – incrementally changing the shape of the organization and formalizing systems, procedures and processes.

The transition from small to medium-sized requires the founding entrepreneurs to adopt new attitudes, new modes of behaviour and high-level management skills, without dropping some of their exceptional entrepreneurial attributes. Some examples are:

- Being a visionary leader.
- Being a business strategist, not merely a tactician.
- Being an information disseminator rather than an information hoarder.
- Devising accessible, reliable management information systems to replace secretive, partial, *ad hoc* sources (principally the founders themselves).
- Diagnosing organizational weaknesses and designing new functions.
- Introducing formal recruitment practices, rather than hiring someone's best friend through informal networks.
- Developing a nascent management team (who probably don't have the skills or knowledge for the job).
- Delegating responsibility for delivering outcomes to trustworthy people.
- Paying serious attention to human processes rather than solely to tasks.
- Putting emphasis on developing employees' knowledge and skills.
- Being a mentor, coach and people developer.
- Dealing with difficult situations and underperformance.
- Handing over the biggest and best customers to a professional key account team.
- Negotiating with and influencing people (some of whom you don't really like).
- Achieving positive outcomes from meetings with key people.

How do the founders adopt new attitudes, behaviour and skills, thus mutating into professional managers? Is it in fact desirable that they should do so? By making the change, they are bound to sacrifice some of their strengths. Would it not be better to hire in a professional general manager, or even a new CEO? The ability to identify weaknesses in their personal armoury of management competences and set about plugging them with the right amount of skill and knowledge is a key turning point in the successful transition from small to medium-sized. The founders must recognize that they cannot 'go it alone' because they lack the competences that will take the business into the next phase of growth.

The relevance of management theory to growing businesses

In considering the management needs of growing businesses, we must take into account the great diversity of business organizations and their individual situations and characteristics. Can we simply apply the standard, large-company management approach to smaller, growing businesses? In other words, are growing businesses simply large ones writ small? No, there are distinct differences that give rise to the need to modify standard management theory as it applies to growing businesses.

Motivation of the founders

The presence of the founders (or their progeny) provides a central clue to the way the organization functions and how it behaves; its industry 'personality', so to speak. Entrepreneurs are generally thought to be abnormal people – the black sheep of the business community – whose autocratic management style and 'Victorian' business philosophy are considered an anachronism in the modern business world. Box 1.1 lists some of the special characteristics of entrepreneurs and their putative behavioural effects.

Some of these characteristics do not fit well with modern management theory. For example, a 'bias for action' could be considered synonymous with a lack of analysis, 'knee-jerk' undisciplined response and whimsical decision making, leading to costly mistakes. Management thinkers prefer a planned, orderly, systematic approach to business decision making in order to control risks. Yet it is crucial to understand the motivation, values and ethics of the founders. They constitute the dissatisfied minority who are not usually tolerated in large organizations. Driven by a high 'need for achievement' (managers in large organizations have a high 'need for power and affiliation'), they eschew hierarchical reporting structures (indicative of power) and extra-mural social activities (affiliation), preferring to work long hours to ensure that customers' orders are fulfilled on time and quality standards are up to scratch.

Managerial competence

Business founders are not normally professional managers. They are typically specialists in sales or technical areas; yet they still need the skills of general management. Many do not understand the nature or relevance of key functions that could hinder successful growth, for example marketing (as opposed to promotion and advertising) and human resource development (as opposed to personnel). Paradoxically, they have an extravagant view of their capabilities, which can get in the way of evolutionary change. Nor do they have a managerial role model to learn from; in contrast, most managers in large organizations have access to excellent role models in the shape of senior managers and directors, as well as to advanced techniques of management development, including mentoring and coaching.

Box 1.1 Twenty characteristics of successful entrepreneurs

	Characteristic	Behavioural effects
1	Drive and energy	Hard working over long hours
2	Self-confidence	Ability to generate confidence and trust among customers, suppliers and employees
3	Long-term horizon	Willingness to stick to business creation over the long term
4	See money as a measure of achievement (not an end in itself)	Conserve money at the start; accept low salary and deferred gratification
5	Persistent problem solvers	Persistence in overcoming seemingly intractable obstacles
6	Clear goals	No wasteful decision making
7	Controlled risk takers	Ability to instil confidence in investors
8	Dealing head-on with failure	Not easily put off, learning from failure
9	Bias for action	Rather do things than talk about them
10	Take personal responsibility	Don't pass the buck
11	Efficient resource users	Get the most out of every scarce £
12	High self-imposed standards	Strive to achieve high quality for customers
13	Internal locus of control	Willingness to take the blame, confidence in taking on achievable tasks
14	Tolerance of ambiguity and uncertainty	Decisiveness
15	Commit own money and personal resources	Total commitment to the venture, disciplined decision making
16	Creativity and innovativeness	Generate 'out of the box' solutions
17	Self-reliance	Ability to solve all problems
18	High regard for people	Willing to show trust in others
19	Reliable, honest, ethical	Win trust of stakeholders
20	Financial awareness	Confidence in negotiating

Sacred cows

Founders cocoon themselves in the cottonwool of unsubstantiated myths, assumptions and beliefs, which they deem necessary for survival as independent business owners. These flimsy beliefs can become 'sacred cows' that, if not challenged objectively, will ultimately cause the demise of the business. Some classic sacred cows are:

- An unsubstantiated but long-held belief in the profitability of the largest customer or best-selling product (whereas if detailed records of profitability were to exist, they might suggest differently).
- The suitability of tried-and-tested marketing and sales methods for existing and new markets (whereas close inspection reveals out-of-date literature and verbose copywriting more suited to the 1980s than to the twenty-first century).
- The loyalty and therefore assumed effectiveness of long-serving staff (whereas sane people consider them to be hopelessly out of touch and error-prone).
- The adequacy of quarterly management accounts as the main source of control on profit and cash (when in reality accounts are late, do not reflect current trading and are incorrectly and inconsistently presented).

Inseparability of ownership, investment and management

Proposals for managing the growing business should take into account the implications of having owner-investors actively engaged in running the business:

- Business founders often remortgage their homes and invest their savings in the venture, only to discover that in the early years net worth can actually decline to the point of technical insolvency. This can render decision making unduly risk averse, which is inimical to sustained growth. It does have the advantage, however, of ensuring that major decisions are taken by shareholders who have a lot to lose if things go wrong.
- The multiple roles of shareholder, worker, manager and director, which give the founders a special insight into the workings of their businesses, can limit their effectiveness as business developers. For example, as a shareholder you might have to relinquish outright control if an injection of external equity capital is needed (even though this might threaten the very essence of your motivation to go it alone, viz. the desire to control your own destiny); and as a director you need to take a long-term view, which can conflict with the roles of manager or worker, focusing on day-to-day tasks.
- The owners can view the business as a personal possession with concomitant emotional as well as financial strings, which makes it difficult to drag them away from day-to-day 'worker' tasks to take on a loftier 'strategic leadership' role.
- The family dynasty might depend on the business as its sole source of income and wealth (and, indeed, social status), with implications for management succession: the respective roles of the founders, their progeny and outsiders, and the need for professional managers. It is not easy to fire the CEO when he or she owns the business!

Undercapitalization

In combination with negative attitudes to third-party equity capital, undercapitalization is a potent force for instability in the small growing business. It arises from inadequate founding capital combined with over-optimistic forecasts of profit and cash (which don't materialize). On top of this, there is a tendency to milk the business when cash is available and to depend too much on short-term lines of credit (overdraft and suppliers). The problem of inadequate capital can cause decision making to focus unduly on generating or preserving short-term cash at the expense of profit and long-term investment. Without the latter, there can be little prospect of stable long-term growth, and none at all of building a delegated management infrastructure, which is a necessary requirement for the founders to take a more strategic view of the business.

Customer, market or product dependence

This arises in part because of the relatively small number of customers needed to sustain a successful business and produce a good living for the founders, and also because of a lack of strategic marketing capability – the ability to identify and evaluate opportunities and threats in existing and new markets and to take the business into new growth areas with appropriate organizational competences. Moreover, it might not be realistic to move into new markets or widen the customer or product base if the strength of the firm is its market focus.

Many small businesses are very successful at 'keeping their eggs in one basket' because of a sharp focus on a market niche where customers' changing needs can be closely monitored; or they are nimble enough to move into new areas of opportunity when they emerge – a reactive approach to business development. Whether nimble or not, financial performance can be highly volatile in the short term, with the business moving from profit to loss in months. These consequences have implications for forward planning: why plan ahead when a rapid change of direction is practicable and within the scope of existing resources, or when you can't influence demand anyway?

Market powerlessness

Small businesses are unable to influence the market because of their lack of market power. Their markets are often idiosyncratic niches and generally they do not compete head-to-head with large competitors. An important consequence of this feeling of powerlessness is that owner-managers do not consider business planning to be a fruitful activity, in the way that large organizations do. Planning is regarded as the preserve of large firms, which engage in it as a means of reducing uncertainty and aligning resources with the needs of the market. Planning and power to influence the market go together. If planning is to be useful as a management tool in the smaller business, it should be seen to perform different but still appropriate functions.

Managing effectively and efficiently

Sustained, profitable growth cannot be achieved without paying proper attention to the need for greater *effectiveness* (doing the right things, which ensures that everything gets done to an appropriate standard) and *efficiency* (doing things the right way, which ensures that tasks are undertaken in the right sequence and completed in the optimum time). While in the early years of a business sheer enthusiasm and hard work will eclipse inefficient practices, the successful transition to a medium-sized business demands greater attention to effective and efficient management and to the formal systems and procedures that need to be in place to ensure that this happens.

As complexity increases and an organizational hierarchy starts to emerge, the founders can come under pressure to add new functions and roles (the dreaded overhead!) to ensure that customers' needs are met at *high and rising* levels of service, while giving themselves space to stand back, plan the future and pay more attention to leadership processes. A typical example is adding a marketing department incorporating not only external communications, but also strategy, market research, product development, customer feedback, etc. In the early years parts of this function are performed by the founders, but to improve the effectiveness and efficiency of marketing, full-time marketing professionals will have to be recruited. The same overhead growth applies to other emergent areas, such as human resource management, product development, research and development, information systems and financial control activities.

At this point in the organization's development, informal, word-of-mouth methods of passing on working practices and procedures start to break down. When a handful of people perform a task, it is easy enough to brief them about the goal (desired outcome) and how it is to be achieved. When there are teams of people performing diverse, interdependent tasks, briefing becomes more complex – one or two key managers soon find it impossible to brief, train, monitor, give feedback to, motivate and lead increasing numbers of new staff, most of whom are taking on new jobs in unfamiliar surroundings. Thus task and team effectiveness starts to erode as tried-and-tested working procedures are neglected or short-circuited. If not nipped in the bud, these inefficiencies soon compromise quality, with the consequent defection of long-standing customers.

There is a similar problem with efficiency: informal ways of communicating information suit existing employees who have the ability to identify improvements, i.e. short cuts in working practices, because of long experience in the job. But with frequent infusions of inexperienced new blood, unless there are adequate safety nets in place (training, monitoring, feedback, supervision, motivation, leadership), high standards of service delivery can falter as the learning curve starts to take effect (Figure 1.1). This can stall the process of falling unit costs (curve B) – caused by errors and inefficiencies – when ideally the business needs to travel over time down learning curve A to take advantage of lower unit costs.

Many small organizations try to plug this hole by shoring up the teetering informal system with formal procedures such as those covered by ISO9000 accreditation, which ensures that quality management systems are recorded and that people adhere to them rigidly. In a curious way, formal recognition of quality systems can corrupt the culture of the organization – its belief systems – because high-quality service is ingrained in people's beliefs and working habits, rather than conforming slavishly to a quality manual. Rapid growth can undermine culture and managers

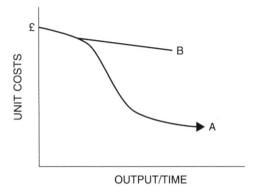

Figure 1.1: Business growth and the learning curve.

should respond by reinforcing and building on the positive things that grew up with the business.

Setting realistic goals

The motivation to found a business is sustained by a need for achievement, self-reliance and personal fulfilment, although one or more negative 'push' factors might also be a cause, e.g. redundancy, lack of alternative job opportunities or changes in personal circumstances. But once the initial 'buzz' of starting the business is over and the initial goal has been achieved, what is in it for the founders? Psychic and emotional goals (sense of independence, control of your own destiny) can conflict with economic ones, such as growth in income and net worth. For instance, founders often express their motivation (goal) in terms of 'controlling their own destiny'. Arguably, this is true only in the context of their initial career choice. Once the business is under way, the job of owning and managing it is like any other and soon control of one's own destiny is subverted to the demands of customers, suppliers, employees and bank managers. The owner-manager will soon feel that outsiders are controlling his or her destiny.

What are realistic goals for the founders as the business grows, and why change? Explicit, measurable objectives should be formulated and the first should probably be net profit margin (net profit before tax as a per centage of sales), framed with future growth in mind; growth in net worth might be a secondary objective (set it as a specific percentage uplift on the previous year), with an eye on future external financing needs. Being explicit about goals gives everyone something concrete and achievable to aim for – the founders cannot expect increasing numbers of new employees to buy into their nebulous personal goals and ambitions, even if the original loyal staff, much smaller in number, might be willing to continue to do so, because of their close emotional connection with the founders from day one. Few people will commit to a goal that seeks to build the founders' egos, or helps define the meaning of life for them!

Synopsis of the book

In this book we deal with the job of managing business growth successfully. We do not accept that growth (or rapid growth) is a foregone conclusion, even when there has been growth in the recent past. Markets can change rapidly and customers can be fickle. Each situation needs to be examined and the decision to grow or not to grow taken on its merits. Monitoring and assessing business performance and periodically evaluating existing strategy and future strategic options are crucial activities for directors; leading and managing people to implement the chosen strategy effectively and efficiently are crucial activities for managers. The following ten chapters tackle the fundamentals of directing, leading and managing a growing business: setting business strategy and getting performance from people.

We begin in Chapter 2 with business strategy, on the grounds that everything else follows the lead question: 'in which direction should the business be going?' By 'direction' we mean the market segments into which you choose to sell and the mix of products and/or services on offer in the chosen markets. We examine strategic options and techniques for making defensible choices that produce the optimum strategic fit between markets and organizational competences, thus ensuring that managers have every chance of implementing the chosen strategy profitably within planned financing limits.

We follow with further market-related issues in Chapter 3, which deals with day-to-day marketing and sales decisions. This involves more than merely advertising and printing brochures. What frameworks are available to ensure that you can meet the needs of your customers effectively and efficiently? How can you communicate effectively with your chosen markets and generate profitable leads? This chapter also deals with the development of a complete marketing function that includes the usual promotional and website roles as well as the increasingly vital ones of gathering market and customer feedback data, competitor research, product development and customer care.

Chapter 4 provides a general outline of organizational design and development. Effective and efficient organizational change is at the core of successful business growth – managers need the skills of diagnosing organizational problems accurately to ensure that proposed changes will align structure, people, processes and systems more closely with the existing and emergent needs of customers.

Having put in place the right organization to deliver the strategy, in Chapter 5 we discuss the management skills required to get teams of people to perform their tasks effectively and efficiently. Once overall corporate objectives are communicated to team leaders, they in turn can brief their teams clearly, set achievable goals for individuals, monitor progress towards these goals and provide constructive feedback on achievements. These, with an understanding of motivation and demotivation, are the essential skills of managing people at work.

Managing people effectively and efficiently requires much more than these essential skills, however. In Chapter 6 we discuss the role of the leader who understands delegation and who can apply the 'situational leadership' model to teasing out superior performance, thus distinguishing ordinary teams from excellent ones. Striking the right balance of contributions to team performance through specific team roles (and recruiting for these roles) is one aspect of effective team leadership; another is building and developing the team through performance appraisals.

Few growing businesses thrive without the 'magic' in their culture that sets them apart from competing organizations. Chapter 7 deals with the beliefs and assumptions held by people about their organization: the way they do things that is different to their competitors. Small, dynamic, growing organizations have a special aura about them – a 'can do' culture – that initially sparkles without much explicit burnishing by managers. Yet these special features can go unrecognized and therefore be neglected in the dash for growth, with unintended damage to the human fabric of the organization.

Moving from the human side of enterprise to the financial side, Chapter 8 explains profit and loss accounts, balance sheets and cash-flow statements, not from the standpoint of the accountant but rather from that of managers faced with making the right business decisions; every decision has a direct or indirect impact on profitability and cash flow. So managers should understand clearly where and how profits are made and how effectively finance is used in their business. To this end, we analyse the accounts using common financial ratios, applying them to day-to-day as well as strategic decision making.

Chapter 9 deals with management information systems and financial controls: the systematic provision of financial, market and operational information for effective decision making, and the controls needed to ensure that financial targets are met. The quality of internal information is usually poor in growing businesses, and none so poor as profitability data on individual customers, market segments, projects and products. The emphasis is on practical information systems needed to monitor and manage the business and on the fixed and working capital controls needed to make efficient use of available long- and short-term finance.

Bringing it all together is the theme of Chapter 10, which introduces the essentials of strategic and operational business planning. The pressure to produce business plans with ever-increasing complexity is immense as the business grows, although given the rate of market change, the powerlessness of the small business and the lack of high-level management resources to implement plans, it is understandable that *plan* nowadays is considered an undesirable four-letter word! Our treatment of the topic is entirely practical: plans can be useful documents, but they must meet certain minimum standards. We provide examples of the different types of business plans in the appendices.

Our closing words in Chapter 11 are devoted to the hazards that lie innocuously in the path of the unsuspecting founder-director or key manager. Whether appointing a successor, dealing with nepotism or seeing off the 'sacred cows' of business growth, it is important to recognize them as potential obstacles to progress and to confront them head on by examining alternative options and making decisions based on an informed choice.

Making Sense of Strategy

CHAPTER 2

Key issues dealt with in this chapter are:

- The meaning of business strategy.
- Distinctive and core competences as the basis of competitiveness.
- The techniques for reviewing and setting strategy.
- The available strategic options and how to choose a direction that will maximize profits over the longer term.
- Organic growth vs merger or acquisition.

Strategic issues: Setting the scene

Strategy as applied to business is a recent phenomenon. The term 'strategy' derives from military science and describes how a general deploys his forces in battle with the objective of achieving victory by defeating the enemy. Business strategy describes how you organize your business (deploy your resources) to compete for the attention of customers in your target markets (achieve your objectives), faced by competitors and other external factors that present threats to your business (defeat the enemy, so to speak).

Business strategy addresses the following questions:

1   *Customers and markets* – which customers (and markets) should you target?
2   *Products and/or services* – what should you sell to these customers?
3   *Organizational resources and competences*, such as people, processes, structure and systems – how should you organize your business to get these products/services to your customers?
4   *Finance*, both working capital and long-term capital – how much money will be needed to make the strategy happen and to achieve corporate objectives?

Here are some fundamental propositions about strategy that explain its relevance to managing today's growing business.

1   The essence of business strategy is to compete profitably by identifying a target market with specific unmet needs (*opportunity*) and to sell products and/or

services in it, exploiting your organizational distinctiveness (*strengths*) at a price that will return the optimum level of profit, while making continuous improvements to those parts of the business that don't work well (*weaknesses*), in the face of competition and other unfavourable external factors (*threats*).

2   This seems straightforward in a period of slow, steady growth. However, strategy erodes quickly in rapidly changing times because yesterday's competitive strengths that successfully underpinned past performance cannot be automatically expected to do the same today and tomorrow. Customers, competitors and other exogenous factors will not allow it. New unique or special strengths have to be found and existing ones revamped simultaneously to ensure that profitability is maintained or increased.

3   Business strategy is a total concept embracing every function in the business: customers, products or services, research and development, marketing, production, purchasing, logistics, operations, administration, personnel, information systems and finance. Most of all, it is concerned with the way these functions are brought together to generate profits: the sharper your focus on the needs of your customers and the closer the alignment of your organization with these needs, the higher the rate of profit.

4   Customers have choices: they can buy from you, from a competitor, or, if they prefer, defer their purchase temporarily or even permanently. Competitive action and reaction are always at work, whether implicitly or explicitly. Thus customer behaviour is fundamental to business strategy. It is a moving target, continually changing its shape and composition. And as a result, it is not easily influenced in the short run.

5   Business strategy does not have to be written in a business plan to exist. All businesses have a strategy, even if it is implicit, since they have:

- Customers to whom they sell and markets in which they compete.
- Products or services that they sell in these markets.
- Organizational resources that are deployed to make these sales.
- Financial resources that underpin all this activity.

So the key questions are: What is your strategy? How well is it working? Are corporate objectives being achieved? Can profitability be raised by refining strategy and focusing resources more effectively on the right customers? Directors of growing small and medium-sized businesses generally admit that they could be more profitable. The only question is: How?

The *Titanic*: A salutary lesson in strategy

The story of the *Titanic* is widely known. The giant passenger liner was considered indestructible, embodying all the latest technologies in marine engineering, and was finished to a luxurious standard. Everything about it was top class: construction, engines, food, music, furnishings, décor, bed linen, service and crew. Nevertheless, on its maiden voyage it hit an iceberg in the North Atlantic and sank with substantial loss of life.

   The point about this tragic event is that there was more focus on the internal trappings of luxury than on the external strategic picture. In other words, the crew's attention was focused on arranging the deckchairs, the waiters' on serving meals and the musicians' on tuning their violins, when there should have been more attention paid to what was happening off the ship – in the sea, to the elements, to other shipping nearby. In particular, was this the right course? Was this the right ship for this course? If more attention had been focused on threats to the safe passage of the ship (and to the lifeboats, of which there were not enough for all the passengers), the outcome would have been less tragic.

This can be used as a metaphor for business performance. There is no point in concerning yourself with tactical matters, e.g. checking brochure copy to improve communication with your market (*Titanic* equivalent: arranging the deckchairs), when you are threatened by head-to-head competition or defecting customers (*Titanic* equivalent: steaming into dangerous waters).

The captain of the ship should have put strategic considerations before tactical ones. Look out for icebergs before arranging deckchairs or tuning violins! In other words, make sure that you have a long-term outlook (at least two or three years for a normal business) with clear objectives, and that your business is organized to keep in view the principal influences on what happens over this period. Then organize your resources in pursuit of these objectives and make day-to-day adjustments as the situation demands.

Or think of business strategy and business tactics as a jigsaw puzzle: the straight pieces at the edge seal the fate of the inside pieces by forming a boundary beyond which the inside pieces cannot stray. It is much easier to assemble a jigsaw by putting the edges in place first, because they dictate the position of the inside pieces. So it is for business. Strategy comes first.

Strategy should not be the preserve of only the owners and directors. Everyone constructing a jigsaw should be able to see the edge pieces. In business, everyone in the organization should know and understand the chosen strategy in its broadest terms. This will give meaning to their jobs and place their work goals in context. Communicating strategy to all staff and helping them see their jobs and goals in context is an important source of individual and team motivation, as well as being good management practice.

Review of current performance

As with any journey, it is vital to know your starting point. Implementing a successful business strategy starts with knowing where your business is at the moment (where profits are made, and why), since a solid platform is needed on which to base future business strategy. This requires a careful review of the business, the objective of which is to establish the rationale for business strategy and identify which areas of the business should be developed (where the focus of attention should be), which should be eliminated or cut back and how development should proceed.

The review should be undertaken by the senior team responsible for strategy, including not only owners and directors but also key managers; indeed, anyone who has a view or experience of *internal strengths and weaknesses* as well as *external opportunities and threats*. Ideally they should also have some familiarity with financial performance and, above all, should understand the link between distinctiveness and profitability (see below).

The strategic review should start by answering the question: Where do profits come from? There is clearly no sense in developing those parts of the business where you are either losing money or just breaking even. Resources must be focused on the parts demonstrating the highest levels of profit, while taking action on the least profitable parts. For example, the British computer manufacturer Apricot identified its main source of profits late in the day, with unfortunate consequences (Box 2.1).

Box 2.1 Case study: Apricot Computers

In the mid-1980s, the British computer manufacturer Apricot found itself competing fiercely against Amstrad, IBM, Apple and other makes for a growing share of the lucrative PC market. Profits were under pressure and the company had to make major decisions about which parts of its business to expand and which to contract or close down.

At the time the parent company ACT was not only selling computers, but was also servicing and repairing them, as well as designing, selling and supporting financial software. There were three major divisions to the business: making computers, servicing them, designing and selling software. So where were the problems? It was felt that ACT was principally in the manufacturing business, but getting rid of manufacturing was unacceptable because the company believed that maintenance and software sales derived principally from customers who owned Apricot computers. Besides, what was ACT without its flagship product, Apricot computers? Profit in the maintenance and software businesses was dependent on sales of Apricot machines, it was thought.

A breakthrough came when a closer analysis of the data revealed that new sales of maintenance contracts and software were increasingly to non-Apricot customers. So a careful analysis of the sources of profits (where profits came from) enabled Apricot to come to the conclusion that PC sales were no longer a vital component of overall business profitability and that the other two businesses could stand on their own.

This realization enabled ACT to change its strategy, reduce dependence on PC sales and eventually dispose of the manufacturing operations to Fujitsu.

You will need to collect, collate and analyse internal sales and cost data to establish clearly where your profits come from. Gross sales data are not sufficient and can even be misleading. The markets and products with the highest sales values could be the least profitable parts of the business, e.g. when pursuing sales revenues at the expense of margins.

Having profitability data available on a continuous basis at all levels of the business should provide a powerful platform for decision making. For example, profitability data on different market segments, different product or service lines and different channels for reaching and servicing market segments allow resources to be focused on customers in these segments. This should raise overall margins. The quality of financial reporting, including profitability data for each customer (where appropriate), market segment, product/service, marketing channel, branch, country, etc., can only be as good as the comprehensiveness of your management information system (covered in Chapter 9). The example in Box 2.2 illustrates how detailed profitability data can aid considerably in strategic decision making.

Box 2.2 Profitability by market segment

Company A manufactures car components and sells in three geographic markets. Which is the most profitable? Sales values, costs and margins are as follows:

	UK (£000)	%	USA (£000)	%	Asia (£000)	%
Sales revenue	355	100	560	100	205	100
Cost of sales	199	56	342	61	105	51
Gross profit	156	44	218	39	100	49
Sales and marketing overheads (direct)	39	11	83	15	43	21
Contribution to indirect overheads and profit	117	33	135	24	57	28

On the surface, i.e. considering sales revenue only, it appears that the USA, being the biggest market, is probably the best one to be in. At the gross profit level, this is again true if gross values are the measure.

However, the gross margins (%) tell a different story: Asia is the most profitable (49%), followed by the UK (44%).

At the contribution level (before indirect overheads), the UK (33%) ranks first with Asia (28%) second and the USA third.

This indicates that the USA is the least profitable contributor and business strategy adjustments would need to take this into account. Which market would you prefer to be in?

Analysing competitive forces

The aim of having a winning strategy is to be able to compete effectively to make profits. Analysing the way you compete is therefore an important part of reviewing and setting strategy.

Michael Porter,[1] the eminent Harvard professor, proposed five competitive forces that could erode profitability, as follows:

1   The actions of existing competitors. Are your existing competitors likely to introduce new products as a direct threat to yours?
2   Substitute products or services. Can your customers replace your products or services easily?
3   New entrants into the industry. Will new competitors be attracted by your success?
4   Bargaining power of customers. How powerful are they?
5   Suppliers' bargaining power. How powerful are they?

To these five, we should add the effects of PEST factors (political, economic, sociological, technological).

Your job in reviewing your strategy is to examine each of these factors, both for the present as well as for the immediate future (the next two to three years), identifying direct competitors and coming to a view about the probability of threats from one or more areas. Your strategy should reflect the probable impact of these threats and your business plan should contain actions to counter them. For example, if you have spotted an opportunity in a new market that is currently served by only one or two entrenched suppliers, your approach, either in what you sell or how you sell it, should incorporate specific features to contain the threat from existing suppliers.

Market segmentation: Defining customer behaviour

Different customers have different needs, each with their associated mix of quality, service and price. For instance, some customers are not interested in comparing prices at all, preferring top quality every time; many shop around to secure the best deals; and others are prepared to pay a premium to get their purchases immediately. It is therefore important to segment the market and record profitability by market segment.

The process of identifying customers by the attributes of their buying behaviour is called *market segmentation*. The idea is to align the business with individual market segments and, where feasible, to operate separate business units or teams serving each segment (see Chapter 4 for examples of organizational alignment with market segments). The example in Box 2.3 illustrates this for an IT systems supplier.

Box 2.3 How segmentation determines operations

Segment 1: London merchant banks

Products: back-office systems, consultancy, engineer support

↓

Marketing and sales: seminars in City, brochure, hospitality, calls and visits

↓

Organization: Sales manager, IT-literate people, finance or banking backgrounds, location in Square Mile

Segment 2: European finance houses

Products: front-office dealing systems, consultancy

↓

Marketing and sales: promote through local distributors, events, calls and visits

↓

Organization: European sales manager, local partners, people with German and French language and culture skills, IT skills, travel and subsistence, support literature

Customers with identical or similar behaviour should be assigned to the same segment, on the grounds that finding, communicating with, selling to and servicing them require a standardized approach (and the same or similar direct costs).

What is meant by customer behaviour? Since it is so complex a phenomenon – there are psychological, sociological, economic and other reasons for different kinds of behaviour – it is not surprising that it creates difficulties. We tend to look for superficial characteristics that allow us to group customers in a practical way, depending on whether we are selling to business markets or consumer markets. So we normally group customers by one or more of the characteristics in Box 2.4 (this is not a comprehensive list).

Box 2.4 Checklist: Segmentation characteristics

Business segmentation	**Consumer segmentation**
Geographic location	Geographic location
Industry sector	Occupation
Profitability	Household disposable income
Size	Lifestyle
Growth rate	Educational attainment
Functional development	Sex and age
Legal status	Ethnic group
Memberships	Religious affiliation
Products/services purchased	Products and services bought
Quality preferences	Quality preferences
Prices paid	Prices paid
Service-level preferences (e.g. speed of response, frequency of delivery)	Service-level preferences (e.g. speed of response, frequency of delivery)
Other specific characteristics	Other personal qualities

The ideal is to be as specific as possible to ensure that all organizational, marketing and operational activities can have focus. For example, a pharmaceutical producer selling to retail chemists through wholesalers could characterize its market as in column A in Box 2.5, whereas retail chemists would target consumer segments as in column B.

An alternative method is to take your existing customer base, examine the sales and profitability of each customer, rank them by profitability and finally examine the ranking for patterns or characteristics. You should find out something that you didn't know before! Further issues of practical day-to-day marketing are discussed in Chapter 3.

Strategic marketing analysis

Strategic marketing analysis refers to the process of choosing which customers to sell to, rather than the specific marketing methods of attracting their attention. Its general objective is to identify customers who satisfy one or more of the following criteria:

1   Unable to operate without your products/services.
2   Faced with the fewest alternatives.
3   Most predisposed to buy from you.

Box 2.5 Examples of business and consumer segmentation

Column A **Business-to-business segmentation**	Column B **Business-to-consumer segmentation**
1 Pharmaceutical wholesalers	1 Families with children in south-east London
2 Selling to independent retail chemists	2 Children aged 5 to 16 years in state schools
3 London and Home Counties	3 Household gross income >£40 k p.a.
4 Employing up to 250 people	4 Home owners (mortgage)
5 Growing at more than 10% p.a.	5 Main breadwinner in white-collar occupation
6 Privately owned	6 Lifestyle – technophiles, keen computer users
7 Buying team led by director	7 Shop on the Internet
8 Member of trade association	8 Aware of health and dietary issues
9 Progressive, formal marketing department	

A customer satisfying all three conditions would:

1 Need the benefits you had to offer.
2 Be prepared to pay almost any price.
3 Contact you (meaning that your selling costs would be low).

So who are your most profitable customers? It is now time to undertake your own strategic analysis by segmenting your existing customer base along the lines suggested above: follow the steps outlined in Box 2.6. Your management information system should produce customer profitability data in sufficient detail, but if not, you should be able to calculate *ad hoc* profitability data from your files and accounting system.

Box 2.6 Summary: Steps in conducting a strategic marketing analysis

As a first step in reviewing and setting strategy, undertake a strategic marketing analysis of your customer base.

1 Examine the profitability of each customer in the current year (and previous year for good measure).
2 Rank your customers by profitability (express gross or net profit as a per centage of sales).
3 Examine the rankings for patterns – who are the most profitable?
4 Group them into clearly identifiable types by aspects of their behaviour or specific characteristics (see examples of segmentation criteria above).
5 Alternatively, start with step 4, then go through the steps from 1 to 3.

Distinctive competence

Customers must have a reason to buy from you. You compete for their attention by endeavouring to make them a 'distinctive' offer (thereby differentiating your business from the competition), which ensures that you can charge a price that makes a satisfactory margin. The more distinctive the offer, the less likely are your customers to be able to compare prices on a like-for-like basis (unless, of course, your distinctiveness is based purely on price).

Successful growing businesses achieve this distinctiveness by getting really close to their customers and understanding their most idiosyncratic needs, then meeting them as effectively and efficiently as possible. The source of this distinctiveness is one or more special or core competences, which must be actively developed.

The origins of distinctiveness lie in the special skills, knowledge and technologies – or *competences* – that businesses develop over time. The special competences that set the business apart from the competition are grouped together and called *distinctive competence*. Identifying your distinctive competence is critical to finding a competitive strategy. However, you need evidence, not merely beliefs or assumptions. The way we do this is to ask customers this key question:

> Why do you buy from us (rather than from our competitors)?

On the face of it, this seems an easy question to answer. But it can turn out to have daunting implications and you might feel that it could open a can of worms! In fact, customers generally welcome a discussion along these lines, because it gets to the heart of their trading relationship with you. Nevertheless, customers do not automatically think of their buying decisions in crisp, black-and-white terms. An effective researcher will elicit the right answers and establish one or more of the sources of distinctiveness listed in Box 2.7.

Hygiene factors

Distinctive competence should be distinguished from *hygiene factors*. These are buying decision criteria that a prospective customer uses to ensure that potential suppliers are good enough to be on the 'approved' list, i.e. in the decision-making frame. For example, price is often a hygiene factor rather than a distinctive one. If you are not within the right price range, you do not even get on to the shortlist from which the final buying decision is made (Box 2.8).

It is impossible to overstate the importance of gathering objective, up-to-date information on distinctiveness, because distinctiveness lies at the heart of competitiveness, which in turn is what business strategy is all about. So when interviewing customers, bear in mind the practical points in Box 2.9.

Box 2.7 Distinctiveness and competences

Source of distinctiveness		Business competences
1	Unique products – providing more functionality than competitors	→	Technical product development R&D function
2	Technical/technological leadership – providing the highest technical standards	→	Ability to commercialize innovations and inventions R&D function
3	Immediate availability or wide range	→	Large inventories Highly efficient logistics Large physical capacity
4	Speed of delivery/response – servicing customers more rapidly than the competition, e.g. responding to enquiries, taking and delivering orders, after-sales service, dealing with complaints	→	Large resource availability Highly efficient and effective operations Very efficient management
5	Excellent service levels – capability to provide the highest standard of service demanded by customers	→	Outstanding customer care Close relationships with clients Excellent market information
6	Competitive price – either the same as or lower than your closest competitors	→	Lowest-cost producer High volumes Low overheads
7	Expert knowledge/skills	→	Recruitment/retention of talent Training/development systems
8	Aesthetic appeal	→	Design values Design skills/talent

Box 2.8 Example of distinctive and hygiene factors

You want to buy a new business suit. You consider Marks & Spencer, Moss Bros, Cecil Gee, John Lewis, Next and one or two smaller outlets. They sell suits within your price range, £200–£400, whereas Harrods, Harvey Nichols and other high-quality boutiques sell suits in the price range £600 upwards. Price is a 'hygiene' factor in your buying decision, i.e. your outfitter must offer it or you would not be interested at all. Ultimately, you will settle on a shop that sells the particular style and colour you want; these are the 'distinctive' factors.

Distinctive factors	Hygiene factors
Design (quality)	Price (must be in range)
Range (choice)	Location (not too far away)
	Service (must be competent)
	Tailoring (for adjustment)

Box 2.9 Tips: Interviewing customers about distinctiveness

1 Check your distinctiveness by sending key managers, not sales people, to talk to customers. There are two reasons for this: one is that valid conclusions could be difficult to reach if sales are influenced by personal relationships and the person doing the researching is the sales person; a second reason is that the researcher needs a broad strategic as well as tactical grasp of the company's operations to interpret the answers and probe for meaningful responses. Sales people do not normally have a well-developed sense of strategy.

2 Watch out for glib answers, such as 'excellent product', when you know that most products have the same features. This sometimes masks 'lowest price' as the real factor and few customers will readily admit that they buy on the basis of price. Watch out particularly for the answer 'your reputation' – probe this response until you are satisfied that you have a usable answer, such as 'reputation for rapid delivery and outstanding product quality'.

3 Select customers in a structured way, sampling from different market segments. A small sample should be sufficient to provide reliable evidence.

4 Just as valid is the related question 'Why buy from our competitors and not from us?', which you could address to a small number of ex-customers and those who have asked you to quote or have approached you, but without making a purchase. In these cases, you will find out a great deal about the competition and provide accurate data on which to decide your future positioning in the market.

5 As a final check on the responses, ask yourself the question, 'Isn't that the same response given about my competitors?' If the answer is 'yes', then you have a hygiene factor, i.e. all the main players must have that feature of their businesses to be in the customer's decision frame. If the answer is genuinely 'no', then it is likely to be a distinctive factor.

Defining core competences

Having identified the distinctive and hygiene factors that make up your competitive advantage, you should now determine what core competences give rise to them. A core competence is the combination of skills, knowledge and technologies that you employ in your business that ultimately gives you a competitive edge. The example in Box 2.10 illustrates the difference between distinctive and core competences.

It should be straightforward to devise a strategic business development plan around these critical issues. The main focus of development activity for management should revolve around the distinctive competences in manufacturing (e.g. flexible technology, short runs, efficient workflow, skilled machine operatives), design (e.g. people's creative skills, interpreting customer needs, market awareness), resourcing (e.g. capacity, scheduling, training, interpersonal skills) and company values (e.g. recruitment policies, teamworking, skills and knowledge).

In this model (Figure 2.1), distinctiveness is supported by the three main core competences, which are key departmental functions in this tile-manufacturing business. By identifying the distinctive and core competences, the task of developing

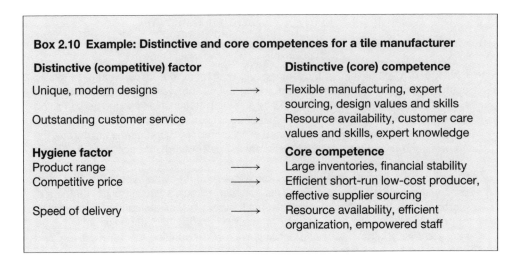

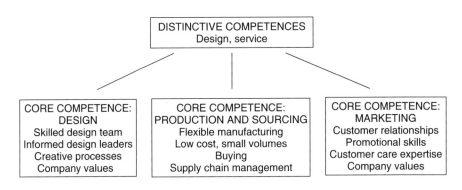

Figure 2.1: Model of distinctive and core competences (tile manufacturer).

the most important parts of the business has a clear logic to it and limited resources can be focused on those factors that will bring the greatest return.

The core competence model can be used effectively to plan ahead.[2] To identify the options for taking your business into new areas of opportunity, you should be asking the question: Where else can our distinctive and core competences be deployed? This is illustrated in Figure 2.2. An explanation of this model follows.

Drive for efficiency and effectiveness (slow growth)

In this quadrant, you should sharpen the focus of existing core competences in existing markets. At times when there are few significant opportunities for growth, competitiveness remains the key to achieving profit objectives. What better way to improve competitiveness than by cleaning up and improving existing operations, including, for example, a drive to raise skill and knowledge levels for the whole organization? The main focus for such activity should be raising customer service

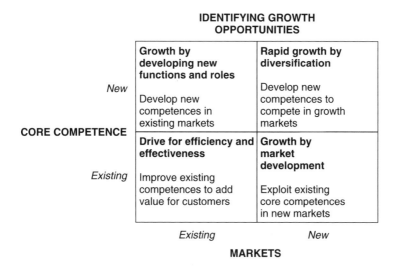

Figure 2.2: Using core competences to establish growth options.

standards and adding value at every point in the customer – supplier interface, with the ultimate intention of maintaining or raising profitability.

Growth by developing new functions and roles

In this quadrant, you should radically improve existing competences and develop new ones to add significant value to existing and new customers in existing markets. Typically, this requires you to add new functions and roles to your existing organization (e.g. introducing a professional marketing function quite separate from sales or a buying department) as well as committing new resources to developing people's skills and knowledge (e.g. formalizing the personnel function or seeking accreditation to the Investors in People[3] standard) and adding new technologies, to exploit perceived growth potential in existing markets. The risk here is that by growing overheads rapidly (which is what is implied in this option), you run the risk of losses in the early stages of growth if productivity, sales and margins do not materialize rapidly. This can be compounded by overambitious business plans and optimistic forecasts of both profit and cash (see Chapter 10 for ways to alleviate this problem).

Growth by market development

In this quadrant, you should take existing competences into new markets (preferably into contiguous ones to reduce commercial risk – options involving significant commercial risk should be analysed together with the product/market choices discussed below). Clearly, this involves much greater risk than a cleaning-up operation and commensurate returns should be expected. But be careful: the risks of venturing into new markets, sometimes without an effective marketing function, constitute one of the hazards discussed in Chapter 11.

Rapid growth by diversification

In this quadrant, you should develop new competences and simultaneously take them into new markets where significant growth opportunities are known to exist. This option should be analysed carefully in conjunction with the diversification option discussed below under product/market choices, because it involves the highest level of risk – but, enticingly, the highest potential returns!

Once core competences are identified and growth choices analysed, project teams (or individuals) can be assigned to them, improving those in existing markets or developing new ones for existing and new markets, depending on the chosen strategy.

Completing the strategic review: SWOT analysis

Identifying and examining the factors that underpin your competitive performance are traditionally done by undertaking a *SWOT analysis* (strengths, weaknesses, opportunities and threats). SWOT has been around for many years and it remains a favourite technique for exploring the dimensions of strategy, whatever the size or complexity of the business. An effective strategy uses SWOT in the following way:

- Match internal *strengths* (especially distinctive and core competences) to external *opportunities*.
- Remedy internal *weaknesses*.
- Counter external *threats*.

The analysis proceeds along the following lines:

- *Strengths:* Where are you strong (vs competition)? What works well?
- *Weaknesses:* Where are you weak (vs competition)? What is not working well? Where are the bottlenecks?

Strengths and weaknesses are internal factors. Use the checklist in Box 2.11 to conduct a strengths and weaknesses analysis, looking ahead over the next one to three years. You may need to adjust the headings to allow for the idiosyncrasies of your own business, e.g. a manufacturer should expand the 'production' heading, a retailer should add shop-related headings, etc.

Looking outside the business to opportunities and threats, the analysis should focus on specific customers and markets, and also on wider environmental (PEST) factors:

Box 2.11 Checklist: Strengths and weaknesses analysis

Business area	Strengths and/or weaknesses
Products/services	Quality of products and services Features of products and services New product development (R&D)
Production/operations	Quality and capacity of plant, equipment, premises Production methods and technology Production staff/management Sources of supply Supply chain management Operational efficiency (working practices)
Marketing/sales	Customer base Pricing policies Promotional activities Sales Distribution/logistics Staffing Market research/customer information Sales and marketing management
Organization/people	Skills, knowledge and qualities of staff, managers, directors Functional structure/roles Human processes (communications, teams, etc.) Systems Quality of administration Culture and morale Attitudes and loyalty of staff
Finance/controls	Capitalization and gearing Working capital Profitability Management information and control systems

- *Opportunities:* What external opportunities are likely to surface over the next one to three years? An opportunity is brought about by a qualitative or quantitative change in the market, typically by a change in demand or supply conditions. Change can be very general, e.g. growing public awareness and concern for the environment, or quite specific, e.g. growth in demand for ecologically sound detergents. Do not make the mistake of claiming a strategy as an opportunity, e.g. launching a new product is not an opportunity itself, but rather a strategic response to an opportunity.
- *Threats:* What threats are likely to surface over the next one to three years? Like opportunities, a threat is brought about by a significant change in the market, typically by factors potentially reducing demand, such as new competition, a rise in interest rates or new legislation.

Use the checklist in Box 2.12 to discover opportunities and threats.

Box 2.12 Checklist: Opportunities and threats analysis

Factor	Examples
Existing customers	Changes in needs of existing customers Growth or demise of existing customers Changes in strategies of existing customers
Existing markets	Changes in needs of potential customers Growth or demise of potential customers Changes in strategies of existing competitors Emergence of new competitors Changes in supply factors
New markets	Changes in needs of new customers Growth or demise of new customers Changes in strategies of new competitors Changes in supply factors
Politics/laws	New government (local/national/foreign) New policies New legislation
Economics	Structural or cyclical change Interest rates Exchange rates International factors
Society	Demographic change Cultural and social change Lifestyle change
Technology	Improvements in technology Innovation and invention

---

One technique that you could try is *brainstorming*, which requires you first to list all conceivable ideas without being judgemental, allowing the inclusion of even those ideas thought by some to be 'off the wall'. Then you should evaluate each idea in turn, prioritizing them by probability, profitability, growth potential, closeness to your existing products and markets and other factors that you consider are relevant to your business plans and that have an impact on risk. Ultimately, the viability of each idea will depend on the probability of each opportunity and threat materializing in the time span required to introduce a new strategy.

Setting strategy

You should now have at your fingertips all the relevant information to allow you to explore future business strategy and make your strategic decisions with confidence. In summary, these are:

1   Comprehensive market segmentation.
2   Detailed data on where you make profits and losses (which customers, markets, products/services, marketing channels, etc.).
3   An up-to-date analysis of distinctive and core competences.
4   An up-to-date analysis of competitive strengths and weaknesses.
5   An up-to-date analysis of opportunities and threats.

Setting strategic direction is best approached in two phases, each calling for a different way of thinking and working.

Phase 1: Setting out the options

A brainstorming and exploratory style is appropriate here, encouraging lateral thinking and deliberately aiming to move away from tunnel vision. It is worthwhile allowing people to entertain 'odd' ideas alongside more obviously sensible ones; even if the odd ideas turn out to be unworkable, they can spark off a fresh perspective on more realistic options.

It is important to make sure that you set out all the options. Don't forget that your options always include (from most pessimistic to most optimistic):

1   Cut back or eliminate parts of your business mix that do not match the core business that you want to develop, or that lose money (analysed earlier when you looked at the profitability of each segment). Remember, small can be beautiful and more profitable too!
2   Do absolutely nothing, except react to any problem or opportunity that might surface. However, this is probably the reactive type of management that you have eschewed.
3   Consolidate your present position and do not seek major new development. Essentially do more or less the same as before, except generate new business and clean up operating efficiency and effectiveness to eliminate key weaknesses, thus raising profitability by a few per centage points.
4   Within the confines of your financial resources (though including short-term borrowing), set out a strategy for modest growth that seeks to develop incrementally new products or new markets.
5   Go for rapid growth by setting a new strategy that embraces major changes in products and/or markets, as well as radical organizational change. This option might require new finance from external sources, including an injection of new equity capital.

From a practical point of view, it is unlikely that you will be considering all these options at once. In addition to your own risk profile (the amount of risk you are willing to bear), your recent business performance (profitability), the nature of your distinctiveness (uniqueness) and the results of your SWOT analysis (optimistic or pessimistic) should tell you how upbeat you can afford to be.

To focus on the specific opportunities and threats identified in your SWOT analysis, you should investigate each product and market option, basing your analysis on:

- The experience of your key people and external advisers.
- Results of customer feedback and market research.
- Forecasts of profit and cash including breakevens, based on key assumptions.
- A strong dose of common sense!

The product/market matrix[4] (Figure 2.3) is a useful tool for testing whether you have considered all possible strategic options.

The practical value of this matrix lies in working out the potential profitability and level of risk associated with each quadrant and systematically evaluating each option before reaching a decision.

1   Market penetration strategy – risk scale = 1

Selling your existing products/services to more customers in existing markets. This caters for cutting back, doing nothing or making modest changes with minor expansion through gaining new customers. If you know your markets well, winning a few new customers will not be costly, nor will your product range need costly development. This is the most compelling strategic option for all businesses, unless there are strong reasons for pursuing other options as identified in the SWOT analysis, e.g. serious weaknesses in the organization that will affect competitiveness, major new opportunities emerging in new markets, or major threats to your hitherto comfortable relationships with existing customers.

2   Product development strategy – risk scale = 2

Selling existing and new products/services to existing markets. This caters for growth through incremental development of new products/services. You should know the emerging needs of your existing customers well (you should be close enough to them to discover their unmet or unexpressed needs), so the cost of developing new products should be quantifiable, depending on your type of business. Your analysis should turn to how to manage new product development risk, e.g. sourcing new products from existing suppliers, piloting new products

| | **PRODUCTS AND/OR SERVICES** | |
	Existing	*New*
Existing	1 Market penetration	2 Product development
MARKETS		
New	3 Market development	4 Diversification

Source: Ansoff Matrix, 'New Corporate Strategy', John Wiley & Sons Ltd.

Figure 2.3: Product/market matrix.

with cooperative customers, securing orders or commitments from customers in advance of large-scale expenditure on new product development, or partnering with suppliers to reduce financial exposure.

Considering the unfavourable odds on new product failure (some studies have put the failure rate of new products at over 90 per cent), the further you veer towards total innovation, the more risky your venture becomes. So you should be very clear about the reasons for pursuing this option and the key sensitivities. Check your SWOT analysis carefully and review the evidence in support of this option, commissioning new customer and market research where existing data seems inadequate. Identify organizational strengths that can reduce the risks, e.g. a successful history of new product introduction, as well as weaknesses that can exacerbate it, e.g. lack of project management skills. In particular, confirm growth assumptions and review possible threats to your existing products/services from competitors or customers.

3 Market development strategy – risk scale = 4

Selling existing products and services to existing and new markets. This caters for growth in new markets while simultaneously keeping existing customers satisfied – a very difficult task. To make this option a reality, you should know your existing markets well and your marketing function should be a major strength (check your SWOT analysis), so developing new markets, although costly, should be quantifiable. The risk is therefore controllable. New markets can include contiguous geographical markets, e.g. moving into the French or other global markets, or new industry sectors, e.g. selling to food wholesalers as well as to caterers.

Considering the unfavourable odds on new market failure, the further you steer away from your existing markets, the more risky your venture becomes. You should be crystal clear about the reasons for pursuing this option. Check your SWOT analysis carefully and produce reliable evidence to support your case, conducting new customer and market research where existing data seem inadequate. Be prepared to commit resources to test marketing in new areas. You should have identified major marketing and selling strengths in your organization (you could hardly venture into the unknown without the comfort of strong marketing and sales functions) and significant new opportunities in new markets, rather than merely dire threats in existing markets.

4 Diversification strategy – risk scale = 16

Selling existing and new products and services to existing and new markets. This represents a leap into the unknown on product and market fronts, holding out the prospect of large profits, which necessarily must accompany high risk. To make diversification work, you should be confident not only about your marketing and selling skills (a smoothly functioning department headed up by a senior marketing person with proven skills in delivering sales in new markets), but also about your operational capability. You should have full confidence in your new product development and supply chain management functions, which should together work harmoniously with marketing and sales. You should have a clear idea of product development costs and alternative scenarios, if delays or problems were to occur. Your SWOT analysis should have identified many more strengths than weaknesses in all major functional areas, and you should have analysed comprehensively the opportunities and threats inherent in the new markets, conducting customer and market research in detail.

However, you can be left with having to launch potentially costly expeditionary marketing into new areas where customer behaviour is difficult to fathom. To control the risks, you must secure orders or commitments to buy from prospective customers. Otherwise, stay well clear of diversification!

In practice, your options are never as extensive as the product/market matrix suggests, because the risks of moving into new areas are too great for most small and medium-sized businesses, given their limited resources of finance and people. The missing component in failed growth businesses is almost always management. The existing owners and managers somehow fail to assess the management needs of the changing business, often extrapolating from existing needs. It takes a fully delegated management structure to make a rapidly growing business work successfully, and building such a structure is a long-term affair.

Phase 2: Evaluating the options

The evaluation process is simply to take each of the options (quadrants) and systematically enquire how effective a strategy it represents for moving towards your business objectives. In evaluating the options, the first question to ask is: How far can we get as we are?

Having completed your SWOT analysis, the answer will be partly dependent on your evaluation of the relative weightings you have given to your competitive strengths and weaknesses, and in particular to your analysis of the following factors:

1   The distinctiveness of your business in the minds of your customers (which must be founded on hard evidence, not the product of your beliefs alone).
2   Your key strengths *vis-à-vis* your weaknesses (the former should outweigh the latter comfortably and your plans to eliminate or ameliorate the latter should be actionable without exceptional cost or organizational energy).
3   Countervailing forces in the market (which should not pose an insurmountable threat).
4   The probability of opportunities and threats affecting your business within the timescale of your business plan (this might require further research or investigation).

Unless there are many factors in this analysis forcing you to change the way you do business, you should be in a strong position to maintain your present strategy, while making the usual marginal improvements to take action on the key points in your SWOT analysis; in other words, to improve profitability by making the business more efficient and effective. The main benefit of this penetration strategy is that you can focus resources on the things you do best, allowing more time to look after existing customers, while continuing to build the business by organizing to win new customers in existing market segments. While this should necessitate a modest amount of reorganization, it does not constitute a change in strategy and is therefore the least risky option.

On the other hand, your analysis might force you to consider cutting out parts of your business. Changes might encompass small-scale cutbacks to sales territories, or swingeing changes to product lines and market segments, with internal resources being retrenched at the same time. If your management information system is sufficiently detailed (otherwise you will have to resort to *ad hoc* costing and profitability calculations), you must cut out those parts of the business that lose money and focus resources on those that generate profits. The net effect is an increase in overall profitability, although a decrease in terms of sales value. This could be a prelude to a later 'go for growth' strategy.

If your SWOT analysis points to one of the three 'growth' strategies as a serious option, it should be evaluated more thoroughly. A methodical approach is called for, testing each option against the same set of criteria, as follows.

1   Is there a market for it now?

- What are the characteristics of the market, including the need?
- How closely matched are you to these needs?
- How large is the market in terms of units, value and growth?
- What market share can you expect and over what time period?
- What are the key features of customer buying behaviour (preferences for products and services, price sensitivity, seasonality, frequency and volume of purchase, substitute products/services, channels used)?
- How strong is the competition?

2   What are the required features of the product/service?

- Design and packaging features.
- Size and weight.
- Pricing points.
- Development and testing issues.
- Piloting or test marketing.
- Costings.

3   Market and customer research

- If any of the above areas are weak, what research is needed and how soon can you secure objective data to fill the gaps in your knowledge?

4 How much will it cost to reach the market and make target sales?

- Produce a draft marketing plan and budget.
- What are the breakeven sales figures on key sensitivities ('what ifs'), e.g. higher overheads, lower gross margins?

5 What resources will be required?

- Competences – does your team have enough knowledge and understanding of new markets, new products/services and competition?
- Does your team have the skills to reach and sell to new markets or to develop and launch new products/services?
- Do you have appropriate technologies to support development?
- Contact networks – do you have access to market and industry networks?
- Do you have the necessary organizational structure and administrative systems to support proposed new developments?
- To produce to the necessary standards, do you have the right technical, production and purchasing expertise?
- What equipment, space and technology are required?

6 What would it cost you to provide the resources you lack?

Do not overlook hidden costs. If the answer to 'do you have the resources?' is 'yes', who will be taking time and attention away from other parts of the business to bring the new activity on stream?

7 Financial

- Do you have the finance? Produce forecasts to establish how much finance is needed for the new strategy.
- Can you raise any shortfall? What is the attitude of shareholders to selling equity?

8 Strategic sieve

- How much money will the new strategy make?
- What is the payback period (how long it will take the new activity to make the profit to pay for the investment)?
- Will it improve overall business profitability?
- How long is the profitable life of the strategy? (What competitive action is likely? What environmental effects are likely?)
- What additional opportunities does it open up?

- How does it help you exploit and build up your distinctive competence? Is there synergy with the existing business (see Chapter 4)?
- Does it provide opportunities for your people to develop?
- What is the nature of the complete business with which you will end up? Will the new strategy cannibalize the existing business?
- What could stop it working? What are the business-critical factors and what are the probabilities of their happening? What is the worst-case scenario and can you deal with it?

The chosen strategy

The final outcome of the process of setting out the options and evaluating them methodically is a short statement of strategy, illustrated in Box 2.13 (an extract from a completed strategic business plan is given in Appendix 1). Each target market and product group must contain projected sales and profit margins.

Box 2.13 AR2 business strategy

Target markets — existing

The company will continue to target markets that have demonstrated their profitability in the past and are expected to show rising demand for staff at all levels from 2003–2005:

- City of London banks (c 250 main players)
- City of London investment managers (c 50 main players)

Target markets — new

After a period of consolidation in 2003, the company will investigate growth in the insurance investment sector for 2004/2005:

- Lloyds insurance market syndicates (<100 main players)

Products/services — existing

The company will continue to place permanent, contract and temporary staff in the following jobs:

- Operations managers (perm)
- Operations staff (perm + temp)

Products/services — new

Opportunities for introducing new positions will be exploited in 2004 as demand grows for permanent, contract and temporary staff in the following jobs:

- IT managers and staff (perm + contract + temp)
- Accountants/audit staff (perm + contract + temp)

We can summarize the entire process of reviewing and setting strategy (Box 2.14) in ten simple questions and answers.

Box 2.14 Business strategy checklist

Question	Answer
1 How can you generate more profit?	Check that you have the right business strategy and that objectives are realistic
2 How do you check strategy?	Analyse your sources of profits (and losses) and distinctive and core competences
3 On what basis do you analyse profits?	Segment your markets (and products) and examine profitability in each segment
4 How do you analyse distinctive and core competences?	Ask customers why they buy from you – distinguish distinctive from hygiene factors and identify core competences
5 What action do you take to focus resources on the right strategy?	Align your distinctive and core competences with profitable market segments
6 How do you work out the detail of alignment and where your priorities should lie?	Undertake a SWOT analysis and add some common sense
7 How do you evaluate the strategic options facing your business?	Use the product/market matrix to set out options and calculate profit and finance for each option
8 How do you assess the risks of the chosen strategic option?	Use the strategic sieve
9 How do you turn the chosen option into reality?	Produce a strategic business plan
10 How do you get the plan to work in practice?	Get people to produce departmental action plans and budgets; monitor and review the plans monthly

Stretching your organization

The process of setting strategy has to be conducted speedily in today's fast-moving markets. Employees who are customer- and market-facing have real-time data to inform business strategy – this is more effective and efficient than having to gather data from secondary sources – so do not restrict strategy setting to senior people only. Encourage involvement by the whole organization, especially people who spend their time close to customers and out in the marketplace. Think about strategy in terms of new ideas and creating new markets, or at least redefining existing markets. Try to 'stretch' your organization's goals and get everyone to do the same by imagining how they could achieve more for your customers.

To do this effectively, you should be trying to develop a strategy that puts people at the centre of your business, as Anita and Gordon Roddick have done at the Body Shop for many years (Box 2.15).

Box 2.15 Analysis of Body Shop success

Controlled growth ⟶
1 Testing idea in known market slowly
- Local market in Brighton

2 Expanding in UK through franchise route
- Preserves capital
- Exploits local market knowledge
- Uses motivated manager/owner

3 Use of owners' strengths
- Financial control (Gordon)
- New product development (Anita)
- PR/promotion (Anita)

4 Moving with market sentiment
- No animal testing
- Exploited green issues

5 No strains
- No strain on finance
- No strain on management

Conclusion	**Analysis**
1 Built on strengths (new product development, control, market demand)	1 Marketing develops over time in UK, later moves into foreign markets
2 Controlled expansion = stability	2 Emphasis on new products (not price) beats competition (distinctiveness)
3 Difficult for competition to keep up	3 Play to strengths – personality/skills of the owners; commitment of people
	4 Finance not a problem (franchising)

Strategic issues

Markets	Expanded in existing then tested new markets before moving abroad rapidly
Products	Continuous development of product range related to market needs (core competence)
People/organization	Focus on staff development (university) Staff committed and sympathetic to ethos Local, committed management (franchisees) Strategic functions covered by owners
Finance	High R&D and marketing costs (barriers) Cash from franchising

Organic growth vs merger or acquisition

Once you have settled your business strategy, the next question is how it is to be achieved, given limited or scarce resources. If projected growth rates are modest and achievable within existing resource limitations, then natural organic growth, topped up judiciously with new resources to build competences in key areas, should be the way forward. However, can you achieve your growth targets in this way, bearing in mind the speed at which new resources need to be employed and integrated with the rest of the organization? The success of rapid organic growth depends in part on how effectively and efficiently your organization is presently functioning (check your SWOT analysis) and whether you have a delegated management structure already working smoothly. If resource recruitment and deployment are down to the owner-manager, high rates of growth are unlikely.

If rapid growth is the goal, what are the options for stepping up the pace of resource acquisition and market penetration? Where does a strategic alliance or partnership fit in? Is it possible to gain access to new markets or acquire new products and technologies through a joint venture with another business? What are the advantages and disadvantages? Should you be looking to acquire another business to boost capacity rapidly and to expedite immediate market access? Or would a merger be a better idea?

These means of achieving growth targets have their advantages and disadvantages. The mechanics of a merger or acquisition should be thought through very carefully and planned with the help of external advisers. The main points to bear in mind when considering a merger, acquisition or strategic alliance are much the same as those discussed in this book. For example, in the case of a merger or acquisition, it would be appropriate to run the strategic sieve over the proposed combined business, apart from rigorously producing a business plan exploring profitability and cash generation for the different options.

Much of business history is littered with examples of failed mergers and acquisitions, despite thorough analysis and planning. Evidence suggests that the main hazard limiting successful integration of merging organizations is, unsurprisingly, the internal dynamics of the organizations themselves – a lack of real synergies in the areas of structure, people, processes and systems (see Chapter 4). Different business cultures get in the way of successful mergers and, in the case of small and medium-sized organizations, allegiances and loyalties to the founders also play their part. So if you decide to reject organic growth (slow growth) in favour of a merger, acquisition or joint venture (fast growth), be sure to plan the approach and the resultant organization thoroughly, ensuring that you have the necessary skills, knowledge and qualities in your management team to bring about a successful transformation.

Notes

1   Porter, M. (1980) *Competitive Strategy*, Free Press, New York.
2   Adapted from Hamel, G. and Prahalad, C. K. (1994) *Competing for the Future*, Harvard Business School Press, Boston, MA.
3   Investors in People is the UK's national standard for training and developing people in line with business objectives and has been specially adapted for use in small to medium-sized businesses. Details can be obtained from your local Business Link or from www.iip-uk.co.uk.
4   Ansoff, H. I. (1988) *New Corporate Strategy*, John Wiley & Sons, New York.

Further reading

1 Porter, M. (1980) *Competitive Strategy*, Free Press, New York.
2 Johnson, G. and Scholes, K. (1999) *Exploring Corporate Strategy*, Prentice Hall, London.
3 Hamel, G. and Prahalad, C.K. (1994) *Competing for the Future*, Harvard Business School Press, Boston, MA.

Marketing for Profit

CHAPTER 3

Key issues dealt with in this chapter are:

- The importance of market segmentation, distinctiveness and positioning.
- Techniques of practical marketing: the marketing mix.
- The role of customer feedback and market intelligence.
- Developing your marketing capability.
- Marketing plans: monitoring and measuring effectiveness.

Marketing is an approach to business that starts with the customer. It encompasses the activities of finding, winning and keeping customers and is a 'whole-company' concept, not confined solely to the marketing and sales department.

Marketing decisions can be divided broadly into:

1 *Strategic* marketing decisions – how to compete effectively over the long term in target markets.
2 *Tactical* marketing decisions – how to reach, communicate with and sell to customers on a day-to-day basis.

We dealt with strategic decisions in Chapter 2. We now go on to deal with tactical marketing decisions.

Customer behaviour

Marketing starts with a clear idea of who the customer is. We group customers into market segments (or niches) as defined by their buying behaviour. Researching, observing, collecting, recording and analysing data about customer behaviour are fundamental tasks for marketing people. If we were to trace buyer behaviour back to its roots, we would find a range of psychological, sociological, economic and even physiological factors at work (Box 3.1).

Not all buyer behaviour can be easily categorized and certain kinds of human behaviour lie outside the bounds of rationality. Some buying motivation is hidden below the level of consciousness. For example, most people don't like to take risks with their purchases, so they tend to buy the same proven goods and services from

Box 3.1 Dimensions of buyer behaviour

Underlying factors	Measures	Buying behaviour
Psychological	Feelings of guilt, anxiety, loss Need for power or status	Extravagance, secrecy, impulse, price insensitivity
Sociological	Belonging to a particular social group	Product features, supplier preferences, price sensitivity, volume, frequency, timing, quality and service preferences
	Family and household composition	
Economic	Personal/household disposable income	Price sensitivity, product features and preferences, supplier preferences
	Inherited or accumulated wealth	
Physiological	Physical stature	Size and volume preferences, product preferences, convenience, buying channels
	Health and fitness	

the same proven suppliers, rather than transfer their loyalty to new, risky ones. This is partly because they don't want to waste money, but also because they don't want to look foolish. This complicates the problem of finding out what people actually want.

For these reasons, customer behaviour and market segmentation analyses are more concerned with the following overt practical features of buyer choice (although they are mindful of the hidden ones):

1 Who are the customers? Who makes the buying decision? Who recommends? Who influences? Who else benefits from the purchase?
2 What do they buy? What kind of product preferences do they have?
3 Why do they buy? What benefits do they want? What does the product mean to them?
4 Why do they choose one product and/or supplier over another? Quality? Price? Service? Reliability? Convenience? Habit? Less rational reasons?
5 Where do they buy? Place? Channels? Competition?
6 What volumes do they buy? When and how frequently are purchases made?
7 What prices do they pay? How sensitive are they to price changes?
8 Where does product/supplier information come from? What media do they read, view or listen to and what kind of information influences their buying decision?

Because an understanding of buying behaviour is so critical to business success, we will use a short case study to illustrate key issues and their implications, with the specific objective of assisting in the improvement and development of your marketing capability (Box 3.2). ABCO could be any small to medium-sized

Box 3.2 Case study: ABCO Systems Ltd

Andrew Barclay, MD of ABCO Systems Ltd, considered his good fortune. Sales had grown by 26 per cent to £2m in the year to March 1998 and profits were at £200 000. Not only were the directors able to pay a dividend, even the bank manager was happy.

ABCO's products were aimed at the banking and finance industry in the City of London, with a number of sales coming from smaller corporates in other sectors. ABCO's software engineers had developed a niche software product that made back-office transactions highly efficient. The full service comprised a networked computer system including hardware, software, cabling, training, maintenance and support.

Sales leads were mostly generated by Sue White, sales director, getting out and about to meet decision makers at seminars and City events. She led a small field sales force who regularly performed demos.

ABCO was widely known in its market for rapid response and high quality, but it was thought to be cold, uncommunicative and not very innovative. Some put this down to Sue's computer engineering background.

Events leading up to March 1999

Andrew had one niggling concern: ABCO was dependent on three banking customers, who accounted for 78 per cent of sales. Another 40 smaller customers made up the balance. The former insisted on very tough delivery deadlines and bug-free software ('right first time' quality standards were essential in the banking sector), but they paid their bills on time and the sales staff found them easy to service.

The small accounts were the opposite: the 'hassle' factor was higher (they typically wanted a customized service without paying a commensurate premium) and they took up a lot of time arguing about the bill. Although credit procedures were rigorously enforced, payments were very slow and there was a persistent bad debt problem.

Sue White had drawn up a marketing plan, which she agreed with Andrew, to reduce dependency on the large customers. In October 1998, she mailed every bank in the City of London, as well as banking and finance companies headquartered in Zurich and Frankfurt. A sprinkling of UK insurance companies and financial services companies was included for good measure.

The existing lists produced a few leads, but only three responses came from the new ones. Sue attributed this to seasonal factors and tried again in November, with equally poor results.

Competition started to affect existing business. Previously six sales leads on average produced a confirmed order. Although the number of leads had risen, more estimates were necessary to achieve the same level of confirmed orders. Regular customers continued to demand lower prices and the company responded by offering discounts on orders received before March. In this way, it hoped to retain these customers' loyalty.

In January 1999, Andrew and Sue went to see the new prospects in Zurich and Frank-furt and to their delight were given a trial order by a Frankfurt bank. Some customization was required and, although they had to give away margin to secure the order, they felt that getting a toehold in Europe would help to reduce their dependence on London.

Unexpected development problems arose with the Frankfurt order, which ran late, so there was no question of invoicing the customer yet.

The position at 31 March 1999

ABCO reported sales up by just 2 per cent for the year to 31 March 1999. Worse still, the company lost £123 000.

The directors met to discuss their problems and review the marketing actions they had taken during the year.

organization; try to imagine it as your own. (You can ignore the case study if you wish – its use is simply to facilitate the connection of theory to practice.)

Where should the analysis begin? The simplest solution would be to list all ABCO's problems and trace each one back to its underlying cause (Box 3.3). Let's see what marketing issues the list of problems throws up . . .

When we examine these problems and causes carefully, we find that they can be grouped into two 'root' causes, as follows:

Box 3.3 ABCO's problems

Main problems	Likely causes
1 Large loss in year to 3/99	High costs of product development and marketing; deep discounting to secure new business
2 Perceived dependence on a few large customers	Lack of confidence in customer relationships (or incorrect analysis?)
3 Existing small customers are price sensitive and slow/bad payers	Focus on price-sensitive segment; lack of appropriate financial policies and controls
4 Threat of competition	Lack of current marketing information; no market research function
5 Lack of marketing knowledge	Directors' technology background; business has outgrown simple sales function
6 Inappropriate range of marketing actions	Lack of effective segmentation; lack of marketing knowledge by directors
7 Mailshots to new markets received poor response	Inappropriate marketing methods, based on wrong assumptions
8 Company image was cold, uncommunicative, not innovative	Technology background of directors; lack of current marketing information
9 Price cutting to retain existing customers	Perceived threat of competition; lack of market information; wrong assumptions
10 Product development problems	New customers = different needs; lack of resources to manage product development
11 Lack of a viable marketing plan	Poorly articulated strategy; lack of market research
12 Marketing (to new customers) not aligned with internal operations	Lack of marketing organization; lack of planning for changing needs
13 Invoicing and payment held up	Product development problems; lack of financial monitoring and controls
14 Reactive management (dealing with problems when they occur)	Lack of management information systems; poor planning

1   The directors failed to understand the idiosyncratic needs and buying behaviour of their various groups of customers, both existing (which had changed in the course of the year) and new (about whom they knew little). In short, they failed to *segment* their markets effectively and assemble available information around each market segment.
2   They failed to grasp the significance of changing direction from focusing on an existing market to targeting existing and new markets, i.e. changing *strategy*, and the implications of such a change for marketing and operational activities.

Market segmentation

We have already stated that the first step in effective marketing is to understand customer behaviour. This means gathering information about customer behaviour by grouping customers according to their specific buying characteristics. This is *market segmentation*: dividing up the whole market into segments (or niches) based on the way that customers actually make their buying decisions (see the eight questions above). Please refer to the discussion about segmentation in Chapter 2.

How should the directors of ABCO segment their markets? A common-sense approach would be to use geography (because of language and culture), business sector (because of different types of organization with different needs) and customer size (because of systems complexity), as follows.

Existing markets

- UK – London banks and related financial institutions.
- UK – small corporates.

New markets

- Europe – banks and related financial institutions.
- UK – London insurance companies.
- UK – London financial services companies.

Once market segments are identified, we arrive at the main conclusion that ABCO's marketing should be reorganized to meet the specific buying behaviour of each segment (Box 3.4).

A few simple questions about ABCO's marketing approach should clarify the importance of accurate segmentation:

1   Would a European bank have been prepared to purchase a costly new system from a British company (expert though they might have been) without some endorsement from a known source, e.g. through existing channels?
2   What language did ABCO use to contact European banks? Using English to contact certain European customers could produce a much lower response than using the vernacular.

Box 3.4 ABCO: Market segments

Segment	Characteristics and buying behaviour
A Existing markets	
1 UK – London banking and finance institutions (78 per cent of sales)	Geographic concentration in the City Complex and diverse needs Insist on tough deadlines Demand high quality Easy to work with Slow decisions Prompt payment
2 UK – small corporates (22 per cent of sales)	Dispersed through London and major cities More simple but diverse needs High hassle factor Price sensitive Argue about discounts Quick decisions Bad debts
B New markets	
3 Europe – banking and finance sectors	Not much known! Customized systems Need several quotes More hassle (concern about fit with their needs) Foreign languages and cultures
4 UK – London insurance companies	Not much known
5 UK – London financial services companies	Not much known

3   Why did ABCO employ a mailshot and telephone follow-up to reach European banks? Does it necessarily follow that established methods will work effectively in new market segments? A foreign-language mailshot and follow-up would have been a low-cost approach, though an alternative would have been to send sales people to visit European prospects, a more costly but more effective method than a mailshot.

It is evident that very little quality information was available about European banking and finance markets, and it is not altogether surprising that the sales director ended up making unsupported assumptions to justify her marketing approach. Marketing should have been more focused and more effective, with the right up-to-date information elicited from customer feedback and research into new markets.

Profiling the customer

To segment markets accurately, a profile of each customer should be built up from known information. Any gaps can be filled in from customer research. Try the profiling exercise in Box 3.5 for your own customers, grouping together all those with the same or similar profiles to form a segment. Then give the segment a name.

Box 3.5 Profiling exercise

1   Select your customers in turn from the most profitable to the least profitable. Describe their buying behaviour under the following headings:

Business profile
- Business activity
- Size (employees or sales)
- Location
- Financial performance (vs competition)
- Positioning in market/market share
- Person(s) making purchasing decisions
- Person(s) influencing purchasing decisions

Buying behaviour
- Preferred products/services
- Motivators/demotivators (reasons for buying/not buying)
- What influences them to buy (price, delivery, quality, service)
- Price sensitivity (low, medium, high)
- Volumes bought
- Purchasing frequency
- Where they hear about the products/what influences them to buy

2   What market segment title describes this customer?

The profiling exercise should produce accurate market segments, each defined by different aspects of customer buying behaviour. The idea is to group all the same or similar customers into these segments and give them a common title, e.g. UK publicly quoted companies in the heavy engineering industry; or small companies within the M25 in the travel industry employing up to 50 people with a website but not more than 25 networked computers.

If your business sells direct to consumers (individuals, households, families, communities), use a consumer profile for this exercise (see Chapter 2, Boxes 2.4 and 2.5 for criteria).

Competitor analysis and distinctive competence

Turning from market segmentation to competitiveness, ABCO's problem was that its distinctiveness in the market was diluted by mismanagement of its main strengths, i.e. quality product and fast response, and an unsympathetic external image, i.e. not communicative, not innovative.

The evidence suggests that it was competing on price in an attempt to win new business in its existing market segments, with a consequent loss of profit margin. Unless it was able to secure higher volumes, it was bound to lose money – which it subsequently did. As we discussed in strategic analysis (Chapter 2), sustained profitability depends on being able to identify which market segments produce the highest profit margins and why (and conversely which produce the lowest and why), which permits the marketing effort to be refocused on the former and promotional marketing and selling activities to be planned in a logical, cost-effective way.

Rational customers will have a clear reason for preferring one supplier to another – purchasing is not normally a random affair. It is the task of the marketing department to find out what these reasons are (which points to *distinctive competence*) and what *competitors* are offering, and it is the role of the directors to bring the organization into alignment with the market's needs. (Refer to the discussion about competitiveness in Chapter 2.) We might conclude that these basic tasks were not carried out very effectively at ABCO.

Market positioning

'Positioning' simply means how a business is positioned against (differentiated from) its competitors in the minds of its customers. The clearer the positioning, the easier it is for customers to make their buying decisions. The key, of course, is to ensure that your positioning meets your target market's buying preferences on all major criteria, e.g. price, quality, service, proximity, availability, range, etc.

The positioning concept is important because:

1   It implies giving up customers (or potential customers) who are not in the target market.
2   It makes marketing activity more focused, and hence more cost-effective.
3   It expedites customers' (those in your target market) buying decisions and therefore makes selling much easier.

We saw that ABCO was poorly positioned against the competition in its main market segments, which left the directors with only one realistic option, the ultimate competitive tool – lower prices! ABCO was strong in some areas, but its strengths were not developed, nor were they communicated clearly to the market. Instead it was considered cold and not innovative.

These negative feelings by customers, combined with a lack of attention to ABCO's strengths, resulted in inferior positioning against better-organized competitors. The consequences were (they aren't revealed explicitly, but we can infer them from the evidence):

1   Existing customers left ABCO for the competition.
2   Failure to attract new customers and convert leads into orders.

3   Low levels of response to promotional activities, e.g. mailshots.
4   Ultimately, pressure on prices resulted in lower margins.

The more distinctive your market positioning, the greater the opportunity for premium pricing, because customers are normally prepared to pay more for an offer they can clearly understand with unambiguous benefits. The consequences of blurred positioning include the loss of traditional customers and a failure to win new customers in new market segments (see Box 3.6). Distinctive positioning also allows promotional marketing to achieve greater focus, so highly targeted messages can be communicated to the market more cost-effectively.

Box 3.6 M&S: Example of blurred positioning?

When it comes to buying certain types of clothes, Marks & Spencer (M&S) has always been positioned clearly in the British consumer's mind as number one relative to competitors, because of the store's distinctive offering of price and quality and the comfort of being able to return purchases for a hassle-free refund. This has always enabled us to make our buying decisions without undue anxiety!

At least, this was the case until the 1990s, when M&S's *positioning* became increasingly blurred. What did M&S stand for? Was it value for money? Was it a fashion shop? Consumers' tastes had changed, whereas competitors' quality and range of merchandise and service levels had caught up and their prices were sometimes keener than those of M&S. So why pay more to shop at M&S? Indeed, why buy there at all?

Improve your competitiveness and marketing effectiveness by using the positioning statement exercise in Box 3.7. Consider your customers' point of view – try to get into their shoes!

Positioning statement explanation

1   *Target market*. Consider one of your markets and describe (profile) the customers therein. Try to get into their shoes when producing personal and business descriptions, identifying aspects of their needs and behaviour that influence their buying decisions. (Refer back to the profiling assignment.)
2   *Distinctive competence*. You may not be able to answer the question without doing some preliminary customer research. Try this out on a few loyal customers first, moving to more infrequent customers later, e.g. those who buy from competitors mainly, using you as a second source. Ask them why they buy from your company, rather than from specific competitors. They won't feel offended! Indeed, by and large most customers like their suppliers to ask them these questions, because the answers can help resolve sticky situations or even open up opportunities. Your customers are more likely to applaud your efforts to open up communication channels, rather than complain about your interference. Remember to distinguish between truly distinctive factors and so-called hygiene factors; the latter include all those features of your organization

Box 3.7 Exercise: Positioning statement

1 Target market

Write a customer profile for your main market segment.

2 Distinctive competence

Why do these customers buy from you, rather than from your competitors?

3 Benefits

What benefits are these customers looking for from your products?

4 Primary selling proposition

What single message about your offer is most likely to make these customers buy from you?

5 Positioning statement

How is your business positioned in the minds of these target customers, i.e. how do they think of you in relation to the competition?

6 Action

What actions need to be taken to sharpen up your company's positioning?

and offering that you must have just to get into contention, i.e. to get on to the shortlist or be on the tender list. They are not enough to win the order, but you must have them to be in the decision frame in the first place.

3 *Message*. The single most important thing you can say about your product needs to relate to your distinctive competence and the benefits sought by your customers. This single statement is likely to form the basis of your positioning, e.g. value for money, never knowingly undersold, the caring company, etc. The difficulty is to say something meaningful without it sounding corny, clichéd or arcane.

4 *Positioning statement*. This needs to set you apart from your competitors in the customer's mind. It requires you to get inside the customer's mind to connect with their motivations. The statement should be clear, concise and intelligible.

One of the important things to emerge from this assignment should be a better understanding of how you compete. Make a list of improvements needed and enter them into your marketing plan for action during the year.

The marketing mix

Different market segments require a different mix of marketing approaches. This seems entirely logical – a 'one size fits all' approach may be simpler and cheaper, but it would fail to generate a satisfactory response. For example, ABCO's directors did not understand that the marketing mix must vary according to the targeted segment; sending out mailshots might work in the UK, but might not be an appropriate method to use in European markets (see Box 3.3). Other marketing problems were quality assurance of new products, deep discounting of prices to secure sales, lack of market information, ineffective marketing planning and no market research function. We call this combination of tactical marketing factors the 'marketing mix'.

The marketing mix is normally divided into a number of 'Ps'. They can be regarded as a set of tools to be used judiciously to achieve marketing and sales objectives:

- *Product* – consists of existing and new products or services in all their manifestations.
- *Packaging* – how these products are to be presented in the market. Includes size/numbers, packaging, labelling, copy and design.
- *Price* – how the product is priced in relation to others in the range and to those of competitors, including discounts and premiums.
- *Place* – how the product is sold into its market, i.e. distributed through channels or delivered direct to the marketplace.
- *Promotion* – how information is conveyed to the customer.
- *People* – the organization and people involved in the process, their skills, knowledge and qualities.
- *Plan* – how marketing (and selling) activities are brought together in a coherent whole and implemented over time, including budgets.

Products, product differentiation and packaging

Customers make a specific purchasing decision for a number of reasons, even when at times their choices seem (on the surface) almost irrational. The reasons are linked closely to product *features*, which in turn are matched to *benefits* sought by customers. These *quality, price* or *service* features are the basis of *product differentiation*.

Product (or service) is typically at the top of the marketing mix agenda. Differentiating or changing the product is seen as an immediate and viable option when trying to make a competitive offer.

Some basic rules of product differentiation are:

1 Customers buy the product application, i.e. the benefit it brings, and not the product itself. Customer benefit is an uneven mix of product quality, service level and price, and differentiation should work with these needs rather than in ignorance of them.

2 The same products at different prices can appear to be different according to customer needs, e.g. an identical jar of branded instant coffee from a supermarket (priced low for regular needs) or from a corner shop (priced high to reflect convenience). Customers and their needs are the sole determinants of how products are differentiated.

3 Product excellence is a function of perceived benefit relative to customer need. Product value is conditioned by customers' perceived needs and the extent to which these are met by competition. The more urgent the need without any comparable product on offer, the higher the price.

4 Products have life cycles, which depend on customers and competition. No product is assured everlasting life. As soon as business organizations focus on their product rather than on customer needs and wants, they ignore the possibility of these needs being met in different and preferred ways. There is no guarantee against product obsolescence. If a company's own research does not make a product obsolete, another's will. Therefore the basis for differentiation today is not necessarily going to be the basis tomorrow, because of change. Developing new products, through invention, innovation or just incremental improvement, is an important contributor to dynamic product differentiation and product enhancement.

5 The advent of innovative product packaging, including accompanying advertising and promotional activities, can superficially help to differentiate products and services and create higher gross profit margins.

The key differentiating features of products and services are normally expressed in a *unique selling proposition (USP)* to assist with clear positioning, enabling the customer to differentiate one product from another, and to facilitate the writing of advertising copy for promotional campaigns. In this way, the promotional 'P' of the marketing mix is linked with the product 'P'. The role of advertising and marketing agencies is to convert the most prosaic product features into an appealing USP, which makes the consumer choose one particular product over other quite similar (or even outwardly identical) ones.

Product differentiation sounds excellent in theory, but the business does have to make a profit from both existing and new products. Measuring the gross profit margin on each product and group of products will provide information about which products require greater differentiation (Box 3.8).

Box 3.8 Gross margin and product differentiation

Where:

Sales
−Cost of sales (production costs and purchases)
= Gross profit

$$\text{Gross profit margin (\%)} = \frac{\text{Gross profit}}{\text{Sales}} \times 100$$

Product A			**Product B**		
Sales	£100 000	100%	Sales	£90 000	100%
Cost of sales	£33 000	30%	Cost of sales	£22 500	25%
Gross profit	£67 000	67%	Gross profit	£67 500	75%

In the example in Box 3.8, product A has a higher sales value than B (£100 000 vs £90 000), but a lower gross margin (67% vs 75%). This could be the result of competitive pressure on price in A's market, linked to an undifferentiated product (why pay more for the same product?). The profitability of product B is higher than that of A and should prompt an examination of A's differentiation with a view to developing (enhancing) the product and raising gross margin. Note that this could include reducing unit production costs, or raising unit price, or both. It could also include changing any elements of the marketing mix that would lead to a higher gross margin, e.g. packaging, sales channels and selling methods. So successful product development can depend on knowing what is happening with gross profit margins.

Pricing

Deciding how much to charge for a product or service is one of the most difficult decisions in business. If you price too high, you lose the sale; if the customer pays your asking price too readily, you feel that you have given the product away!

Setting prices, discounting policies, pricing structures and pricing points (how the product is priced in relation to others in the range and to competitors' products) are partly a matter of science (they can be worked out systematically) and partly a matter of good judgement, which is itself a function of experience and observation.

How much customers are prepared to pay (or have paid) is one of the simplest methods of segmenting markets. Generally speaking, the lower the price, the greater the propensity to buy a product, and vice versa. Sometimes, however, a low price does not create more sales. Too low a price can be taken to mean poor quality; a high price, for example with perfumes, sometimes implies a level of quality that does not really exist. Gross profit margin is directly affected by pricing decisions and cutting prices to raise profit margins can be an illogical step.

There are four main pricing methods:

1 *Market pricing*, pricing according to market conditions, which means charging at, or close to, prices charged by direct competitors. This is a satisfactory method if you can make a profit doing so. Here price is a 'hygiene' factor, and the business has to concentrate on non-price distinctiveness to make higher than normal profits.

2 *Cost-plus pricing*, which requires calculating variable and other direct costs of making and supplying the product or service, adding an overhead contribution (typically by apportioning the overhead), then adding a profit margin and arriving at an asking price. This method suits situations where the seller is ignorant of market conditions, such as in a start-up or entering a new market with a new product.

3 *Customer-based pricing*, which requires being very close to your customers and meeting their specific needs, based on quality and service criteria, and charging a price that properly reflects their relative price insensitivity. This is an ideal method because it has a win:win outcome (both sides feel satisfied with the arrangement), but it can survive only where your relationship is extremely close.

4 *Monopoly pricing*, where demand is inelastic and you are the only supplier, so your customers can't (easily) go to another source. This includes situations where customers are locked into a sale, for example having bought your bespoke software they are forced to buy your maintenance and service contract. You will not normally be able to get away with extortionate pricing for ever, as high prices soon tend to attract competitors or government regulators.

The opportunity to charge higher or lower prices depends very much on the market segment and the level of competition. Many new businesses, as well as new ventures launched by established businesses, are tempted to start off with a price that is too low, aiming to raise it once they are established. This can result in problems. People may only be buying in the first instance because the price is low and they may cease to buy once it is raised. In other words, raising the price changes the customer segment and the selling effort has to start all over again.

Place: Channels of distribution

This is the process of getting the right product to the right marketplace through direct or indirect channels of distribution. Marketing and selling through direct channels means going direct to the end user, e.g. selling your computer software direct to business users by mail-order catalogue; or selling your pottery direct to the public at a local market. The Internet has given many businesses the ability to sell direct to their end-user customers, cutting out indirect channels. Indirect channels include selling through wholesalers, distributors, importers, retailers and resellers. Selling to a wholesale distributor who has the infrastructure to reach many retailers could be a more cost-effective solution than going direct to the consumer. Although you have to give away margin to the channel, you should gain considerably from higher volumes.

When selling through distributors, pricing must reflect the need for each reseller to make an acceptable profit margin, which means knowing not only the end-user price but also how much margin each reseller requires. Promotion should be aimed at both the reseller and the end user, which entails using different promotional methods and therefore much higher cost.

Channels include physical distribution of the product. Cost, speed and quality have to be considered when choosing a method of physical distribution. For instance, customers may not wait for a slow, cheap delivery service, preferring same-day delivery, albeit at a higher price.

Promotion: Communicating the offer

The aim of business communication is to say

- the right thing
- to the right people
- at the right time
- in the right place
- at the right cost.

Saying the right thing involves thinking about what *message* you are trying to convey. The other criteria affect the choice of *media*: where you place the message.

The *cost-effectiveness* of promotion and marketing budgets holds the key to effective marketing. Every promotional £ must work for you. You pay as much for your message to reach someone who is not in your market as to reach someone who is!

To communicate with the *target market*, i.e. the right people, you need to segment your markets carefully. This information can then be linked to the media they will be exposed to, where they are likely to see your message and respond to it. The right person may not be the ultimate consumer: the right person is the decision maker.

The *message* should be presented clearly and simply. Consider image, the elements of the marketing mix (products, price, place), what must be said to get attention (USP) and other discretionary information. Generally, your slogan should reflect 'less equals more' – the less said, the better. Promotional campaigns tend to contain too much information of doubtful veracity, while ignoring the key question that customers would like to have answered: Why should I buy from this supplier (rather than all the others)? (See the discussion of distinctive competence in Chapter 2.)

When choosing the right *time* to deliver the message, decide when the potential customer will be receptive to a sales message. Most advertising needs to be sustained in some form of a campaign over a period of time – not merely a one-off activity – because customers are influenced not only as a result of one specific promotional event, but also by continual communication over time. After all, the information has to coincide with the moment the customer makes a buying decision and this might be difficult to predict.

When deciding which *media* to choose, you should be guided by the information collected at the segmentation stage, e.g. where your customers look for information about your products and services and the media they prefer. Always ask existing customers where they heard about you as part of systematic gathering of information in the course of the pitch or sale.

Above-the-line promotion includes press, radio and television. It is by nature very expensive per lead generated and suffers from the disadvantage that it does not reach potential customers directly, relying on their reading, listening or viewing to absorb any message you might be conveying. Thus this form of advertising is generally used to generate awareness rather than to prompt buying directly.

Below-the-line promotion offers greater focus on the target market. Potential customers can be reached individually and incentivized to read your promotional message. There are many forms:

- The use of mailshots continues to account for a large part of marketing budgets.
- Sales promotions through incentives, e.g. money-off offers, are popular in consumer markets.
- The Internet has grown rapidly as a promotional and selling medium.
- Press publicity is important as a means of making your market aware of your business through editorial content. A press release is a means of reaching your target market directly: you determine the content of the story and you decide which publications would be best suited to your business.
- Corporate image can be vital to success. What image do you want to project in your business or product name, or on brochures and stationery?

Try to relate your promotional messages and design to your distinctive competence. For instance, if you compete mainly on the basis of fast turnaround, then project an image of speed and efficiency, not only in what goes on paper but also in the way that your people communicate with customers face to face, by phone, email or letter.

When deciding on the mix of promotional activities – whether to go for advertising in local newspapers, printing brochures, emailing prospects, designing a website, retaining a public relations consultant or spending a fortune on revamping your corporate image – be guided by your customer-profiling exercise. What media do your target markets actually read, listen to or view to find out about products and services on the market? How do they actually behave when reading, viewing or listening to these media? What kinds of promotional copy, images and design features are most likely to influence them? A great deal of money is wasted on promotional activities because marketing people are forced to guess the behaviour of the audiences with which they are trying to connect.

Some solutions to the problem of effective promotion are:

- Confirm media preferences and habits of existing customers through customer feedback.

- Confirm media preferences and habits of new customers and markets through primary market research (doing your own original research).
- Confirm media preferences and habits of new customers and markets through secondary research (using other people's published research, e.g. from the medium itself).
- Set out to observe customer media preferences and habits (rather than ask people about them).
- Test market your promotional ideas in selected media in order to confirm media preferences and habits.
- Make initial sales through known channels and research media preferences and habits of these customers before launching into the wider market.

People: Organizing the marketing function

The next 'P' features people in the organization, the structure within which they work and the effectiveness of the marketing function. The general principles of organizational design and development are discussed in greater detail in Chapter 4. They apply as much to marketing as to the rest of the organization.

The entire organization has to be geared to customer needs through close alignment with its market segments. In this sense, marketing cannot be left to the marketing department alone, although the marketing department should take ultimate responsibility for all marketing activity in the organization.

To meet customers' needs to the standards they require, the entire organization must view itself as a customer-creating and customer-satisfying organism. Analyses of 'excellent' US companies[1] and 'winning' UK companies[2] emphasize the importance of staying 'close to the customer' – having a strong customer focus as the best means of understanding and satisfying their needs.

Marketing structure and roles

How you organize the marketing function depends on which key functions or activities should be represented and how much resource needs to be applied to each basic activity (Box 3.9).

Once all the elements of the marketing function have been defined, they can be combined in a logical way to form distinct marketing roles and tasks. These can be broadly divided as follows.

1 Providing strategic information

Tasks associated with gathering information about customers, markets, competitors, environmental factors (threats and opportunities), products and costs to inform strategic decision making. Typical duties include:

- Organizing a marketing information system, including margin analysis from the accounting system.
- Market research and analysis (external data collection, analysis, reporting).

Box 3.9 Marketing functions and tasks

Finding and identifying the customer	Winning the order from the customer	Retaining and caring for the customer
• Planning • Market intelligence and segmentation analysis • Market, competitor and product analyses • Customer feedback analysis • Defining customer needs and buying behaviour • Defining the target market • Implementing a marketing management information system	• Product mix decisions: product, price, place, promotion, publicity • Sales activities: new business, existing business • Organizing people	• Following up • Relationship marketing • Key account management • Retaining loyalty of existing customers • Organizational development

- Customer research and analysis (internal data collection, analysis, reporting, customer surveys and systematic feedback, segmentation).
- Marketing and sales activities analysis (lead generation, sources of leads, conversions, etc).
- Database management.

2 Product development

The tasks associated with product research, costing, competitor product analysis, R&D, supplier relations, new product search and sourcing, copyright and patenting. Typical duties include:

- Monitoring existing products and services (data collection, analysis and reporting).
- Monitoring competitors' product activities.
- Generating new product ideas (data collection, analysis and reporting, supplier liaison, sales liaison, production liaison, R&D, idea-generation methods).
- Managing new product development (much of the above, copyright and patenting).

3 Marketing communications

The tasks associated with communicating with and influencing the marketplace. This typically subdivides into specialist roles, e.g. advertising, sales promotion, public relations and press publicity, Internet marketing, database marketing, events. Typical duties cover:

- PR and press publicity.
- Advertising and copywriting.

- Database marketing, including mailshots.
- Telemarketing.
- Corporate identity and image.
- Brochure and sales literature design and production.
- Direct marketing.
- Sponsorship.
- Corporate hospitality.
- Web design and management.

People: Key skills, knowledge and qualities

Not surprisingly, people are the key to marketing success. Does your marketing department have the skills, knowledge, attitudes and qualities needed to make the marketing function work smoothly in pursuit of the agreed objectives? For instance, are your marketing people naturally inquisitive types? Do they have effective listening and interviewing skills and detailed knowledge of the major players in the market?

It is clear that certain skills, knowledge, attitudes and qualities are needed to perform a marketing role and that these competences are different from those for (say) sales or production roles. To determine these competences and the type of people best suited to the role, you should:

1   Undertake a *job audit*, which requires you to identify all the tasks associated with the marketing role. These tasks should include existing tasks as well as those that are not currently seen as relevant to the role, but are necessary to perform it to an agreed standard.
2   Produce a *job specification* for the role, which should clearly state the overall purpose of the job, agreed objectives, tasks (what actually needs to be done) performed in pursuit of each objective and performance standards relating to each task.
3   Produce a *person specification* setting out succinctly the type of person who could best perform the job, in terms of their skills, knowledge, attitudes, qualities and any other requirements.

A more detailed discussion of roles and the advantages of producing job and person specifications can be found in Chapters 4 and 5. Chapter 6 discusses recruitment procedures in more detail. An example of a job specification for a marketing position can be viewed in Appendix 3.

Human processes

How well communication works within the marketing department and between marketing and other functions is bound to be important. For example, how will the marketing department collect customer and market data from other departments such as sales or customer services if it does not communicate effectively or does not have a robust relationship with them? (See Chapter 4 for a detailed discussion of human processes.) To check internal processes for robustness, undertake a marketing review, as follows:

1 Intra- and inter-departmental communication. How effectively is information passed from its source to where it is needed for decision making?
2 Interpersonal relations. How well do people get on with each other at an individual level?
3 Teamworking and leading. How well do teams function, how effective are their members as team players and how effective are their leaders?
4 Personal development. How well matched are people's skills, knowledge, attitudes and qualities to the work that needs to be done? Does performance management work well and how effective is training and development?

Systems

Check that marketing systems for collecting, analysing and reporting information are effective. Marketing information is covered in detail in Chapter 9.

Relationship marketing

A market focus strategy requires constant attention to target markets and close personal working relationships with customers. Relationships have to be managed systematically to generate real benefits for both sides and this realization has led to a fundamental move away from transactional marketing in recent years. The differences between transactional and relationship marketing are summarized in Box 3.10.

Think back to ABCO's problems. As a result of the company focusing attention and skilled resources on a very small number of customers, it must have had close working relationships with key accounts. In sharp contrast, the ill-conceived drive into European markets used impersonal approaches such as mailshots, a departure from ABCO's 'relationship' approach. Could the weakness of the new approach have been foreseen?

One of the driving forces for focusing on long-term relationships rather than short-term transactions has been the relative cost of retaining existing customers compared with winning new ones. Research has shown that it typically costs more than five times as much to win a new customer than to retain an existing one. Furthermore, it has become evident that the real needs of customers can only be ascertained with confidence over the medium to long term and it requires a close working relationship to winkle these needs out of the customer; many are so hidden that even the most skilled salesperson finds them hard to uncover. These unarticulated needs can be explored more effectively through close working relationships between customer and supplier and are often a source of the next generation of new products. Successful, profit-oriented organizations do not rely solely on meeting overtly expressed needs and wants, because over time these will lower profit margins. High and rising profit margins require continuous invention or innovation of products and services.

Box 3.10 Transactional vs relationship marketing

Criteria	Transactional marketing	Relationship marketing
Timeframe	Do the deal quickly, returning only to take new orders and disappear	Negotiate a win:win sale and provide on-going support to mutual satisfaction
Price	Emphasize price as the main benefit	Promote value to the customer and other non-price benefits
Segmentation	Find, win and develop new customers or new markets	Maintain existing customers, developing new business by supporting emerging needs
After-sales support	After-sales support and service are seen as a cost to be minimized	After-sales support and service are seen as an investment in the relationship, amortized over the long term
Incentives	Reward sales people for doing deals, with commission rated on the sales value	Reward sales people for maintaining and growing relationships and revenue, with remuneration based on salary or account profitability
People	Appoint sales people who are skilled at closing the deal	Appoint account management people who are skilled at developing relationships
Cost	High transaction costs by allocating resources to new customer acquisition	Low long-term transaction costs by retaining existing customer loyalty

The main benefits of close working relationships are as follows.

Cost reduction

- Reduced marketing costs through higher customer retention. Marketing activities to find, win and keep new customers are much reduced in scope and scale because existing customers are spending more. This also allows the search for new customers to be more selective, focusing on related segments that are likely to know and appreciate your company's reputation. Greater focus of marketing expenditure helps to concentrate resources in key areas and thus also improves the ratio of wins to expenditure.
- Reduced operating costs through more efficient organization. By means of concentration of effort internally and a focus on key people (a team) to maintain and develop customer relations, efficiencies reduce the costs of operations. Improved teamworking is another by-product of the approach, leading to greater effectiveness and efficiency.
- Reduced R&D costs through customer involvement in product testing. By maintaining a close working relationship with customers, they are more likely to

see the benefits of involvement in the testing of your new ideas where constant monitoring and accurate, valid feedback can accelerate 'time to market'.

Higher sales revenues

- Higher volume and margins via more cross-selling opportunities. Through closer working relationships and account planning you have an improved understanding of the customer's business and the customer's market, which gives rise to more opportunity for selling existing and new products. This opportunity includes managing the product mix proactively to achieve higher average margins.
- Higher volume and margins through winning new customers. Though a small contributor, close relationships with existing customers give rise to a higher level of referrals and recommendations, which bring in new customers. (NB: There is no particular benefit from the account management approach in winning large numbers of new customers. A different marketing approach is needed for this strategy.)
- Higher volume and margins through new product development. Close relationships with customers give rise to an improved flow of ideas for innovation, new products and product enhancements. Account planning encourages customers to reveal their own plans for growth and change while knowledge of customers' own markets tends to produce ideas to promote customers' profitability. Customers are more likely to be involved in the new product development process.
- New income opportunities through feedback and research. Systematic, open and sincere working relationships produce valid on-going feedback, which becomes an automatic part of the partnership arrangement. Market research, evaluation of new ideas and testing of prototypes and pre-launch products can be introduced into the relationship more readily at marginal cost.

Customer relationship management (CRM)

The capabilities required to manage a business successfully in partnership with customers place a heavy emphasis on personal qualities and on interpersonal and communication skills. However, technology has an important role to play in the growing organization, because data can soon become unmanageable as the number of key accounts and sources of new data increase. The 'mining' of databases to produce accurate profiles of customers down to their most idiosyncratic needs and behaviour has permitted suppliers to meet these needs more precisely, thus providing added value for their customers.

The development of smartcards and loyalty cards as mechanisms for collecting data about customers has contributed substantially to making CRM an important marketing tool. Relationships no longer have to be solely at the interpersonal level; the information about needs and behaviour can now be collected and analysed electronically.

Suppliers interact with their customers in many ways, so there are many points at the supplier–customer interface where developing closer relationships could radically improve marketing and financial performance. The following customer service, sales and marketing capabilities have a strong influence on positive customer relationships:

1 Making it easier for customers to contact you.
2 Attracting and retaining the best service and sales staff.
3 Developing sales skills in all staff.
4 Fairly compensating and rewarding sales, marketing and service personnel.
5 Developing and executing an effective channel strategy, e.g. selling through distributors, agents, resellers, etc.
6 Using information systems and technology effectively.
7 Using high levels of customer service (partnerships) to generate sales.
8 Pricing products and services to maximize returns.
9 Sharing customer information throughout the organization.
10 Producing and implementing marketing and sales plans.
11 Measuring customer service effectiveness against objectives.
12 Accurate and timely invoicing of customers.

The exercise in Box 3.11 enables you to diagnose your own marketing and sales processes in order to identify areas for improvement and consolidate the relationship side of your marketing and sales functions. The overarching objective should be to improve customer retention through higher levels of customer satisfaction at every point of their contact with your organization.

Customer feedback

To ensure that your strategy is based on sound market data and that you make the right tactical marketing decisions, marketing information should be sought from the following sources:

1 *Existing markets/customers*. What factual market information do you have about market size, trends and your share of the markets in which you operate? Which customers are most and least profitable? What are their existing and future (unarticulated) needs and are these being met? What are their feelings about your company in relation to competitors (positioning)? How sensitive are they to price changes? What are their future business plans?
2 *New customers in existing markets*. Who do they currently buy from? Who are likely to be most and least profitable? What are their existing and unarticulated needs and how do they regard your company in relation to existing suppliers? What are their future business plans and what would persuade them to move to you? How sensitive are they to price changes?
3 *New customers in new markets*. You need new market information to help the planning team decide on future strategy. What information do you have about new markets identified in your SWOT analysis, in terms of market size, trends,

Box 3.11 Diagnosing marketing and sales processes

1 By identifying each point of customer contact using the diagrammatic example below, examine how marketing and sales take place with:

   • existing customers
   • new customers

2 Now either interview a few customers, or put yourself in your customers' shoes, examining each contact point. How well does each work? Where are the weak points? What needs to be done to ensure the entire marketing and sales experience meets your customers' required standards of performance?

Progress of a sale through the business

prices, marketing channels, barriers to entry, etc.? Who do potential customers currently buy from? Who are likely to be most and least profitable? What are their existing and unarticulated needs? What are their future business plans and their buying behaviour, and what would persuade them to buy from you? How sensitive are they to price changes?

4   *Competitors in existing markets.* How do they compete and how successful are they? Why do their customers buy from them (rather than buy from you) and how might they respond to your strategic actions?

5   *Competitors in new markets.* How do they compete and how successful are they? Why do their customers buy from one rather than another and how might they respond to your entry?

6   *Other market-influencing factors.* What economic (e.g. interest rates, exchange rates), political (e.g. government policies, laws), technological (e.g. computing power, product development), social (e.g. people's leisure choices) and environmental (e.g. effluent rules) factors are likely to emerge in the planning period? Are these likely to give rise to opportunities or threats?

There is a welter of market information available from public and private sources, but none is likely to be of any use without the essential data provided by existing customers. Most companies do not realize how much data lies untapped in their sales and operations records, and what useful new opportunities (or indeed threats) might be identified by examining and analysing this readily available data.

The organization of effective, systematic feedback from customers about current deliveries and existing levels of service is of prime importance. Although large amounts of information can be gathered in the normal course of carrying out sales or marketing duties, it is surprising how many businesses fail to seek direct feedback from customers before, during and after a sale. The result is that customer satisfaction can never be gauged accurately (and suppliers are left with unsubstantiated assumptions about their service); even worse, the opportunity to engage in serious heart-to-heart dialogue is passed up in the interests of getting on with the next job. Customers like to be consulted. They frequently complain that their suppliers do not communicate enough with them, except when they want another order.

We cannot place too much emphasis on an effective marketing information system that produces accurate and up-to-date data as the by-product of a well-organized customer relationship process. Typically, this involves planning each key account or each group of key accounts to permit the collection and recording of data by salespeople in the course of their duties; but it also requires periodic bursts of feedback collection by marketing people, who can extract objective feedback because they are less likely to be affected by close customer relationships.

The ABCO case illustrates the point. Mistakes were made as a result of not fully understanding the basis for making sales to existing market segments. Surely if the company had had this information, it would not have moved into European markets without first examining its options (Box 3.12)?

Box 3.12 ABCO: The need for market intelligence

ABCO displayed little coherence in its approach to the market, partly due to a lack of effective planning. Comprehensive, accurate, relevant and up-to-date information lies at the heart of effective planning, but there was no systematic *feedback process* to extract information about buying behaviour from existing customers, nor any serious attempt at gathering data through *market research* into new markets.

Therefore the directors had to base their decisions on assumptions and beliefs about existing customers' needs and buying behaviour, the nature and strength of competition, how ABCO was perceived in terms of its distinctiveness, strengths and weaknesses, and the needs of geographically new market segments, rather than on well-researched facts.

Market research

Market research is the process of collecting, analysing and presenting information about markets, both existing and new. Research surveys should consider how best to ask the questions in Box 3.13 in everyday language to maximize response rates.

Box 3.13 Important market research questions

Questions	Key marketing issues answered
1 Who are the customers? Who makes the buying decision? Who influences the decision?	Segmentation, targeting, profile
2 What products/services do they buy? What are their preferences?	Product mix, product development
3 When, how frequently and how much do they buy?	Seasonality, capacity, forecasts
4 Why do they buy these products or services? What benefits do they want?	Differentiation, USP, product features
5 Why do they choose one product/supplier over another?	Distinctive competence, quality, price, service, reliability, convenience, less 'rational' issues
6 Who currently supplies them and on what terms?	Competition, competitive factors, channels
7 How much are they prepared to pay and how sensitive are they to price changes?	Pricing
8 Where do they get information about the product? What media do they read, view or listen to and what kind of information influences their buying decision?	Promotional mix, media, message, costs

Once factual, objective information has been sought about real (not hypothetical) behaviour, research can then turn in sequence to:

1   Aspects of satisfaction/dissatisfaction with present/past purchases.
2   Suggested areas for improvement.
3   Attitudes to new or improved products/services on the market.

Asking about the future and about hypothetical matters will necessarily involve a high degree of subjectivity, so customer responses must be treated with caution. Most people are not capable of thinking creatively and constructively about their needs without proper guidance and support. In this case *focus groups* might provide a more thorough and flexible method of collecting data from existing and potential customers (though they should be organized and facilitated by a professional researcher).

There are a number of survey methods to consider, each with its own advantages/disadvantages (Box 3.14).

Box 3.14 Market research methods

Method	Advantages	Disadvantages
Telephone survey	Large numbers	Low quality
	Speed	Low data volume
	Allows probing	Not very personal
Street survey	Face to face (data quality)	Low data volume
	Targeting	Low response
	Allows probing	Time-consuming
Postal or email survey	High data volume	Low response
	Medium-quality data	Suspect statistical validity
	Targeting	No probing permitted
	Low cost	
Personal interview	Great depth of data	High cost
	High-quality data	Time limit
	Spin-offs	Low number of responses
	Relationships	

When designing a survey questionnaire, be sure to test it out with a pilot study before launching into the main survey. You are certain to want to change questions when you observe how respondents actually reply. There are many useful lessons that can be learnt from undertaking research surveys, the main ones of which are presented in Box 3.15.

The marketing plan

A marketing plan serves the specific purpose of bringing together all the marketing reasoning (the arguments for a specific course of action) and associated marketing

---

Box 3.15 Tips: Collecting market data

- To collect information about existing markets, select customers and non-customers in a structured way, sampling from different market segments. Also include ex-customers and those who have approached you but not yet made a purchase.
- When asking a question about distinctive competence ('why do you buy from us rather than from the competition'?), for those respondents who are not customers, ask why they buy from the competition and not from you.
- Do not necessarily accept the first answer, probe for more information about buying decisions to get to the root of buyer behaviour.
- Select your researchers carefully and brief them about the task in detail. If budgets permit, you could brief an independent market researcher to collect the data for you. The advantage is that external researchers are disinterested in the buying decision; the disadvantage is that they know little of the strategic and other business-critical factors. The answer lies in part in a comprehensive briefing.

---

and sales actions that will achieve your business objectives. The plan should be short on words though long on figures, and it should contain appropriate indicators of marketing success to enable you to judge its effectiveness on a continuous basis, i.e. at weekly sales meetings and monthly marketing meetings.

As a preliminary assessment of your marketing capability and the areas on which your plan should concentrate, try out the marketing capability test in Box 3.16. It should point to the areas where you might wish to concentrate scarce resources.

From the questionnaire that you have just completed, what actions can you identify to improve your marketing? These actions should be incorporated into your marketing plan. It is the responsibility of the marketing director (or someone in the company looking after the marketing function) to draw up a marketing plan containing the following essential elements (see a completed plan for ABCO in Appendix 2).

Marketing review

Review the past year's results (sales, margins) and undertake a SWOT analysis to establish current marketing strengths and weaknesses, opportunities and threats. The findings of this analysis will form the basis of a marketing strategy (see Chapter 2).

Objectives

The review leads to a statement of principal objectives (sales, margins, market share, etc.).

Box 3.16 Marketing capability test

Answer the following 12 key questions about your marketing capability.

How accurately do the following statements describe marketing in your company? Score on a 1–5 basis, as follows:

1 = negligible (hardly exists)
2 = poor (exists but no thought given to it)
3 = mediocre (exists but *ad hoc*/unsystematic/unplanned)
4 = quite good (but needs lots of work)
5 = excellent (achieves objectives every time)

Marketing capability factor	Score
1 Driven by customer needs rather than by a need to sell existing products/services	_____
2 A carefully planned and sustained approach using all appropriate marketing methods to retain the loyalty of existing customers	_____
3 A carefully planned and sustained approach using all appropriate marketing methods to find, win and keep new customers	_____
4 Continuous reassessment of the needs of existing customers through systematic feedback and research processes	_____
5 Continuous market feedback and review of key assumptions about customer behaviour	_____
6 Continuous flow of new and innovative ideas to meet the needs of existing customers	_____
7 Systematic comprehensive recording, monitoring and analysing profitability of all markets, customers and products/services	_____
8 Periodic reviews of marketing strategy (which markets and what products to be in) involving key people	_____
9 A written marketing plan and budget regularly reviewed to meet the changing needs of customers and the market	_____
10 Periodic appraisal of marketing competences: skills, knowledge and capabilities to enable marketing to function smoothly	_____
11 A strong focus throughout the business on high levels of customer service through planning and managing customer relationships	_____
12 Continuous customer service training to raise awareness of each person's contribution to meeting customer service goals	_____

Total

Scoring key

 0–20 Marketing in poor shape – needs a complete overhaul if you are to survive another six months!
21–40 You might survive, but not without careful attention to several key areas of your marketing
41–50 You are nearly 'marketing capable', but sort out your priorities
51–60 Your marketing is excellent – but don't be complacent!

Strategy: Target markets

Who are the customers (by market segment) that you are planning to reach? How many are there in the market (existing/potential)? Why should they buy from you?

- What are the characteristics of the target markets in terms of location, age, income, gender, needs, benefits sought, etc. (for domestic customers) and type of activity, location, decision maker, decision criteria, benefits sought, etc. (for business customers)?
- Once these have been identified, how do the customers behave, and particularly how do they make their buying decisions?

Sales and gross profit forecasts

The forecasts should be based on a realistic assessment of what is achievable (how many customers are likely to buy from you, do you have the capacity to deliver these sales, what are realistic gross margins?). The forecast should consist of:

- Monthly/annual unit sales and gross margin by market segment and product or service.
- Unit price.
- Total sales and gross profit.

Marketing mix

How will you use the tools of the marketing mix to meet the needs of your target markets (organized by market segment)?

1   Product plan

- Products/services offered.
- Product features matched to customer needs/benefits.
- How are they different/unique to competitors' products?
- Product development plans.

2   Packaging plan

- Details of packaging and costs.
- Design issues.
- Customization for different segments.

3   Place plan

- Channels of distribution.
- Physical distribution of products.

- Selling methods.
- After-sales service.

4   Pricing plan

- Customer price sensitivity.
- Pricing structure.
- Effect of competition on prices.

5   Promotion plan

- Key points of appeal that will influence customers to buy.
- Media and costs for informing customers about product/service availability.
- Messages to be used in these media.
- General publicity/PR.
- Schedule and action plan.

6   People plan

- Marketing function (structure/roles).
- People responsible for marketing/selling activities.
- Organizational and administrative support for marketing.
- Service standards to meet customer requirements.
- Management information systems.

Budget

Once you have considered the optimum marketing strategy and action plan, the budget can be set (then incorporated into the projected profit and loss account). The marketing budget should include:

- Direct costs associated with selling and marketing, e.g. printing, media advertising, sales promotion, mailing, events, travel, entertainment, hospitality, commissions, etc.
- Indirect costs associated with sales and marketing, e.g. salaries, telephone, other office costs, general corporate marketing, etc.
- Capital expenditure directly associated with marketing and selling activities, e.g. purchase of laptops, sales aids, vehicles, etc.

Monitoring the plan

What monitoring and review arrangements have been made to ensure that the plan is being implemented, e.g. weekly and monthly meetings, management information systems?

These are the main components of an effective marketing plan, but no amount of planning will necessarily generate profits unless there is the involvement of all relevant people in the planning process. Since we made the point at the beginning that marketing is a whole-company concept, it stands to reason that everyone should be involved in the plan in an appropriate way. Customer-facing people should be consulted individually; back-office people should be involved through their team leaders. People with a strategic orientation should be engaged on the planning team, whether or not they are in the marketing department.

Postscript: Action on ABCO's marketing problems

To illustrate how a thorough marketing review can help to solve problems and put the organization back on track for profitable growth, the key questions that should be asked of the directors of ABCO are as follows.

First, explore strategy.

1   Is ABCO targeting the most profitable *markets*? What information is available about profit in each market segment to help with this decision?
2   What are ABCO's *distinctiveness* and *positioning* in each segment? Are they closely aligned with customer needs and buying behaviour?

Then go on to consider the marketing mix.

3   Are the *products* right for each segment?
4   Are they *packaged* (presented) in the right way?
5   Are they being sold at the right *price*?
6   Are the right *channels* being used to reach each segment?
7   How effective is *promotion*? Are the right *media* being used to reach the market segments and the right *messages* communicated?
8   How effective are the *people, processes, systems* and *structure*?
9   Is there a *marketing plan* to guide the business towards its chosen market segments and what arrangements are in place to permit monthly monitoring?

Recommendations to ABCO's directors should centre on the following sequence of actions:

1   Undertake a business review including a strategic marketing analysis and produce a strategic marketing plan. The purpose of this is to set direction (target markets and product mix) over the chosen planning period (three years in outline is ideal) and clarify vital marketing ingredients such as distinctiveness and positioning against competition.
2   Produce a thoroughly researched and detailed operational marketing plan for the next 12 months setting out target sales, gross margins and the marketing mix for each segment chosen in the strategic plan, and marketing actions with costs on a month-by-month basis. The directors need to meet departmental managers to discuss the plan and how it coordinates with those of other departments.
3   Produce a monthly marketing budget to accompany the plan and communicate the plan to the marketing team together with individual contributions.

4 Convene monthly marketing meetings using the marketing plan as the roadmap. Make periodic adjustments to the plan and budget to reflect changes encountered or anticipated during the year.

Notes

1 Peters, T. and Waterman, R. (1982) *In Search of Excellence*, Warner Books, New York.
2 Goldsmith, W. and Clutterbuck, D. (1997) *The Winning Streak*, Orion, London.

Further reading

1 Peters, T. and Waterman, R. (1982) *In Search of Excellence*, Warner Books, New York.
2 Kotler, P. (1999) *Kotler on Marketing*, Free Press, New York.
3 Postma, P. (1999) *The New Marketing Era*, McGraw-Hill, New York.

Developing an Organization that Delivers the Strategy

CHAPTER 4

Key issues dealt with in this chapter are:

- A framework for understanding how organizations work: the basic components of organization and how they fit together.
- How to overhaul an organization to diagnose and rectify pressure points and problems.
- How organizations begin.
- Designing the structure and processes that will underpin growth.
- Shaping the roles that the business competence model needs, and specifying jobs that match people to purpose.

Understanding organization

Is your organization in shape to make your chosen strategy happen and deliver your business goals? Are all the necessary resources in place to translate the competences you have identified into effective action? Are there weak points in the organization? Even if things are working well at present, are there areas that will come under pressure if you do more business, or do business differently?

You need to be able to analyse how the organization works and to foresee and plan for the adaptations necessary to meet future challenges. Piecemeal adjustments made in response to pressure of work – enlarging a role here, adding new people there – can easily throw an organization out of kilter and lead to more problems than they solve. It is important, therefore, to have an appreciation of the functioning of organizations.

What is meant by the term 'organization'? It is a common enough word, but its meaning is quite difficult to spell out. Dictionaries come up with definitions such as 'organizing or being organized', 'an organized body or system or society' – which gets us no further than that an organization is organized. But it is worth looking further into the shades of meaning here. The term comes originally from a Greek word for a tool or instrument, from which we take our word *organ*, which can denote an instrument or a part of the body. We have the word *organism*, which denotes a living body with connected interdependent parts (organs). So to *organize* means to form into an organic whole, a functioning body made up of connected, interdependent parts that share life – an *organization*.

This exercise reveals some important points. First, organizations are organic – the parts are interdependent and they operate as a whole – so not only can a problem in one part affect the functioning of the whole outfit, but also when we change or reorganize a specific area, the consequences can be widespread.

Secondly, organization has more than one connotation: we can think in terms of tools and instruments and get a concept of an organization as a machine; or we can focus on the idea of an organization as a living body, an organism. We often want our organizations to work like machines. A good machine consists of well-coordinated components, tirelessly and reliably carrying out their appointed function and getting the job done; switch it on and it does the job, predictably. But machines have their drawbacks: however sophisticated, they can only perform to specification and are always limited. Living organisms, in contrast, are capable of flexibility, adaptation and growth, and brainy organisms are capable of reasoning and imaginative response. When we see our organization as a brainy organism, we recognize that it is made up of human beings, each with an individual personality and the potential to enhance or undermine the working of the whole.

A well-functioning organization combines the reliability of a well-oiled machine with the intelligent responsiveness of a brainy organism. Get the balance wrong, and instead of enhancing the benefits of each concept you magnify the problems: the rigidity of machine-like procedures can stifle initiative or responsiveness to customers; enthusiasm and bright ideas that are not channelled systematically can lead to disruption and conflict.

Organization maintenance and development

Work organizations do not stay the same. Indeed, even if it were desirable, it is probably not possible for an organization to stand still. There are a number of reasons for this:

- Business strategy: responses to shifting opportunities and threats in the environment call for a realignment of the way the work is done.
- Technological changes necessitate revision of working patterns.
- The people in the organization themselves change. Some people leave and are replaced by others who are different; people who stay may grow and develop wider skills and greater maturity, making them capable of a bigger role; or they may stagnate and not turn in the performance they once did.

So organizations need conscious attention and maintenance. Clearly, when new strategic initiatives are to be pursued, the organizational adjustments needed to deliver them have to be thought through in advance of action in the marketplace. But even when the requirement is for business as usual – carrying on with the same strategic direction – there needs to be a regime for organizational fitness, so that emerging problems are nipped in the bud and performance is kept on track. Organizational issues can easily be neglected in growing companies: there are always more pressing demands on management time and attention until a crisis looms, and the inclination and skills for working with the firm's own people are often subordinated to customer and task orientation.

The origins of an organization

Organization is seldom a preoccupation in a newly founded business. The emphasis is on finding customers and getting orders, then doing whatever has to be done to supply them. At the very beginning, business founders may do everything themselves. As sales expand, people have to be brought in to get the work done. This necessitates some kind of definition of the roles that employees are there to carry out: administration, selling, producing. Often role definitions are vague, and people may not be fully trained or qualified for the work they are doing. The firm consists of a band of people, all directly linked to the boss, who get on with whatever needs to be done, without bothering too much about whose job it is to do what. There appears to be little in the way of procedure: people make up in enthusiasm for what they may lack in expertise or efficiency, acquiring the skills they need as they go along. Communication lines are direct – people are often all in the same room – and everyone knows what's happening.

At first sight, an apparent lack of structure and formal order in such operations might lead to the belief that this is not an organization at all, merely people mucking in together. However, closer analysis reveals an organization 'cell' that meets the definition given above and that can be highly effective. It is structured like a spider's web, with the boss at the centre of everything (Figure 4.1). Reporting and communication strands radiate out from the centre, but there are direct lateral communication lines between each strand as well.

People who have been part of this stage of development of a firm often look back to it nostalgically, with good reason. Things were accomplished, there was a sense of achievement, people helped each other out and everyone took responsibility for satisfying customers. Often bosses attribute the effectiveness of this stage of organization to its informality, and they can be reluctant to put in place more clearly defined structures and working practices, fearing that this will make the company soulless and 'bureaucratic'. However, a deeper look at what it is that makes a spider's web organization work well is likely to reveal the following factors:

1 *Common purpose.* Everybody wants the business to succeed and will do their part to make that happen.
2 *Goals and work standards are clear.* Each person knows what they are there to do and takes responsibility for doing their bit well enough.
3 *High level of motivation.* People want to do well, feel a sense of responsibility, see their contribution make a difference to results, experience job satisfaction, experience team spirit, rise to challenges and learn how to do new things.

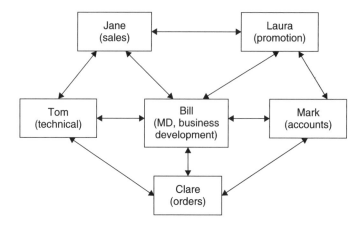

Figure 4.1: Organization cell structure: The spider's web.

4   *Task commitment.* All of the above add up to a determination to get the job done and see things through.
5   *Group cohesion.* People don't merely get on with their own work in isolation, they cooperate, support their colleagues, make sure that they exchange the necessary information and give someone else a hand to ensure that important tasks get priority.
6   *Structure.* Although people may help colleagues, each has their own role and knows what their central function is, and they understand what the central functions of their colleagues are. There are no problems about levels of authority – the boss is in charge and everyone else is on a level.
7   *Work processes.* The work flow (from getting an order to getting an invoice paid) is straightforward: people get used to working with one another and routines for doing so emerge that provide coordination of the 'normal' part of the firm's work. Communication is fast and direct. There will be a simple method for ordering priorities and sorting out bottlenecks, probably by referring them to the boss.

These features produce an effective bond between the *leadership* of the unit and its *membership*. The boss exercises leadership by setting direction, and by aligning the members of the organization to be able to deliver its purpose in the work they do. The boss is 'hands on', and people are likely to find him or her working alongside them. The effectiveness of the match between leader and members is likely to be further strengthened by the processes of recruitment and such training and induction as exist – all of which are likely to involve the boss directly. We can sketch a model of the features that make this organization work (Figure 4.2).

In fact, the set of factors that makes this organization effective is quite sophisticated. Furthermore, all of the factors are interlinked. When an organization is operating well, strong performance stems from the way in which each key part of the organizational model works to reinforce the effectiveness of the other parts. However, a change that affects just one part of the model will have a knock-on

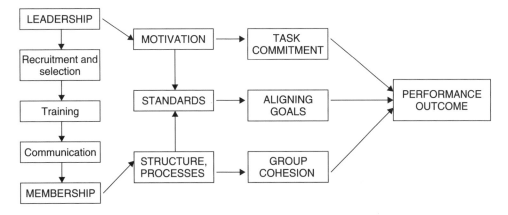

Figure 4.2: Key features of organizational effectiveness.

effect. A change in leadership, membership, motivation factors or structure can disrupt the positive functioning of the organization as a whole.

As the business grows and more people are needed to do the work, the shape of the organization will have to change, as will some relationships between roles – there is a limit to the number of people who can be directly coordinated by the boss. Factors that are important to making the embryonic organization work well can and should be translated to the enlarged organization in a manner that will fit its new shape. This requires conscious processes of diagnosis, to discover what in the existing organizational model works well and what needs to be improved, and design, taking the whole of the organization into account.

A closer look at the anatomy of organization will help us understand how to maintain organizational fitness, and what is involved in developing and retuning the organization in line with the demands of strategy.

How organizations work: Structure, people, processes and systems

Looking into an organization to enquire how it works, we can see that it consists of a set of *people*, carrying out various roles that fit together into a *structure*. The structure relates people's functions to one another and to the firm's environment. Everything is coordinated and kept moving by organizational *processes* that integrate the parts and provide impetus. In a well-developed organization, *systems* will be in place to give direction and maintain order and control.

These are the main parts of an organization, each of which contains its own further set of components. These components can be assembled in various ways. The art of organizational design is to fashion and combine the components so that the interaction between them is conducive to effective performance of the whole organization in realizing strategy. The checklist in Box 4.1 summarizes these four components of organization.

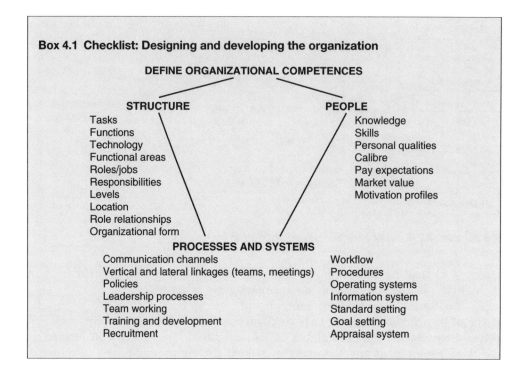

Box 4.1 Checklist: Designing and developing the organization

DEFINE ORGANIZATIONAL COMPETENCES

STRUCTURE   PEOPLE

Tasks	Knowledge
Functions	Skills
Technology	Personal qualities
Functional areas	Calibre
Roles/jobs	Pay expectations
Responsibilities	Market value
Levels	Motivation profiles
Location	
Role relationships	
Organizational form	

PROCESSES AND SYSTEMS

Communication channels	Workflow
Vertical and lateral linkages (teams, meetings)	Procedures
Policies	Operating systems
Leadership processes	Information system
Team working	Standard setting
Training and development	Goal setting
Recruitment	Appraisal system

In the following sections we look in turn at the building blocks of organization: structure, people, processes and systems. In practice, though, all of these aspects have to work together, so when overhauling or designing an organization we cannot simply deal with each building block sequentially – we need to bear the others in mind.

We create organizations in order to enable people to work together in pursuit of a purpose; an organization is first and foremost its people. Getting performance from those people begins with getting a good match between the jobs to be done and the people doing them, and ensuring that the jobs that people are asked to do are viable. Remember, a badly put-together organization can actually impede rather than enhance people's capability. So before we can put people into the organization, we first have to consider what they are needed for and how the work of the organization can best be structured.

Structure

Organizational structure is essentially the scheme of how individual roles in the organization relate to one another. In designing structure, you are aiming to divide up the work between jobs in the manner that gives people doing them the best chance of collectively delivering strategic competences. You need to be able to set the scheme of roles out in a chart, so that each person in the organization can see where he or she fits into the whole.

The first step is *matching competences to tasks and functions*. What *key tasks* have to be carried out for the company to operate its business? Whatever the nature of your business, they are likely to fall under the broad headings in Figure 4.3.

This broad task analysis reveals the *key functions* that have to be performed in the organization, and provides the cornerstone for specifying the *roles* to be carried out by people, most of whom will specialize in a particular aspect of the company's work.

In a larger organization, each of the functions denoted here, and probably others, would be delineated as separate departments, each headed by a member of senior management. However, in a smaller organization this is often not practical. We can take the personnel function as an example. If you have, say, 40 staff and low staff turnover, you do not need a personnel department, but you do need to ensure that the personnel function is carried out and that it receives proper attention at senior management level. So whoever has responsibility for personnel management is likely to combine it with other functions: a managing director might take responsibility for personnel policy and coordinating recruitment, delegating personnel administration to an administrative assistant, who works with the finance department on payroll matters. Some functions are split between a number of

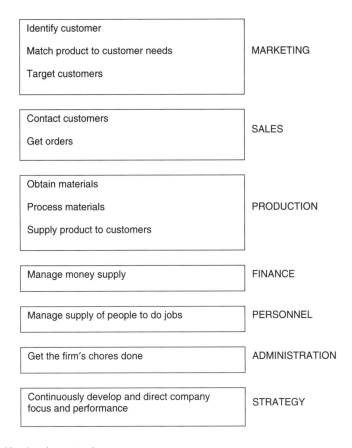

Figure 4.3: Key business tasks.

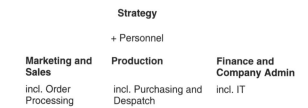

Figure 4.4: Mapping main functional areas.

areas – administration typically is – and this can throw up tricky decisions as to where certain tasks are controlled. Salesforce support, order processing, despatch, IT coordination, company secretarial responsibilities – these are all administrative functions that can be located within other main areas.

Bearing in mind the particular strategic competences that your firm needs to be set to deliver, you will need to work out how tasks can best be grouped in your own organization and what the main *functional areas* are to be. You might map them out something like Figure 4.4.

Your map thus begins to indicate what roles will need to be specified. It also starts to show where one type of work needs to tie up with another, requiring particular attention to integrating processes and systems.

Step two is *defining roles to deliver competences*. We now need to move from the overall scheme of things to specifics. A job specification for each type of role within the structure will have to be outlined. Before this can be done, some important questions have to be posed about the work in each functional area:

- How do tasks most appropriately group together into *roles for individual job holders?*
- What *technology* is to be used?
- What *results* have to be achieved in each area for the company's strategic competences to be enacted?
- What *standards of performance* have to be met?

Answering these questions will help indicate the answers to the next set:

- What *levels of expertise*, responsibility and authority are required?
- *How many job holders* will be needed to get the work done?

Now, consider how roles will interrelate:

- What interaction is needed within areas and between areas?
- Will the location of functions or the layout of premises have an effect?
- Which roles carry external relationships?

When the scheme of individual roles and the relationships between them is clear, a *job specification* can be produced for each type of job. The job specification sets out the purpose, objectives and performance standards for each role. It is a key tool for channelling individual purpose and performance into the company as a whole. (A detailed example is given in Box 4.2.)

The form of the organization

What form of organization provides the best map of the way the roles in the organization fit together and indicates the basis for coordinating the flow of work? Your organization chart need not be tidy, as long as it is clear and representative of what actually needs to happen. There are several basic models of organization, ranging from a hierarchy with clearly demarcated departments to much looser forms where staff are brought together into temporary project groups including contract or freelance elements. You need to decide which model best suits your organization, the work to be done and the kind of people who will be working in it.

Most people, when they think of organization charts, think first of all of a traditional hierarchy. In this model, functions and levels are clearly defined and separated. People get their instructions from the person above them. This can be very efficient if the firm's business is routine and predictable. But – and it is a big but – all decision making and communication between functional areas happens at the top, so messages and questions have to be referred up the line and instructions passed down the line, with obvious disadvantages for speed and flexibility of response.

It is more likely that one of the other organizational models shown in Figure 4.5 will be suitable for the modern small to medium-sized firm.

People

It is people who provide the energy and spark that give a company its edge. And people are individuals, so when we build up an organization by bringing in more people to get more work done, there is an opportunity to increase the organization's strength and capability, as new individuals add to the range and depth of skills and outlooks available. That said, we are not going to want to hire just anybody. How do you get the right people? It is often difficult for a small firm to attract high flyers. Therefore the firm needs to find the best people it can to do the work it needs, and then cultivate the art of getting the best performance possible from the people available to it.

Having clarified roles and structure, we now need to ensure that the people in place are able and willing to carry out their jobs as specified. One way to do this is by defining the ideal characteristics of the person required for each job.

Starting with the question of ability, how should the person in each particular job contribute to the enactment of the company's strategy? What are the competences that they need to put into practice to play their part? This comes down to identifying key components of *knowledge* and *skill*.

By *knowledge* we mean the mental framework that provides the basis of someone's expertise. Even simple jobs require knowledge, and if we try to perform them without the appropriate knowledge we can go badly wrong. A cleaner needs to know what materials to use on what surfaces, how the equipment works, how to tackle different types of soiling. An administrative assistant must know how to operate the PC and work with the software that goes with the job; he or she is likely to perform more valuably with knowledge of how to develop a filing system or set

Box 4.2 Example: Job specification

Name: Jean Jones

Job context
Title: Account manager   Reports to: Client Services manager
Department: Client Services, London

Central purpose of the job
To manage and develop existing company clients in a manner that meets the current and future needs of these clients, according to an agreed account plan for each client.

Main job objectives
1 To produce and implement an effective plan for each client
2 To meet client sales and contribution targets agreed from time to time
3 To develop effective and efficient client working relationships, including keeping clients informed of company activities
4 To contribute effectively and efficiently to company and team meetings and other internal communications
5 To maintain and enhance personal effectiveness through training and development

Main tasks	Performance standards
1 Produce a client account plan and agree it with manager	Comprehensiveness, relevance, timeliness, accuracy
2 Adjust plan as client needs change	Accuracy, currency
3 Plan client visits rota	Realism, efficient use of time
4 Monitor client sales and contribution by product (actual against plan)	Accuracy, currency, comprehensiveness, meeting budget
5 Set up cross-selling opportunities for sales/take orders (where appropriate)	Speed, accuracy, excellent client feedback
6 Establish a close working relationship with each client	Company-agreed style, excellent client feedback, satisfactory peer feedback
7 Visit/telephone clients on agreed rota	Company-agreed style, excellent client feedback, appropriate frequency
8 Resolve client problems and deal with complaints	Excellent client feedback, satisfactory problem resolution, speed of response
9 Inform client about new and existing products and relevant activities	Comprehensiveness, currency, excellent client feedback
10 Complete client contact reports weekly	Comprehensiveness, accuracy
11 Gather client feedback and information and add to account plan/database	Comprehensiveness, accuracy, currency
12 Pass on product development leads to appropriate department in company	Quality, timeliness, relevance of leads, new sales won

13	Prepare for weekly/monthly individual and team meetings with manager	Clear, specific information, constructive recommendations
14	Meet with manager weekly/monthly	Quality of contributions, positive feedback from manager and peers
15	Identify own training needs and arrange training with manager	Positive peer feedback, improved job performance

Responsibilities and relationships

Staff reporting to job: None
Other resources responsible for: None
Budget responsibility: None

Key internal relationships

Client services manager, product sales managers, helpdesk, account coordinators, junior account executives

External relationships

Clients

Terms of employment

Annual appraisal and salary review with client services manager
Other terms as Employee Handbook

up a bring-forward system. For every position, we can define what type and level of knowledge the job holder must have, as well as that which is desirable (industry knowledge, technical or professional knowledge, languages, practices, whether a recognized qualification is necessary).

Skill is the heading under which we look at what people need to be able to do effectively. This goes beyond theoretical knowledge and is about practice. The administrative assistant may be required to prepare many documents for presentation to clients, and will need keyboard skills (able to type fast and accurately) and maybe layout skills (able to arrange titles and text clearly and consistently so as to convey meaning and enhance readability). All administrative assistants need the skills of clear oral communication and managing competing priorities and scheduling workload. In specifying skills, we need to consider not only technical and task skills, but also personal and interpersonal skills. For all skills that are central to competence in the job, we need to specify the *level of skill* required to perform the job to standard.

In looking at the abilities needed to do the job, we have so far considered only part of the job holder. Just as important as what they know and are able to do is the issue of how they approach the job, which is influenced by personality factors. It is seldom appropriate to try to classify the personality type needed for the job, but what we can do is identify those *personal qualities* that will help a person fit into their role and into the organization so as perform in a way that chimes with the firm's distinctiveness.

1   **Traditional hierarchy**
    Clear separation between functions, with coordination between functions coming from
    the top. Can be highly reliable in action, but inflexible.

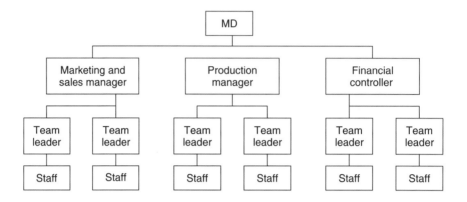

2   **Hierarchy with liaison groups and project teams**
    The clear separation of functions and reporting lines is retained, but mechanisms are
    brought in to provide coordination between functions at lower as well as senior levels.
    Standing liaison groups are maintained for coordination of routine activities between
    functional areas. Cross-functional teams can be brought together temporarily for special
    projects.

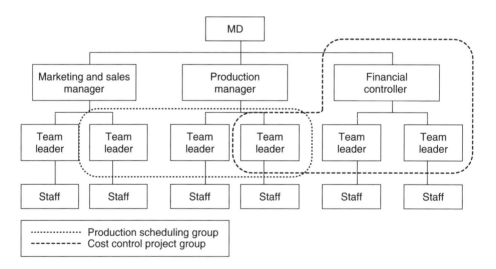

Figure 4.5: Forms of organization.

3 Matrix organization

Functions are organized along two axes. One axis is market facing, the other consists of functions provided across the whole company. On the market axis, staff are organized in groups focused on a specific area of operation (e.g. a specific market sector). Staff on the whole-company axis are grouped by function. Out of this formation, cross-functional working at all levels can take place, so that operational and company-wide perspectives can be balanced without the need for constant senior-level intervention.

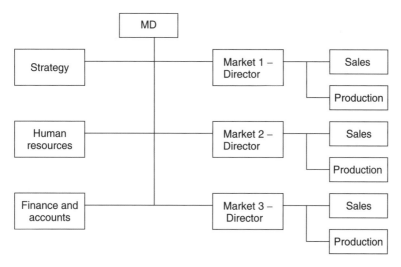

4 Project team organization

All operations are handled through project teams, with staff being deployed according to suitability and availability. The organization will need some kind of establishment staff to provide basic financial and administrative functions. This very loose type of structure is common in design and consultancy-based businesses, where a high proportion of operating personnel may be freelance.

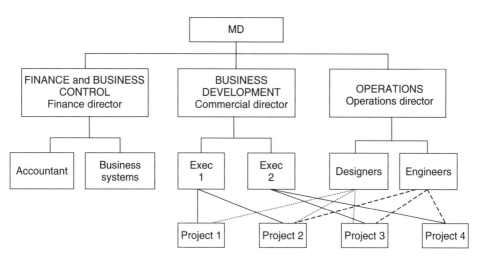

Figure 4.5: (*continued*)

Personal qualities differ from knowledge and skills in that the latter can be learnt, whereas personal qualities are more innate. That said, a person's array of personal qualities can develop over time and can be evoked by changed circumstances or a deliberate act of will. We can see people overcome lack of confidence as they grow in experience, for instance, or behave in a less arrogant fashion after being cautioned about the effect they've been having. It is often by acquiring new knowledge and skill that people are enabled to extend and control the personal qualities they bring to their work.

However, there is no guarantee that such development will happen. We need to be clear about the qualities that will make a difference to how they do the job (no point in putting someone in a customer-facing position if they don't enjoy working with people). So we need to consider issues such as aptitude, attitude, interests and values, as well as a person's manner and way of conducting themselves.

By building up a *person specification* of the knowledge, skills and personal qualities required, we can determine the *calibre* of person for each type of job. This will be linked to *market value*, and will have implications for the *pay expectations* of the job holder.

Will each person perform in the manner envisaged? This raises the issue of the *motivation profile* of the job holder: what are likely to be the factors that motivate the person in this job in this firm? (This is a big subject and is dealt with more fully in Chapter 5.) It is important that person specifications are realistic – there needs to be compatibility between the individual's goals and what the firm can offer.

Processes and systems

The role structure of an organization provides a foundation for making the right things happen – rather like a skeleton – and the people matched to the roles bring it to life. But it is the organization's operating processes and systems that form the parts into a whole and harness the energy and expertise assembled in its different functions to a coherent purpose. However carefully designed, an organization's structure will usually have its faults – the parts that don't join up properly, the roles with bits tacked on that don't really fit but have to be covered by somebody. And the fit between people and roles will be less than perfect – the firm has to run with the people available. It is by attending to operating processes and systems that we can make a creaky set of components run smoothly.

When the organization needs to adapt – as part of a strategic initiative, or to respond to market or technological change – it is often possible to adjust the organization's processes without changing its structure or people. And problems that appear to stem from shortcomings in people are usually best solved by supporting those people with effective working systems, rather than chucking them out and starting again with other people, who will also have shortcomings.

Organizational processes bring parts of the organization together and coordinate thinking and activity. They include:

- *Workflow.* The routing of work through the organization brings different functional areas into contact at certain points.

- *Communication channels.* The pattern of who speaks or writes to whom. It is important to keep up to date and ensure that channels are clear, that the necessary communication is done and that the unnecessary is eliminated.
- *Group and team processes.* The various ways in which people are brought together to coordinate information and work contributions, order priorities, reach decisions: *meetings, project teams, steering committees,* etc. Such processes are used to bring together people at different levels (vertical linkage) – as in a regular departmental staff meeting – and/or people from different functional areas (lateral linkage). It is important to ensure that these processes are kept relevant, that the right people are involved and that the content matches the purpose.
- *Leadership and motivation.* The conscious process by which the person in charge of a team, project or department gives a framework for getting people to perform in line with goals and purpose.
- *Recruitment.* A systematic process for finding people who best fit the organization's needs.
- *Training and development.* Processes for improving the match between an individual's knowledge and skills and the requirements of a role, and for enabling the individual to contribute more effectively.

Systems are put in place to underpin efficiency: they give direction and control – follow the system and it will help you do the right things in the right way. Having effective systems in place means that people have guidance on how to deal with standard situations and do not waste energy and talent reinventing the wheel. Systems complement the more intangible organizational processes described above. They include:

- *Policies* – written statements that clarify the company's approach to handling specific issues.
- *Procedures* – the standard practices to be followed in executing a task.
- *Standards* – including both the defined standards of work that an individual job holder needs to achieve, and the company's quality and ethical standards.
- *Information system* – those communications, reports and analyses that it is useful to circulate regularly to provide people with the information they need to do their jobs.
- *Appraisal system* – complements the processes of motivation and development; enables each individual to align their work contribution with the goals of the organization as a whole.
- *Pay structure* – a scheme for planning pay levels throughout the organization, taking account of internal and external comparisons.

It is important to be aware that some organizational processes and systems will emerge whether they are consciously planned or not – people develop habits and patterns, and these become standard practice. Conscious development of effective processes and efficient systems is needed to ensure that the practices followed are *best* practices.

Specifying jobs and the people to fill them

The organization's job specifications are a statement of how the company's work is divided between people and the part that each job contributes to achieving the company's purpose. It also documents for the job holder what the company's expectations are of their role.

It is worth taking note of a subtle difference between the terms 'role' and 'job'. A role belongs to the organization: it is part of the overall scheme of things and cannot be detached from it. (A role in a play becomes meaningless if it is separated from the text as a whole.) A job, however, has a job holder. There is a sense in which a job belongs to the person who does it, and people usually treat their job as part of their identity (how often do we ask people socially what their job is, to help us know who we are talking to?).

Giving somebody a job is giving them a role in the firm, a chance to contribute to joint achievement. Their job specification sets out a purpose – it is not merely a set of tasks to be carried out. The more clearly a job holder understands the purpose of their role, the better the chance is that they will tackle it effectively.

Will defining jobs lead to demarcation disputes and encourage people to dig in their heels when something is 'not my job'? This idea arises from the misconception that a list of 'tasks' or 'duties' is all that a job specification consists of. It is impractical to try to spell out in detail every action that a job entails. Essentially, every job holder is there to achieve certain results and they carry out tasks to secure those results. So we need to specify jobs in terms of the results required. That means stating the overall *purpose* of the job; the *main objectives* at which the job holder is aiming; and the *standards* of performance expected (see Box 4.2).

Having specified jobs, it makes sense to specify the attributes that the person doing the job needs to have. Effectively, when you draw up a person specification, you are designing the ideal job holder to fit the role, and setting down a series of criteria for knowledge, skill and personal qualities against which real people can be assessed for suitability.

The person specification is necessary for recruiting, but it has a more general application as an important tool for ensuring that the company does not have square pegs in round holes (Box 4.3).

Box 4.3 Person specification

Title: Sales manager   **Reports to:** MD
Dept: Process/Manufacturing   **Based at:** Welwyn Garden City

Knowledge

Sales and market information handling – gathering, analysing, reporting
Surveying and planning approach to new market
Planning and scheduling sales activities
Budgeting, forecasting, account planning, target setting
Structuring work of sales team
Developing and maintaining sales information procedures
Developing sales leads

Literacy
Basic computer skills including e-mail

Skills

Ability to initiate new projects
Team skills – set up new team; manage and motivate – briefing, feedback on
performance, coaching
Leadership
Establish and nurture customer relationships; excellent service
Selling (face-to-face and phone); cold calling
Clear and relevant oral communication, internally and externally
Effective written communication
Ability to understand product and discuss technical issues credibly
Driver

Personal qualities

Solutions-oriented, overcomes problems
Takes responsibility, sees the job through
Responds to challenge
Cooperative attitude to colleagues – team player, flexible
Productive, effective user of time, systematic approach
Initiates ideas
Listener
Willing to travel and spend time away from home
Presentable appearance
Personable manner, not arrogant
Sense of humour; able to thrive in small-company situation
Willing to do own chores

Education/qualifications

Minimum – GCSEs (incl. English, Maths)
Ideal – 2 A-levels

Experience

Consistent employment record
Selling; opening new accounts
Managing people (not necessarily as sales manager)
Budgeting, forecasting, planning
Successful selling in more than one product field

Career expectations

Willing to accept the career path characteristic of a small but growing company, and to
create own development opportunities.

Other influences on organization

Work organizations do not exist in a vacuum and can never be subject to watertight
control. One reason for this is the individuality of the people who form the

organization, each of whom brings with them their own behavioural habits, attitudes, beliefs and values. A second reason is that the organization exists in and interacts with a varied environment – customers, suppliers, the backgrounds of the organization's people, the economy, legislation, political and social factors all impinge on it.

This combination of internal and external factors will influence the organization's culture and have an effect on interpersonal relations. We can think of organizational culture as 'the way things are done around here' – that set of shared assumptions that accumulates when people come together in groups. Managements can have some influence on an organization's culture, but they cannot govern it. What is important is to be aware of it and to take account of how plans to develop the organization may be affected by – and affect – its culture. (These issues are explored more fully in Chapter 7.)

Organizational diagnosis: How to overhaul your organization

Organizational diagnosis is the process of examining the components of an organization and the interrelationship between them. It is a necessary first step to redesigning an organization when change is necessary, for solving problems of dysfunction or seeking improvements. A diagnostic check is also worthwhile to understand how a particular organization works, and *why* it works, and thus to be able to ensure that what is effective is properly maintained.

A diagnostic check seeks to establish the following in relation to the chosen strategy:

- Does the organization work effectively and efficiently at present? (Are company goals achieved? How does performance stand up against that of relevant competition or comparable companies?)
- In what areas is it effective/efficient and in what areas less so? Why? How can effectiveness/efficiency or ineffectiveness/inefficiency be traced to causes in the components of the organization?
- What are the factors underlying ineffectiveness/inefficiency and how can they be remedied?
- What are the factors underlying effectiveness/efficiency and how can they be preserved?

A useful diagnostic procedure is to draw a diagram of the existing organizational structure, laid out to show the functional areas into which the company's people are grouped. Now indicate how the workflow is routed through this structure. Can you identify any pressure points, either occurring already or with the potential to develop?

What are the options for making adjustments to relieve any problems occurring or anticipated? Can problems be resolved through processes or systems, or is change necessary at the level of structure or people? Which of these options would most successfully preserve the positive factors in the organization's functioning and eliminate or neutralize negative factors, as well as ensuring that the organization is aligned to deliver its strategy?

An example of organizational diagnosis is provided in the case study (Box 4.4). Using the checklist provided in Box 4.1, a careful diagnosis of the organization reveals some of the following problems and issues (asking the key questions: What is working well? What is not working well? Where are the bottlenecks? and so on):

- *Structure* – slow decision making, no effective marketing function (including market intelligence), overlap between marketing and sales, roles not clear, some functions more productive than others, lack of effective delegation, structure not aligned with strategy, etc.
- *People* – reactive, autocratic leadership style, interfering managing director, knee-jerk reaction to problems (no analysis), lack of skills to delegate, abdication of responsibility, lack skills in managing difficult situations, etc.
- *Processes* – no meetings, poor information handling, no planning, no skill development, no training to meet changing strategy, no teamworking across functions, lack of interpersonal skills, lack of clear leadership, etc.
- *Systems* – no written procedures, poor information systems (cost overruns), lack of clear policies, etc.

In spite of some real strengths in meeting customer needs in the past, Manufacturing Systems Designers appears to have lost direction (see Chapter 2 for a detailed discussion of strategy) and the organization has also failed to keep abreast of market changes. What has to happen in each of these four areas should follow readily from a comprehensive diagnosis and analysis of the company's problems, digging beneath the surface to discover the root causes. For example, the process could start by drawing an organization chart and diagnosing in which function things have gone wrong before devising a plan to correct them (Figure 4.6).

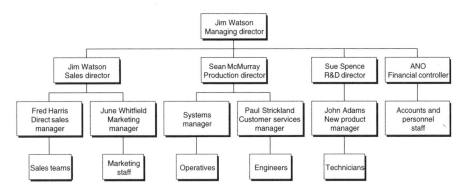

Figure 4.6: Manufacturing Systems Designers organization chart.

Box 4.4 Case study: Manufacturing Systems Designers Ltd

Manufacturing Systems Designers built computer-controlled machinery for the food-processing industry. Prices for its bespoke systems ranged from £180 000 to £500 000. The company's market dominance derived from machinery that produced consistently high-quality food products. Behind this was a policy of working closely with customers by having development engineers on site to solve production problems quickly, thus keeping machine downtime to a minimum.

In the 1990s, competition became intense. Orders were lost on price and speed of delivery. In response, the company cut development time on bespoke contracts while introducing a new 'off-the-shelf' product for quick and easy installation on existing machinery. It was thought that this would maintain at least six months' lead over competitors.

The organization

Jim Watson had been a salesman before rising through the ranks to become sales director. He led a management buy-out in the early 1990s and duly became MD. His management style was thought to be 'autocratic' and people responded by keeping a low profile and leaving most decisions to him.

The management team consisted of Sean McMurray (production), Fred Harris (direct sales), Paul Strickland (customer services), Sue Spence (R&D) and June Whitfield (marketing). A financial controller who had worked with Jim Watson for 15 years ran the accounts and personnel functions.

Jim Watson continued to look after sales and marketing, but marketing took a back seat to sales and tended to consist of periodic reactive bursts of activity when sales needed boosting. There was little effective planning and Jim never arranged meetings ('time wasting', he said) to discuss marketing. The marketing team was often diverted to helping with sales.

Sean McMurray was an engineer with long service in the industry. As long as his team did their jobs well, he let them get on with it. He often walked around the shop floor offering helpful advice and he always supported his managers when they needed him. He knew most people by their first names and was respected by all. Productivity was generally high, with low absenteeism.

Company procedures were informal ('What's the point of writing them down when they work well anyway?' remarked Jim). There were no regular meetings to discuss operational matters, although the production team met together at the local pub once a month.

New products

R&D was critical to the company's continued growth, but mistakes had started to creep into design and development work, with several contracts experiencing overruns and delivery delays. The new 'off-the-shelf' product required lengthy testing, but time was running out as competitors started to launch their own new products. Sales people complained of delays in getting access to the new product and having to disappoint existing customers.

Sue Spence had been spending more and more time 'fire-fighting' and the cost implications were overlooked because there was no system for recording time and allocating costs on product development work.

> **The crisis**
>
> Sales of the new product, introduced to reduce dependence on bespoke systems, were suspended in February when several dealers complained about serious difficulties with programming software.
>
> This was compounded by dismissals of key staff. A new R&D team under John Adams had been set up to work on the new product. John was promoted from the ranks and was given responsibility for achieving a tight launch deadline. As a result of allegedly being drunk at work, two programmers were sacked by Jim Watson without a hearing. Sue Spence was blamed for lack of discipline and John Adams was singled out for censure. Morale in R&D declined rapidly, which soon spread to the rest of the company.

An action plan to deal with problems diagnosed might, for example, cover some of the following areas.

1 Strategy

- Review options and draw up strategic plan (see Chapters 2 and 10).
- Specify the kind of organization needed to deliver the strategy (distinctive and core competences, see Chapter 10).

2 Structure

- Should it be more flexible, delegated (decisions made where they matter)?
- Clarify purpose of all functions and roles.
- Consider new functions, e.g. channel marketing, personnel, new product development department to deal with packaged product.
- Review R&D function.
- Separate marketing and sales functions.

3 People

- Review all roles.
- Review job and person specifications (what skills, knowledge and qualities are needed?).
- Clarify practices for managing people.
- Appoint new sales director.

4 Processes

- Improve information flow through meetings.
- Improve teamworking and interdepartmental working.
- Produce development and training plan.
- Leadership – create and communicate vision, deal with low morale.

5   Systems

- Review management information systems.
- Introduce time keeping and costings.
- Agree and write up procedures.

Further reading

1   Hunt, J. (1992) *Managing People at Work*, McGraw-Hill, Maidenhead.
2   Handy, C. (1993) *Understanding Organizations*, Penguin Business, Harmonds-worth.
3   Morgan, G. (1989) *Images of Organization*, Sage, London.

Getting Performance from People

CHAPTER 5

Key issues dealt with in this chapter are:

- The fundamentals of managing people at work: attention to task and attention to people processes.
- How attention to people processes can improve productivity.
- Understanding motivation: how to work with the factors that lead people to give of their best and avoid demotivation.
- A framework for managing performance: briefing, monitoring, review and feedback.

In Chapter 4 we looked at organizing work in an abstract manner. Designing the organization requires us to stand back from involvement with current pre-occupations and personalities, to come up with the right blueprint to underpin operations. However carefully designed the organization, though, it is the actions and attitudes of its people that decide whether it is effective and successful. People bring the organization to life: they provide the spark, the electricity that drives performance.

Chapters 5, 6 and 7 are concerned with the practicalities of running the organization. They examine the underlying frameworks of knowledge that enable us to recognize issues and diagnose problems with accuracy and insight, and the skills we can develop to enable us to work with people effectively and with enjoyment.

Attention to task and to people processes

A fundamental principle underlies getting an organization – or a team, or an individual – to deliver results: the need to balance attention to the *task* (getting the job done) with attention to *people processes* (how people go about things and what happens between them).

Some of us by nature are *task oriented*. Such people focus on what needs to be done and direct their energy to moving the work forward, tending to ignore or override concerns with people and expect that staff and colleagues will remain positive and get on with what needs to be done. It is important to keep one's eye on the ball and keep things going.

Others may be more concerned with a range of much less clear considerations that have to do with how the *people* of the organization set about things: the extent of their involvement, how they interact, how their contributions and their experience can be improved. Someone who is *process oriented* notices people issues and sees them as important. Writers on organization refer to this set of concerns in various ways: 'maintenance orientation', 'concern for relationships', 'consideration for people' and so on. We will use the term *people processes* when referring to this set of concerns.

For an organization to function effectively, its management needs to pay attention to both the task dimension and the people processes dimension. Think for a moment about running a transport firm. The task dimension calls for vehicles to pick up and deliver loads according to a schedule, maximizing productivity per vehicle. However, if the firm focuses solely on what it does, things will go wrong eventually. How is the firm to continue in business over the long term? Vehicles need to be maintained – which necessitates taking them off the road – and so do the people who drive them. Are the expectations of the drivers realistic and appropriate: are routes and schedules understood and accepted? Could improvements be made? Where changes are planned, will people adapt to them? And so on.

A basic definition of management is 'getting things done through people'. That requires working with both the task and the people processes dimensions. Regardless of personal orientation or preference, a professional manager has to learn to work with both and balance them appropriately.

People and productivity

Even within a well-designed organization, what happens at a human level makes a difference to effectiveness and efficiency, because of the ways in which human factors affect productivity. How often have you observed two people carrying out the same job where one, with a combination of enthusiasm, energy and orderliness, is shifting far more work than the other – and probably creating harmonious customer and colleague relationships at the same time? Why is the other one less productive? Two possible explanations are that the unproductive person has inefficient work habits (what is commonly known as a bad time manager); or that he or she is less positively motivated than the productive worker.

There is a circular relationship between how people experience their work and what they put in to it. If, for whatever reason, someone is not making much headway with their work – not doing it well, not getting results – they are likely, all else remaining equal, to slip into a downward spiral of reducing energy and effort, doing the minimum that can be got away with. The internal logic goes, 'I'm not cut out for this, it's a stupid job, but at least I'm not demeaning myself by putting more into it than it's worth.' Whereas someone whose experience is positive – they are getting things done or enjoying the situation – becomes energized to continue to make the most of what they are doing, and to continue to get results, setting up a 'virtuous circle'.

Personal resources and self-management

The concept of self-management is crucial to getting performance from people. People who come to work are grown-ups who are responsible for themselves; each of us is ultimately in charge of what we put into our work. However, the firm and its management act as catalysts to a person's experience of work and the performance that person turns in.

Before we can expect to manage other people, we need to be able to manage ourselves and our workload. Apart from anything else, it is difficult to command the respect of others if one is seen to be ineffectual.

Each individual brings to work their own set of *personal resources* that constitute their potential for doing their job, contributing to the firm's successful development and developing their own capabilities and position further. These include:

- *Knowledge*.
- *Skills* – both technical skills (task skills) and interpersonal skills.
- *Aptitudes*.
- *Mental processes* of various kinds – thinking reflectively, analysing, calculating, inventing, problem solving. The effectiveness of someone's mental processes in their job is affected by how appropriately they use their mind (different functions call for differing levels of agility, speed, reliability or creativity), and by their level of concentration.
- *Energy* – the amount of energy available is affected by physical fitness and freshness, and importantly by the way in which it is focused.

The way in which these basic resources are applied will be affected by two further, modifying resources:

- *Self-awareness* – affecting people's ability to marshal their own resources.
- *Motivation* – affecting people's willingness to put in energy and apply their resources.

Promoting each individual's ability to make the most of their personal resources, use intelligent work practices and interact effectively with colleagues is fundamental to making the organization work.

Managing priorities and getting things done

The ability to manage workload hinges on the ability to focus on what is important. The clearer a person's understanding of their central purpose and how their role contributes to the furthering of the company's goals, the more effectively they can identify priorities and allocate their time. A useful exercise is to run through this sequence of questions:

- What are you trying to achieve? What is your central purpose at work, what other goals do you have professionally, what else is important to you?
- What standards are good enough?
- What action is relevant to achieve goals and standards?
- In light of the above, how should you be allocating your time, and how are you actually spending your time?

Priorities should be determined by two factors: what is *urgent* and what is *important*. Too often we are driven only by what is treated as urgent; or when someone with a pile of work asks what has priority, they are told that everything does. That merely creates muddle.

Urgent matters are those with an imminent deadline attached to them, things that have to be done now or within a specified short time frame. An important discipline is to specify the time at which things are needed – 'a.s.a.p.' or 'urgently' mean nothing and only create hassle. When we ask the actual time at which something is needed or enquire what it is needed for, we may discover that it is less urgent than other things on the schedule.

Important matters are those that are central to the person's achievement of their purpose and standards of work, and that affect the quality of what they do. Aspects in the important category are often those that make a difference over the long term, such as planning and devising better systems rather than just tackling each task *ad hoc*. One of the ways in which people can get overloaded is by being led to give importance to something that is central to another person's role, but not to their own.

To sort priorities, go through your list of things that ought to be done and rate each item high or low for both urgency and importance. You can position each item in a matrix diagram like the one shown in Figure 5.1. The example given here indicates the type of tasks that are likely to show up in each box of the matrix.

The number in each box indicates the level of priority that ought to be given to the contents. Clearly, anything in box 1 has to be dealt with. But after that, which box do you tend to go to? How much time do you spend in box 2? Many people find that they are drawn instead to box 3, because someone else is applying pressure to deal with these matters.

Not allocating enough time to box 2 concerns – matters that are important, but do not have to be dealt with this minute – is often the reason for items ending up in the urgent categories. Not putting time and thought into training staff who can be delegated to, so that staff are continually raising queries; neglecting to file figures or make out reports before someone else is desperate for them; setting an unrealistic time frame for a project because the plan has not been thought through – habits like this lead to endless fire-fighting. Box 2 is about thinking, planning, developing – about working efficiently, learning from experience and finding ways to do things better. Setting aside time for box 2 – which contains the real concerns of management – enables you to stand back and take control, reducing muddle and making a substantial difference to effectiveness.

IMPORTANCE

	High	*Low*
High	Deadlines Crises Demands of powerful people **ACT** 1	Other people's priorities Neglected routine **DELEGATE OR RESCHEDULE** 3
URGENCY	2	4
Low	Planning Goal setting Systems Training and development Thinking **ATTEND TO**	Habits Trivia Distractions **CONTROL**

Figure 5.1: Establishing priorities.

Understanding motivation

An important function of a manager or team leader in managing the performance of their staff is to enhance motivation. To help understand motivation, we can observe the people we work with and what makes each 'tick'; and we can explore our own responses (you can try doing this in a structured way by working through the exercise in Box 5.3 later). That can help us appreciate just how powerful the pull of motivational factors can be, but it will give a partial view – nobody is typical. To fill out the picture, we can learn from psychologists and researchers. Their work yields a set of principles that provide a framework for managing people with more awareness, giving us a surer chance of evoking the positive and working with, rather than against, the grain of each person's motivation.

We will look first at some of the classic theories, before pulling together the common principles that emerge from them.

One way of understanding motivation is as a drive to satisfy deeply felt needs. Many of us have felt at some time a compulsion to move our life in a particular direction and have seen others similarly impelled: finding a job with more money, moving to the country or getting a job with more decision power and the ability to influence plans and policy.

Abraham Maslow is most famously associated with need theories of motivation.[1] His ideas on a *hierarchy of needs* were formulated in the mid-twentieth century and have remained popular as they make intuitive sense and bear out what we are able to observe ourselves.

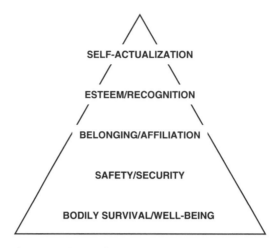

Source: The Maslow Pyramid, 'Maslow on Management',
John Wiley & Sons Ltd. (1998)

Figure 5.2: Maslow's hierarchy of needs.

According to this view, people's efforts are guided by whatever needs they most strongly experience in their lives. If one set of needs becomes satisfied, another order of needs arises that then takes over in influencing behaviour. Maslow identified a series of need categories, which he saw as being arranged in an ascending 'hierarchy' (Figure 5.2).

At the bottom of the hierarchy Maslow places three categories of 'basic' human needs: for keeping our body alive and functioning, for safety, and for belonging, including interpersonal relationships and a place in society. If any of these is not well established or is endangered, the person will be preoccupied with it until the felt need is assuaged.

When these needs are satisfied, people become concerned with the 'higher-order' needs that lead to the development and extension of human potential – the need for esteem (recognition, status, power); and then self-actualization – becoming and living as we are truly able to be. In his later work, Maslow dwelt particularly on higher-order needs and on the development of human potential, suggesting that the pursuit of self-actualization can be presaged by a thirst for knowledge and learning, as well as being linked to aesthetic needs (a striving for beauty and order).

Maslow's thought has contributed to our modern awareness that motivation can change as life proceeds through different stages, and that personal development is lifelong rather than confined to adolescence and youth. Working life can be a major source of learning and growth, both mentally and in terms of our stature as people, and the opportunity for growth can be a powerful motivator.

Whether everyone proceeds through the hierarchy in the order illustrated is questionable. Some people seem to (see the example in Box 5.1), but it does not always work out like that. Maslow himself suggests that there are some people who respond primarily to higher-order needs despite unmet lower-order ones.

The categories themselves are useful. They set out an array of factors that influence what people seek in their lives and work. Different people will be differently influenced. We need to understand what factors are important for each individual we manage and to be ready to see those motivators change with the circumstances of people's lives.

Box 5.1 Applying Maslow's needs theory

We can get a sense of the applicability of Maslow's ideas by tracking somebody through the unfolding stages of his working life.

In his first job, the imperative is to get paid enough to live on, so he's not too fussy about job prospects and takes a series of short-term selling jobs; *survival* needs predominate. Social life is important, so getting away from work is more important than getting on.

Becoming somewhat better established, our person forms a significant *affiliation*. Wanting to set up house with a partner, his *security* needs are activated by the demands of a mortgage, and he has to settle into a permanent job.

Shared income and a stable relationship mean that basic needs are satisfied for the moment, but inner needs are not. Our hero wants to win *esteem and recognition* and seeks to get on at work. His employers encourage him to move into management. This and a move into marketing call for him to invest in *learning*. His employers see him as strongly committed to developing his career with the firm and expect him to take a directorship.

Suddenly, our hero announces that he wants to abandon management and return to selling. With young children and a partner not earning, there is a *resurgence of basic needs* – he wants to be able to maximize income and minimize work commitment. He is persuaded to stay and his financial situation stabilizes; but he is approaching middle age and there is something missing. It becomes imperative for him to pursue his own interests and do things his own way – a need for *self-actualization* has surfaced. He leaves employment to set up his own marketing consultancy.

Another needs-based theory was put forward by David McClelland.[2] He identified three basic categories: need for *achievement*, need for *affiliation* with other people and need for *power*. In this view, depending on which need or needs predominate, different people will require different triggers to bring out their best performance. Someone with a high need for achievement but a low need for affiliation or power (a possible profile of a 'techie' who likes to work alone) has a very different motivation profile from the person who combines a high power need with a strong need for affiliation (who might thrive as a member of management in a large corporation). McClelland was interested in the differences between entrepreneurs and corporate managers, and contended that entrepreneurs were distinguished by a predominant need for achievement and a comparatively low need for affiliation or power.

McClelland's work on achievement needs has contributed to our awareness of the value of individual goal setting for motivating people. He studied the mechanics of the human response to challenge. It is possible to evoke the need for achievement by setting somebody a goal that lies just beyond what they know they are capable of. They rise to the challenge, feel good when they meet it, and are likely to respond to a further goal that will again give them the reward of a sense of achievement.

This process leads to an increasing sense of capability and, as long as the goals are seen as significant, is highly motivating.

However, if the goal is set too far beyond what the person is able, or feels able, to achieve, the result will be the opposite. People are demotivated by failure and so will try to avoid it. Once they believe that a goal is unachievable, people are likely to protect themselves against failure by not trying to reach that goal. If we set people up to fail by giving them goals too far beyond their capability, we diminish motivation.

Positive motivation, dissatisfaction and demotivation

The issue of *demotivation* is a reminder that unthinking or inappropriate management action can trigger the reverse of what is required. As well as understanding how to encourage the positive motivation that enhances performance, managers must also understand the mechanics of demotivation. Demotivation undermines performance, causing enthusiasm, effort and energy to diminish; and it is often catching – one disaffected individual can easily infect others.

Demotivation can arise because of a lack of positively motivating factors, but it can also arise out of dissatisfaction with the circumstances of work. Common demotivators or *dissatisfiers* are:

- Inadequate pay or benefits.
- Poor environment.
- Inappropriate supervision or poor management.
- Unsatisfactory social contact – unpleasant work group, isolation, etc.

These are known as *extrinsic factors* – they are external to the person and the work itself. Problems with any of these factors can lead to demotivation and under-performance. Getting these factors right removes the causes of the dissatisfaction that can undermine performance, but does not, of itself, trigger positive motivation. It merely produces satisfactory work conditions. If there has been a problem with extrinsic factors that is then put right, there may then be a brief surge in motivation and effort. However, people rapidly adjust to take the new circumstances for granted and the surge in performance is unlikely to be maintained. More effective attention to motivation is required to encourage people to give of their best on a consistent basis.

It should also be borne in mind that many people will transcend low levels of pay and conditions if they are genuinely motivated by their work.

Factors that commonly lead to performance-enhancing motivation include:

- Taking personal ownership of work goals.
- Opportunities for and experience of achievement.
- Opportunities to grow or learn.
- Responsibility.

- Recognition and praise.
- Practising a skill or craft.
- Deriving satisfaction from the process of doing the work itself.
- Contributing to something significant.

These are called *intrinsic factors*. They are to do with the person and their relationship with the work itself – much more intimate than the dissatisfiers. This list of factors reminds us that people can and do motivate themselves without outside intervention. When managers and leaders seek to motivate staff, their role is that of a coach helping and encouraging people to respond to their potential.

This way of looking at the difference in kind between the factors that can produce dissatisfaction and those that positively motivate is associated with Frederick Herzberg,[3] though a number of other researchers have taken similar approaches. Famously, he referred to the dissatisfiers as 'hygiene factors', in contrast to motivator factors.

The importance of this view lies in reminding us that working with people to enhance their motivation and encourage them to perform in line with their potential is a personal process. We have to appeal to and get responses from people, we cannot expect to get results simply through the mechanics of pay and conditions.

It also enables us to get the matter of pay into perspective. Pay turns out to be a much less important part of motivation than we might expect. That is not to say it is OK to underpay – people expect to be paid the rate for the job and become dissatisfied when they are not. But their pay level is not a primary motivator for most people. Of course they will often be motivated to work hard to gain a promotion that brings higher pay or to achieve a bonus, but notice that there are other motivators operating here in the form of achievement and recognition. And intrinsic factors can be so powerful as to override money considerations as well as other potential dissatisfiers; there are many instances where people work with dedication despite poor pay and environment.

This awareness is important in small and medium-sized businesses, where owner-managers often suspect that they are hampered in attracting and keeping the best employees by their inability to match larger employers' pay and benefits packages. Nevertheless, any owner-manager can offer an intelligent approach to the personal motivation of staff.

The intrinsic motivating factors that have been identified are not all about striving for achievement. Not everybody wants to be a high flyer, but we still need to be able to get performance from all our staff. Putting people in touch with a sense of capability, helping people feel a sense of responsibility to others and for results, and helping people see the value of the contribution that their well-executed work makes to the firm as a whole are motivators that can be evoked at any level in the organization.

How does demotivation work in practice? Most of us have had sufficient experience of the condition to be familiar with it (Box 5.2).

Box 5.2 Example: Effects of demotivation and positive motivation

When asked to describe how they have felt in a situation where they were demotivated, people of junior management level came up with such responses as:

- Stuck
- Bogged down
- Bored
- Thwarted
- Frustrated
- Resentful
- Inert
- Low energy
- Incapable
- Undervalued
- Low self-esteem

This is not a pleasant set of feelings to have circulating in your company. Everything feels like too much effort for the demotivated person. The feelings of incapability can shade into anger and resentment towards those seen as the cause of the trouble, or depressive feelings of low self-esteem. Those feelings can spread to other members of the affected person's work group, leading to a fall off in productivity out of proportion to the original cause of dissatisfaction.

The good news is that positive motivation can be equally infectious. Asked to describe feelings in a situation where they have been positively motivated, the same people's responses included:

- Energized
- Positive
- Capable
- Can do more
- Enjoying work
- Happy
- Moving forward
- Sense of excitement

The exercise in Box 5.3 puts you in touch with the motivational factors that are important to you, helping you join up your own experience with some of the theory. Being aware of your own motivation profile can deepen your insight – but don't assume that others have the same pattern as you.

Getting performance from people

However ingenious the theorists, none has produced a comprehensive or foolproof scheme for motivating people. There remains no substitute for the basic person-centred approach of endeavouring to discover what a person has to offer – their potential; what their pattern of motivational response is likely to be; what factors will lead them to give of their best; and what is likely to get in the way of their doing

Box 5.3 Exercise: Exploring motivation

Step 1: Demotivation

1 Think back to a situation at work in which you have felt demotivated. What was going on?
2 Jot down words to describe *how you felt* in that situation.
3 Now write down what the *factors in the situation* were that led to your being demotivated.

Take a break before going on to the second part of the exercise.

Step 2: Positive motivation

1 Think back this time to a situation at work in which you felt positively motivated to perform.
2 Again, jot down words to describe *how you felt*.
3 Now write down what were the *factors in the situation* leading to your positive motivation.

Step 3: Compare feelings

Now compare your lists. You will probably notice that the feelings around demotivation are to do with inertia, incapability and being stuck or blocked; they may include anger, boredom, lowered self-esteem, depressive feelings.

Positive motivation feelings are likely to feature energy, confidence, a 'can do' feeling, enjoyment, feeling good about yourself.

You can see how motivation influences productivity.

Step 4: Compare factors

Are your two lists simply mirror images of each other, or do some different factors appear? Most people find that their positive motivation list bears out the theories suggesting that intrinsic factors are what motivate people.

so. That process of enquiry can be as important and rewarding for the employee as for their manager.

What we can draw from the theorists is a set of principles to guide us in this endeavour:

- Develop an understanding of the *motivation profile* of each person you manage (this includes yourself).
- Be aware that this profile may change with developments in life and work.
- In your approach to each person, aim to evoke the motivators relevant to that individual.

Whoever you are dealing with, good motivational practice requires the following:

- Ensure that *goals* are clearly understood and that the person can see their relevance – people need a sense of purpose.

- Ensure that *standards* of performance and conduct are clear and that *priorities* are understood – people need to know what is expected of them.
- Let people face a *challenge* that will stretch them – but one that they are capable of attaining.
- Maintain awareness of each person's *potential* – everyone has some, however well hidden.
- Ensure that the person is *equipped to do the job* – that they have appropriate tools and can get necessary training or guidance.
- Encourage a climate of *open communication* – say what you mean, talk to people adult to adult.
- Give people the *space* to get on with the job – don't breathe down their necks.
- Be ready to give help and *support* when appropriate.

Managing performance: A framework for practice

These basic principles bear out what common sense tells us is fundamental to getting people to do their jobs right:

- Ensure that people know what they're aiming for and what they are undertaking.
- Let them get on with it without unnecessary interference.
- Let them know how they are doing; correct and improve where necessary; build on success and give praise.

Whether you are managing yourself or other people, the management of performance calls for you to coordinate people with tasks within a time frame. That coordination will be clearer if you follow (and are seen to follow) this sequence:

- Get the brief straight.
- Monitor action.
- Review outcomes and give feedback.

Each stage of the sequence provides an opportunity to evoke positive motivation, and needs to be handled in a way that avoids unnecessary demotivation.

Briefing and 'contract setting'

One of the most commonly cited causes of demotivation among staff is *moving goal posts*. People believe they know what direction they are going in and what is important, then find that they have wasted time and effort because priorities have changed. While this is sometimes unavoidable – circumstances and priorities do alter – many such problems can be traced to a lack of clarity in briefing.

Briefing is the process of enabling a person or team to get a clear idea of what they are aiming at and what is expected of them, and of setting work in hand so that it can proceed in a viable manner toward the goal. Importantly, it is not merely a matter of 'getting people started', but of getting them started with an end and a set of performance criteria in view. Briefing also embraces 'contract setting': letting people know what they are taking on and what expectations are held of them, and asking them to commit to these.

Getting the brief straight gives you the opportunity to set up a positive motivational dynamic from the beginning, by putting down markers for achievement and recognition. Encouraging people to take ownership of goals and standards of work appeals to a sense of responsibility; by pointing out how a person's goals relate to and support the efforts of others and the achievement of the firm's plans, you can demonstrate to people the contribution that their work can make to the whole.

The *basic content* of a briefing session will need to include:

- *Goals.* What specific outcome is the work to achieve? Try to set SMART goals (see Box 5.4) and ensure that the *time frame* is clear.
- *Criteria for success.* How will success be measured? What standards of work have to be met?
- *Manner and methods.* How should the task be approached? Are there particular requirements in terms of working practices?
- *Resources.* What resources are on offer? Consider equipment, expenditure, support from other people (including yourself).
- *Information.* What information is needed or might be helpful? Include relevant experience from similar situations.

The brief also needs to be set in *context:*

- *Scope.* In order to get a sense of what is expected of them, people need to understand how big or important a project is.
- *Bigger picture.* Where does this job fit in to the whole – for the employing firm and, where relevant, for the client?
- *Priorities.* Make sure that there is understanding of the crucial aspects of the job. If things get behind schedule, what are the really important things that must be attended to?

Briefing can then move towards setting a *plan of action*:

- *Who does what.* What boundaries of responsibility need to be set so that all the work gets covered without double tracking?
- *Degrees of freedom.* How free is the person to work things through in their own way? Where does approval need to be sought?
- *Monitoring.* What checks on progress and performance will there be? How will you be kept informed on how things are going?

This set of criteria for goal setting is designed to enforce clarity on the job holder and the boss, as well as enabling the job holder to stay focused and to take ownership of the goal.

Box 5.4 SMART goals

<u>S</u>pecific	The more precise and less general the aim set, the more focused the job holder is able to be.
<u>M</u>easurable	How can a person know when their performance meets criteria? Setting measurable goals enables people to assess their own performance and take responsibility for meeting goals.
<u>A</u>chievable	This is where we ensure that we do not set people up to fail. Though it may challenge them, the goal has to be appropriate to the person's level of skill and the resources available to them.
<u>R</u>elevant	Why is this goal worth committing to? The person needs to know how it furthers the company's plans. Personal relevance is important too: will achieving the goal enhance their own development?
<u>T</u>ime framed	What's the deadline? Intelligent time framing does more than identify a final due date. It is usually sensible to identify stages of development to be accomplished at certain points, so that progress can be *tracked* along the way.

As well as ensuring that the content of the brief is clear, the briefing process needs to be effective. Briefing is not something that you do to people while they sit passively by. It needs to be a two-way process of involving them in the planning of a piece of work so that there is agreement and clarity as to what needs to be done, when and how. People need to be encouraged to say when things are not clear and to ask questions. It is well-nigh impossible to work out and convey a foolproof set of instructions. People may in any case have useful suggestions to contribute if they are given space to do so.

Inviting participation usually calls for a little more than merely asking 'any questions?'. By all means invite questions, but in order to check whether the brief has been properly understood a more reliable practice is to get people to summarize their understanding of the goals and what they see as the key points (Box 5.5).

Goals, standards and key points of any important brief need to be written down, so that they can be referred to as work proceeds and when reviewing it. The job specification serves as an overall brief for a person's role, but particular projects will need to be noted, either by the manager or team leader or by the job holder.

Briefing is not just a two-way process, however. It usually needs to be a *two-stage* process. We are seldom aware of all the questions that need to be asked when we first receive a brief, because at that point things are theoretical. When we get down to action, we become aware of more questions, and issues taken for granted at first hearing require clarification. These issues should come up during monitoring. In any event, it is important to allow for subsequent questions. When people feel unable to ask what they need to, time gets lost and mistakes get made.

Box 5.5 SMART and unSMART briefing

Reviewing the last sixth months' accounts, Phil noted that increasing overseas business had brought with it an upsurge in travel costs. The company was now a sizeable client for a travel agent. Could it get a better deal on travel terms, he wondered. He picked up the phone to the newly promoted admin coordinator.

'Wendy, I've got a project for you. We're spending three times more on travel now than last year. Can you see what kind of deal we can get from travel agents?'

'What priority?' asked Wendy.

'Well, as soon as you can fit it in.' Phil assumed that she would have ample time to seek offers from local travel agents by the time he got back from his next trip.

A week later, surprised to find no communication from Wendy about travel terms, Phil rang her.

'Oh yes,' said Wendy, 'I rang the travel agent – they don't do discounts on our kind of business.'

Phil was disgruntled. 'Wendy, can't you do better than that?'

Wendy could have done, if only Phil had first spent a few minutes thinking through what was needed before issuing a vague instruction. *He* knew what he expected, but he failed to convey it to Wendy. Had he thought SMART, Wendy would have appreciated the scope and importance of what she had to do and put more effort into it; and Phil would have set a more realistic timeframe.

Specific goal Obtain information that will enable Phil to decide on the best combination of price and service level from local travel agents.

Measurability (what are the criteria for meeting Phil's standard?):

- Identify which local travel agents handle business travel: who are their customers?
- Interview each to find out what initial offer of terms they will offer the firm to meet existing service levels, at three possible levels of turnover
- Compile information into comparison charts
- Indicate most advantageous offer

Achievability (what limits need to be agreed?):

- Your goal is to compile information as a basis for further negotiation and decision. You are not expected to complete the negotiation on your own. We will agree a framework of questions for you to put to each travel agent.

Relevance:

- Your information will provide the basis for negotiation
- Contribute to control of travel budget and setting standard for a supplier
- Learn the basics of negotiating

Time frame and trackability:

- Within 1 week: List of business travel agents and their customers, draft list of questions on travel agents' terms/service, plan agreed with Phil
- 2 weeks: Appointments set with all travel agents
- 3 weeks: Information in and compiled

Monitoring

Once someone has taken on a job, or a role on a project, most regard it as their own. It is in the interests of their manager that they do this; after all, the idea is that they carry out the function, not that the manager does it for them. So once briefed, people need to be left to get on with things. The manager or team leader does, though, have to have an idea of what they are doing while they are doing it.

The purposes of monitoring are:

1 To gain an idea of how people set about things and their areas and levels of competence.
2 To catch problems and difficulties so that they can be put right and the work can be kept on track.

We therefore monitor people as well as monitoring the task. It is while monitoring that we pick up much of the information that we can make use of to develop and motivate people when reviewing performance.

'Management by wandering around' – regularly going to where the work is being done, chatting to people, asking questions, listening and observing – enables managers to stay in touch with what is really going on, and provides a context for other, more formal means of monitoring. It needs to be done in a non-invasive way, because people are notoriously put off when they feel that someone is standing over them or breathing down their neck. Wandering around also shows that a manager is on hand to give support or assistance where needed.

Sometimes a more formal approach to monitoring is needed: prearranged progress meetings, report sheets, systematic spot checks such as the recording of customer service calls (see Box 5.6). Whatever arrangement is used, the job holder needs to know what it is. It is part of the 'contract' between manager and staff as to how the work gets done.

Importantly, when monitoring you are not merely trying to spot what is going wrong; if all you ever notice is slips and mistakes, you will be cast as a nit picker. You are looking to see *what people are doing right*, information that you can use to give feedback that will motivate further positive performance.

It is easy to assume that the brief has been fully understood if a person appears confident. Healthy scepticism and a willingness to ask basic questions are useful attributes in a manager.

Feedback and review

It is through giving effective feedback to people that we complete the cycle of motivational performance management. Information on where we are meeting expectations and where not, and how our performance is perceived by others, is something on which we can all thrive. Feedback helps staff match what they do to what is needed and so achieve their goals. Not only this, it helps people develop and grow by building on strengths and correcting weaknesses.

Box 5.6 What was understood from the brief? The importance of monitoring

A young man newly recruited to an administrative job was given the task of inputting data into a spreadsheet and summarizing it monthly in a management report, with accompanying diagrams and graphs. He was given training and was expected to become productive within a month.

During the month, his manager asked him regularly how he was getting on with data inputting and learning the spreadsheet functions. He was always positive about his progress and seemed to be in no trouble at all.

At the end of the month, his work was reviewed. Nearly everything was wrong about it. The tables were so badly laid out as to be unreadable and the graphs and diagrams were poorly presented.

The problem was that his manager had failed to ask the right questions – and because the young man sat with his screen facing the wall, it was difficult to catch sight of what was on it casually. So a month was wasted.

What needed to happen was something like this:

Manager: 'How are you getting on with the spreadsheets?'
Employee: 'Fine, it's going really well, thanks.'
Manager: 'That's good. May I see where you've got to?'
Employee: 'Oh, well, I haven't got anything ready to show right now.'
Manager begins to smell a rat.
Manager: 'That's OK, it needn't be finished. But I'm really interested to see how things are coming along. When would you have a section for me to look at?'
Employee: 'Well, er. . . not for a day or two.'
Manager decides to make a firm but friendly intervention: 'Maybe we should take a look on the screen right now.'

Reviewing a piece of work presents the manager or team leader with the opportunity to bring into play and reinforce the following motivators:

- Achievement.
- Growth and learning.
- Recognition and esteem.
- Sense of responsibility.
- Sense of contribution and awareness of value.

So it is crucial to give feedback, and to do it in a way that is effective. Too often feedback is skimped on: we expect people to be motivated and take recognition from vague remarks like 'Well done, keep it up'. Or the sound performer in a section is left to carry on working reliably, while all management attention is given to less capable staff – conveying to the solid performer the message that he or she doesn't matter and the others do.

Reasons for inadequate feedback include lack of skill – people worry about their comments being intrusive or insulting, so they say little or offer vague generalities; and lack of priority – instead of taking time to review a project and help someone learn from it, there is a rush on to the next task (Box 5.7).

Box 5.7 Briefing, feedback and motivation

The managing director of a firm making and distributing natural skincare products had taken on a new marketing executive to prepare the launch of a new, up-market range. The investment required board approval. A week before the board meeting, he asked the marketing executive to prepare a document for the board to help him 'sell' the plan. There was no discussion of the type of document needed.

Understanding that this document was crucial to the project, the marketing executive felt she needed to be absolutely thorough in making the case for launch. She felt under severe time pressure and worked late into the night all week to set out detailed market analyses and forecasts. As she would not attend the meeting herself, she tried to anticipate every question and objection. She finished the 20-page document at midnight and delivered it to the MD the day before the board meeting.

An hour later, she was called to see the MD. 'What's this?' he spluttered. 'I didn't ask for this. It's far too long and you need a dictionary to understand it. These guys aren't interested in wading through all this – they just want the bottom line, something simple that gives it to them in five minutes. The trouble with you is you're a perfectionist and too clever.'

The marketing executive was speechless, hurt and furious. Of course the MD couldn't understand her document – he was too stupid. She went away and within two hours had cobbled together a summary of her work. She then spent the next week doing little but going over this incident in her mind and bending the ear of anyone she could find to moan to about it. The new range eventually went ahead, but the executive was busy pursuing a new job and took little care with it.

How much time and trouble would it have taken to avoid this? The marketing executive was working without a brief. Both the MD and she assumed that she knew what was needed, though she had never met the board or attended a board meeting. There was no touching base once she had started work on the document. As for the MD's feedback, it was negative, critical and personal ('the trouble with you is'), delivering to the executive the message 'your work has no value, and you have no value'.

Feedback comes in two forms: the routine, on-the-job kind given during work in progress; and systematic reviews made at the end of a project and at performance appraisals. Both are important. You need to give feedback on things that come up from day to day, which will be about particular aspects of particular pieces of work and will not always reflect a person's job performance as a whole. For people to retain a sense of perspective about how they are getting on in their role overall, a regular and systematic performance appraisal is necessary (see Chapter 6). Whichever the situation, by following a few basic rules and thinking before speaking, you can tell people what they need to know clearly and straightforwardly.

Rule one: Feedback is designed to help

The purpose of feedback is not to make the manager or team leader feel better by getting things off their chest, it is to build on good and correct weak performance.

So we need to phrase feedback for the benefit of the person receiving it, not to suit ourselves.

Rule two: Avoid triggering defences

Feedback cannot be effective unless the person receiving it listens and understands and sees it as relevant. The snag is that people easily put up defences when they sense that judgement is about to be passed on them. Even when the judgement is complimentary, it may get pushed aside with 'It's nothing, just doing my job'.

People defend themselves against comments they find intrusive and personal, and against criticism. Nevertheless, we need to be able to discuss mistakes and poor performance and deal with issues about which people are sensitive. To do that, we have to keep matters impersonal.

Rule three: Talk about work, actions and behaviour – not personality

This is the fundamental rule for effective feedback. It means that we have to choose our words carefully, not merely say what readily springs to mind.

For example, you need to speak to a customer service assistant about her manner with customers. What comes into your mind may be 'Judy is impatient and rude'. If you say it to Judy just like that, she's likely to feel insulted at being called rude and shrug off the impatience as the way she is, something that she can't change.

You have no right to ask people to change their personalities – that is a private matter. You do have every right, though, to ask people to change or control their *behaviour*. So the message to Judy needs to be different: 'You sounded impatient talking to that customer. It's something I've noticed before. I don't know whether you're aware, but it comes across as rude when you raise your voice and talk over the customer. Yesterday I had two complaints and had to spend my time pacifying your customers.'

Rule four: Enable people to relate to the feedback

To be able to make use of feedback, people need to understand precisely what it is about and to see the significance of it. Therefore make the messages specific and say precisely what you mean; describe the behaviour you want to talk about objectively, rather than giving an opinion; give examples so that the feedback is rooted in reality; and relate it to results – what outcome has the behaviour led to? You can see that the example of Judy above follows this formula.

The formula is just as important when giving positive feedback. People develop by gaining the confidence to try new things, building on a sense of capability. If someone is told specifically what is of value about their performance and how this makes a difference, they can form a clear understanding of how to build on what they are doing right.

Rule five: Balance negative with positive

When there are faults to be corrected, it is often necessary to focus on them in detail. However, the overall feedback message needs to put faults into perspective by pointing out the positive aspects of the person's contribution as a whole. It may be warranted, but if the only thing a person hears is criticism, they are likely to pick up the message that they are not valued and to become defensive or demoralized. If the person is to remain on your staff, they need to know that there are redeeming features to their work, potentially or actually.

Rule six: Build on it

Feedback needs to be constructive. So where there are faults to be corrected, a resolution needs to be reached on the steps to be taken to put things right. The same applies with positive points: consciously plan to build on and extend successes.

Dealing with entrenched performance problems

If someone is performing below expectations and has not responded to normal feedback, we need to understand why before being able to take appropriate corrective action. Likely causes include:

- Poor understanding of the initial brief.
- Lack of knowledge or skill.
- Feeling unable to admit to problems or ask for help.
- Lack of motivation.
- Person not suited to the role.

Explain the performance problems to the job holder (using the rules for feedback) and ask what may be causing the trouble. If the cause is lack of understanding, knowledge or skill, you can take appropriate action to remedy it, clarifying the brief, or offering coaching or training.

Most performance problems are improved by systematic feedback and a clear plan for improvement. However, there are persistent underperformers who do not improve and will brush aside feedback until they are made aware that substandard work puts their job at risk. When a systematic attempt at redirecting work has been tried without result, it is time to make clear to the job holder what the consequences will be of continued failure to meet work standards. To do this you must work within the framework of the firm's disciplinary procedure.

The rules for correcting persistent underperformance are:

- Confront the problem – substandard work – not the person.
- Get support – clear your course of action with superiors and colleagues, ensuring that there will be no appeals over your head.
- Have the facts to hand – have your evidence written down.
- State the problem and its consequences directly and briefly.

- Do not argue – be prepared to restate your message.
- Follow the disciplinary procedure – and spell out that you are doing this.

Feedback, learning and growth

If you build a climate of open communication where people expect, are open to and welcome feedback, there should be little need for confrontation or embarrassment. When feedback is handled straightforwardly, with the clear intention of recognizing and consolidating good work and aiding improvement, people are likely to appreciate it. The most valuable feedback is that which people ask for themselves. Much of the time it can be given as part of a dialogue, engaging the person in assessing their own performance:

Employee: 'What did you think of my presentation?'
Boss: 'It had a lot of good points. What's your assessment?'
Employee: 'Well, I think I got the message across clearly, but I'm not sure they took me seriously, I was really nervous.'
Boss: 'The nerves didn't show. The presentation was clear and easy to follow, the points came across – they could see you know your stuff. You impressed them in the part you'd prepared, it was handling the questions where I had to step in and help. Let's have a look at what you can do to tackle that part more effectively next time.'

Feedback helps people learn. Properly used, it is a means of encouraging people to build on and expand their strengths, helping them gain self-esteem and with that the confidence to correct weaknesses. It is a key process for completing the motivational loop that begins with goal setting, and for developing people who can grow with the business.

Notes

1　Maslow, A., Stephens, D. and Heil, G. (1998) *Maslow on Management*, John Wiley & Sons, New York.
2　McClelland, D. (1967) *The Achieving Society*, Macmillan, New York.
3　Herzberg, F. (1966) *Work and the Nature of Man*, World Publishing, Cleveland, OH.

Further reading

1　Blanchard, K. and Johnson, S. (2000) *The One Minute Manager*, HarperCollins, London.
2　Adair, J. (1996) *Effective Motivation*, Pan, London.
3　Pedler, M., Burgoyne, J. and Boydell, T. (2001) *A Manager's Guide to Self-Development*, McGraw-Hill, Maidenhead.

Leading the Team

CHAPTER 6

Key issues dealt with in this chapter are:

- Building a structure for delegation: empowering others to take responsibility reliably.
- Leadership: a set of learnable professional skills.
- Teamworking to extend capability and increase productivity.
- Aligning people's performance with company purpose: getting results from appraisals.
- Recruiting the right team members.

Power in the growing organization: Making it safe to delegate

Growing organizations often encounter problems in distributing the power to make decisions to a team of managers. The founders and owners of the enterprise have nurtured it from its beginnings and have an enormous personal (and in most cases financial) investment in it. Founders and owners have a perspective on the firm that not all business managers share – and they tend to be regarded as having special authority, by staff, customers and suppliers. There can be expectation on all sides that founders and owners are the only real decision makers.

However, there comes a point where concentrating decision power and control in the hands of the founders restricts the firm's ability to grow. Inadequate delegation can submerge directors beneath a welter of operational problems, holding back the productivity of employees and depriving capable staff of the opportunity to grow into leaders.

For most business founders, a crucial step in developing the firm is letting go of day-to-day operations to a tier of managers who are given the task of running it in line with agreed plans, budgets, priorities and policies. It is important to draw a distinction between the management of routine operational matters and strategic decision making, clearly delineating the role of directors. Their job is to set the strategic direction for the company and exercise responsibility for its financial and other resources. The role of a manager is to implement coordinated action to realize strategic plans. So, once managers are in place, directors exercise their function through the lead they give to managers rather than by fixing things themselves. Their challenge is to hold the vision for the whole company, and to engage operational managers' understanding and motivation in such a way that the company's people and resources are aligned effectively with its strategic purpose and plan.

When letting go of day-to-day operations, those who are steering the growing firm need to make it safe to delegate responsibility. This calls for:

- A redrawing of roles at the top of the organization to separate the functions of operational managers from those of directors.
- Clear definition and communication of performance expectations held of managers, in terms of goals, standards and priorities.
- Structuring the organization's processes, such as planning, budgeting and decision making, to enable managers to make an effective contribution while setting clear limits to authority and ability to commit resources without approval.
- Finding people to fill management roles, either by recruiting or by internal development.

Delegating responsibility for results is a very different matter from merely delegating tasks. When you delegate only tasks, they are often not done as well as you expect, or people have a way of continually interrupting you with questions – because you have delegated the work, but not the responsibility for doing the right thing. You still have to worry about what the workers are up to, so delegating doesn't diminish your workload and seems to add to your problems. True and successful delegation means that somebody else takes over responsibility for delivering a particular result and does so reliably, so that you are relieved of day-to-day involvement in that aspect of work and free to focus on what you should be doing.

Leadership and delegation

Delegating the management of operations to others may require a boss to rethink the practice of leadership. Previously he or she may have used a 'hands-on' approach, expecting to be actively involved in getting things done and solving problems. However, continuing to operate in that way could interfere with the lead that managers need to give to their teams. It is often assumed that effective leadership is 'strong' leadership or leadership from the front – but this is not always what gets the best result. You need to step back and ask what the leadership function is for, before considering how a leader should act.

The practice of leadership is not confined to the senior levels of the firm. Managers lead their departments, within and between which there are likely to be working groups with team or project leaders. All of these people are charged with a leadership function: getting a set of people to pool their individual efforts towards a joint goal and result. In today's organizations, the term 'leader' is increasingly being used in its widest sense, not simply to denote someone at the top but anyone who *takes responsibility for outcomes*. Leaders are expected to link what is aimed at and planned in the company with what actually occurs. They hold and communicate a sense of purpose and, by enabling people to be aware of how their individual roles and goals relate to a bigger context, connect a set of people to contribute to an overarching purpose.

Leadership involves bringing people together to accomplish things. The leader has to be able to engage and draw performance from people, and to ensure that tasks are satisfactorily structured and executed. The function can be stated as that of involving people in a sense of shared purpose, and aligning them in a system to deliver it.

Leadership style

An effective leader is someone who enables a group of people to pull together in a formation in which each makes their best contribution towards achieving the goal. There need be no mystique about it: although some people appear to be 'natural' leaders, this often means little more than that they have considerable self-confidence that they transmit to others. Leadership consists of skills in motivating people and shaping their purposeful interaction on a task, a set of observation, diagnosis, planning and communication skills that can be learned. There is no single right way to lead a team, what matters is getting results. The best way to get results – the most appropriate leadership style to adopt – depends on the nature of the people, the task and the conditions under which it has to be performed. The professional leader needs to be able to adapt their leadership style to the needs of the situation. This is the concept of *situational leadership*, originally formulated by Hersey and Blanchard[1] and now widely influential in management thinking and practice.

The principles of this approach are:

- The leader adjusts their leadership style to suit the needs of the team, taking into account the stage of development of the team and its members.
- The role of the leader is to 'serve' the team where necessary, by providing capabilities that the team has not yet developed for itself.
- The leader encourages the team to grow towards greater autonomy: to develop the capability to run its own work process so that maximum delegation of responsibility can take place.

The practice of situational leadership is based on balancing two types of leader behaviour: *directive* (providing structure and control) and *supportive* (facilitating and encouraging the team's efforts). These correspond to the two basic dimensions of management: *attention to task* and *attention to people*. A leader may pay a great deal of attention to the task dimension and giving direction, or only a little; a great deal of attention to supporting the people in the group, or only a little. Different combinations of high or low attention to task and to people/process issues result in four different leadership styles (Figure 6.1):

1 *Directing* – high on direction, high involvement in the task. Leading by keeping control, breaking the task down into subtasks, allocating them to individuals and giving instructions.
2 *Proactive* – high attention to task, with high support and attention to people issues as well. Sometimes known as the 'selling' style. The leader is fully engaged in all aspects of the team's working.

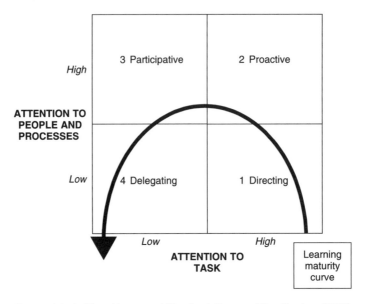

Source: Adapted from Hersey and Blanchard, Pearson Education Inc., (1977).

Figure 6.1: Leadership styles.

3 *Participative* – high on supporting the team's efforts to organize its own work process, low direction. The team is expected to be competent to get the task done.
4 *Delegating* – low levels of involvement from the leader on both dimensions. The team is expected to take responsibility for task execution and organizes its own work process.

Many people have a preference for one particular leadership style. Relationship-oriented people lean naturally to a participative and supportive style, preferring to act from within the group rather than to use authority. Some newly promoted people have this tendency, feeling uncomfortable with setting themselves apart from erstwhile colleagues. Others when newly promoted rely on a directing style, feeling that they must be seen to be in charge.

The style that is probably aimed at by more managers than any other is the proactive, because it appears the safest, with the leader 'looking after' both task and people issues on behalf of the group. However, simply relying on the approach that comes most comfortably can be misapplying the leadership style. Directing can turn into behaving like an autocrat; proactivity can turn into suffocating the group and cramping initiative; participative leaders who merely muck in alongside people can turn into 'groupies' who offer no structure or standards; and delegators who leave the group to sink or swim without adequate preparation have abdicated responsibility.

So how does the professional leader know which style to adopt? The most useful everyday indicator is the level of maturity in the job that the group and its members have achieved.

When people are new to a job, the first requirement is that they learn how to do it and attain technical competence – so this is where the leader needs to focus, using a directing style. The leader keeps control of the task, breaking it down into subtasks and allocating these to people; he or she leads by giving instructions and does the group's thinking and coordination for it.

As technical skill increases, the second stage of maturity is reached. The group (or individual) needs to learn about processes: not only what needs to be done, but how and why. People must to understand how to work most effectively in a team, how to relate to and deal with the rest of the organization – if they do not, the leader will forever have to take care of such issues for his or her staff and will never be able to rely on them to deliver results without close supervision. Therefore, the appropriate leadership style is proactive. The leader still keeps a check on task performance and helps the group structure its work, but actively explains the reasoning behind matters, coaching them towards being able to take more responsibility.

Once people have become adept at the task, i.e. task competent, they are at a third level where the best result is likely to be obtained by enabling them to run the work process for themselves as much as possible – encouraging them to participate in the leading of the team. So the appropriate leadership approach is participative and supportive. The leader is transferring responsibility for control to the group or individual concerned, but is on hand to draw out contributions and facilitate the best use of resources. The group is developing the skills of running its own work process and needs practice in doing this before being left to go solo. The key to this style is asking questions rather than providing solutions.

Only when a group or individual can completely manage effective processes as well as technical output – when the third level of maturity is well established – is it appropriate to proceed to the fourth level and delegate fully. Delegation properly so called is the art of checking signals, ensuring that goals, roles, resources and timing are clear, feasible and agreed, so that the group or individual can proceed reliably without the leader's intervention. The leadership style can be indicated like this: 'Can we check that the goals are clear. . . I believe you know what to do and how to do it. . . When would be a good time to check progress?. . . I don't expect I'll be needed before then, but if there's a major problem I could be contacted (where, when).'

This concept of leadership style is not simply about how the leader should behave, it sets out a framework for developing the reliability of a group or individual in taking increasing amounts of responsibility for their work – for making it safe to delegate. It is concerned not simply with how the leader should behave, but with the dynamic between the leader and his or her staff. Following this model avoids one of the most common disasters in delegation: withdrawing leader support before people have sufficiently developed the practical capability of running their own work process. This typically happens when the third stage of development, participating and supporting, is bypassed. The leader switches straight from proactive leadership – taking responsibility for everything – to delegating, i.e. making the group responsible for everything. The group finds itself thrown in at the deep end, matters that seemed clear when explained turn out not to be understood in practice, and things go wrong.

It is important to work systematically along the maturity curve (see Box 6.1). If the group does not live up to your hopes when you first delegate, then move back to participative leadership. Use questions to find out what went wrong and give support on those aspects of the work next time. If you are using a participative style with someone who then turns out to have failed to master an important aspect of the job, switch back to proactive mode to explain it again.

Box 6.1 Practical example: From proactive leader to autocrat

Tom had been the natural choice to build up the technical department when Tech Services expanded. He struck the MD as someone with natural leadership capability, able to take a project and structure it to be divided between a group of people and to coordinate their work.

Tom enjoyed leading the group of customer service technicians. He had a gift for explaining technical matters and prided himself on being able to bring in people new to the industry and make them knowledgeable customer service technicians. He was also the person on whom the company relied to maintain its cutting-edge reputation in its field, working with one other researcher.

The company's field of operation was becoming more competitive. Even so, Tech Services continued to win new customers. Tom found himself under increasing pressure to keep abreast of technical developments. He had put a great deal of effort into setting up the customer service group, but found that his day was constantly interrupted by staff members bringing him problems and passing difficult customers on to him. In his view, there should really be no need for this – he had compiled a decent product manual for them and they had all had training. They ought to be able to help one another rather than look to him all the time. It was time to delegate, so that he could focus his attention on his own job priority, development work.

At the next weekly staff meeting, Tom explained to the customer service group that from now on he was cutting back his involvement. He assured them that they were fully capable of handling customer service without his involvement. The longest-serving member of the group was to act as team leader. Tom would 'look in' at staff meetings once a fortnight or so, to keep in touch.

Problems broke out swiftly. Tom had always set priorities for the group and they had respected his decisions. When the new team leader tried to do this, people felt free to question him and follow their own preferences. Not everyone had the same level of experience and knowledge, and the more senior found that some people were now coming to them with problems, so that they got behind with their work. They started telling colleagues to work things out for themselves or fobbed them off with quick-fire explanations that were not fully understood.

It was not long before some customers bypassed the technicians, taking complaints direct to Tom. In a matter of weeks, his orderly, competent customer service group had ceased to provide reliable service.

Tom felt really let down. He had recognized the competence of his staff and given them a chance to show what they could do, but they'd lost the plot and descended into muddle. Now he was heavily committed to a research project that he had scheduled on the assumption that he would be able to devote himself full-time to it. He could not go back to the old way of running the customer service group. Nor did he want to. They'd shown that they could not be trusted and needed to be brought under control. His solution was to spend no more than an hour each day running customer services. During that time, he gave instructions on what was to be done and sorted out problems.

He introduced a manual of set responses to frequent problems and devised a monitoring system that enabled him to keep a check on each person's work rate. In these ways, he could keep control without having to get involved.

It was not long before Tom faced a new problem: high staff turnover. People who had previously been motivated by learning and developing their level of competence and getting good feedback from customers now found themselves giving scripted responses under strict control from a distant boss.

Tom's first experiment with delegation had failed. Once he had embarked on autocratic control methods, it took a long time to stabilize things. Another technical expert was brought in – at considerable expense – so that Tom could sort out customer services. Tom lost what he had been trying to protect – his role as the company's technical expert – and the company ended up with a fatter salary bill.

Tom could have avoided this by following the situational leadership concept and preparing the customer service group for delegation using a participative model of leadership. Tom's proactive style of leadership had left the group dependent on his input and unpractised in structuring work for themselves, setting priorities and solving problems. Had they had the opportunity to work out how to do this before Tom took himself completely out of the picture, the transition to delegation could have been much smoother.

Working with teams

Teamworking is at the heart of the modern organization. We talk of management teams, as if it is axiomatic that the managers of separate organizational functions should also constitute a cooperative body of their own. Putting people to work together in teams can be an effective way of coordinating the contributions of different functions at lower levels in the organization too. Larger organizations have shifted their structure and processes away from command-and-control hierarchies in favour of flatter, team-based forms with fewer layers of management. The term 'team leader' is often used in preference to that of supervisor. In smaller organizations, there is likely to have been a phase of development – the single cell or spider's web phase (see Chapter 4) – when teamworking was taken for granted.

A note of caution: 'team' is one of the most overworked and misused words in the workplace. Often what is referred to as a team is nothing more than a collection of individuals who happen to sit together, do similar jobs, or report to the same person. Merely putting people to work together doesn't automatically result in teamwork. Indeed, the misuse of groups can actually waste time and resources.

To get the best from people working together, you need to understand what differentiates a team from a group of individuals, what teams are for, how to constitute an effective team, how to enhance the positive interaction of members and how to spot and deal with factors that can undermine teamworking.

A team is a group whose members cooperate and support one another in pursuit of a common purpose, achieving together a better result than they could with the same number of people working separately. This is what is meant by *synergy*. The work process of an effective team is characterized by a 'virtuous circle' that produces gains in motivation, productivity and quality of results.

Each member of the team is an individual who contributes their own particular skills, aptitudes, experience, outlook and personal qualities. Teams thrive on the increased potential and enhanced capability that differences between people make available. However, profiting from differences requires team members to be willing and able to get on with one another as colleagues. People don't actually have to like their fellow team members, but they need to communicate with them openly and be prepared to deal with conflicts.

Effective teams demonstrate these characteristics:

1   *Common purpose.* All members of the team share a view of what the team exists for, what its priorities are, what really matters to get things right.
2   *Corresponding goals.* Each team member knows what the team as a whole is aiming for and what their own part is in achieving it, i.e. individuals have goals linked in to overall team goals and are governed by the overriding team purpose.
3   *Commitment.* Team members commit to the team and its agenda, not purely to their personal task and its accomplishment.
4   *Cooperation.* Team members support and help one another, such that the team can make the most of the resources available to it at any time. Competitive energy is focused externally (on beating the competition, improving standards, exceeding targets) rather than against fellow team members.
5   *Communication.* The information that people need to do a good job is communicated fast and accurately. Emphasis is placed on giving information clearly, as well as on taking it in attentively. Responsibility for communication is shared.
6   *Climate of openness.* Team members say what needs to be said, including telling a colleague if there are problems working with him or her. It is accepted that conflicts can arise at work and need to be resolved. Team members also feel able to express support and appreciation for one another.
7   *Contribution.* Team members pull their weight and are aware of how their efforts contribute to the achievement of something bigger.
8   *Shared code of practice.* As well as team goals, each team member shares a clear awareness of the team's values and standards and its way of going about things. If any of these are unclear, a team member accepts the responsibility of checking the issue out – they do not wait for someone else to tell them.

The advantages of teamworking

It should by now be clear that simply bringing a set of people together does not produce a team – teams are the outcome of good will, effort and skill. Building a team and getting the best from it require time and attention to be given to communication and processes of interaction. So it is important to ask whether that effort will be justified. Will the team enhance productivity or provide some other worthwhile benefit?

Working in teams can bring benefits in two ways: by expanding the capability to get the job done, and through human factors that improve motivation and make people feel better. Task capability benefits include:

●   Enhanced productivity – getting more or better work outcomes from the resources available.

- Pooling resources – combining a variety of skills, knowledge, experience and outlooks.
- Ease of communication and passing information.
- Coordination of work without the need for cumbersome structures or intervention.
- Learning – members pass on knowledge and skills to one another.
- Generating ideas and refining solutions (sparking off others).
- Testing, checking and spotting mistakes.

Human benefits include these 'team spirit' effects:

- Sharing responsibility and effort, which reduces the burden on individuals.
- Enhanced energy.
- Personal security and a sense of belonging.
- Support from fellow team members, which reverses the feeling of struggling alone.
- Motivation through the opportunity to contribute to a greater whole.

Positive as these benefits may appear, it is important to remember that they are not always required. Some tasks (for example, those requiring sustained concentration, or reliant on a particular type of expertise) are more effectively carried out by people working on their own. What you are aiming for in building a team is to get a better outcome than you would obtain if those people were deployed separately.

Forming a team makes sense to achieve these purposes:

- To coordinate the contributions of a variety of people with differing knowledge, skills and approaches.
- To increase the information available on a problem by pooling resources.
- To generate ideas or explore improvements through brainstorming.
- To promote team spirit and motivation.
- To enable people to deal with uncertainty – group support can make it easier to take risks and enter uncharted territory.

When groups become counterproductive

Forming a productive team creates a working unit that is greater than the sum of its parts. Groups tend to magnify what happens at the individual level and, just as they can magnify energy and motivation, so they can also magnify problems. Using groups for inappropriate purposes, not attending to the composition of the group and failing to set up and maintain effective team processes all result in a waste of time and resources.

Any of the following factors can reduce the effectiveness of a group:

- Insufficient time allowed for structuring the work process (defining problems, sharing information, assigning roles) before attacking the task.
- Members have such different perspectives that they cannot communicate easily.
- One member or subgroup dominates.
- The skills and resources of some members are not fully recognized and used.

- A minority of people have the knowledge necessary for dealing with the problem.
- Numbers are too large for everyone to participate.
- Social interaction takes over from task focus – too much time is given to off-the-point discussion, chat or banter.

Any of the above factors can lead to some people becoming detached from the group as a whole, feeling that they are wasting their time or that their contribution is insignificant or insufficiently valued. This can give rise to resentment and conflict that, if unchecked, can dominate the agenda and block the effectiveness of the whole group.

Conversely, a group can become dysfunctional because people stick together too well, becoming uncritical of the group's functioning and placing loyalty to the group above any other purpose. This can lead to the phenomenon known as *groupthink*. From inside it feels as if the group is working very effectively, because decisions are reached rapidly and without conflict – a great momentum of consensus prevails. However, convinced of its rightness, the group pursues goals and courses of action that are out of line with its official remit or external realities, sometimes with disastrous consequences.

Balancing attention to task with attention to people and processes

When things go wrong in groups and teams, it is usually because attention is being focused on the task dimension, neglecting the social processes between members. All of the pitfalls outlined above can be dealt with, and most of them avoided in the first place, by paying attention to the composition and formation of the team; matching leadership approach to the needs of the team; developing effective work practices; and regularly reviewing the functioning of the group (Box 6.2).

Box 6.2 Basic questions for team formation and review

Purpose – What is the team for? What are its goals?

Functions and roles – What activities are carried out in the team? Should they be carried out in this team or elsewhere? What roles need to be undertaken in this team?

People – Who are the people needed? Why is each person there? Are there people who are needed who are not represented?

Processes – What processes and working practices are needed to get the best from the team's resources?

In most teams distinct roles emerge among the members, some of which are *task* focused and some *people and processes* focused. Task-focused roles are concerned with moving the work forward towards a goal and a *task leader* will provide the driving force. People process roles are concerned with keeping the members of the group together, involved and communicating; with preventing disintegration and splitting, seeking cooperation and consensus and resolving conflicts. In a smoothly running team, the person taking the lead in driving the work forward is able to cooperate with a *process leader* who facilitates the readiness of members to play their parts.

Team roles: Composition of the successful team

The purpose of assembling a team is to make available a combination of skills and aptitudes that is unlikely to be present in strength in any one individual. However, some teams work more effectively than others. Meredith Belbin's model of team roles makes intuitive sense and can usefully be applied in the growing organization.[2] He demonstrates that the most effective teams are those in which members carry out nine key *team roles*. If all of these functions are covered, the team can deal effectively with a variety of remits – from the creatively challenging to the routine – and meet performance demands ranging from searching for new directions to accurate attention to detail. These team roles are solely concerned with team behaviour and the contribution that each role makes to team effectiveness. They are not the same as job roles.

To give an idea of how the roles interlink to maintain team effectiveness, they can be shown schematically (Box 6.3).

Box 6.3 Belbin's team roles

	Task-oriented	People-oriented	Thinking
Initiating Contributing	Shaper Implementer	Coordinator Resource Investigator, Teamworker	
Monitoring Boundary spanning	Completer Finisher		Monitor Evaluator Plant, Specialist

---

Source: Self Perception Inventory, 'Management Teams: Why they succeed or fail', Belbin Associates (1981)

This is what each role denotes:

- *Shaper*. Leads from the front: task oriented, hands-on, driving, challenging, purposeful. Has clearly defined goals and pursues them dynamically, constantly pushing things forward. Often impatient and uninterested in team process, with a tendency to ignore or exclude those who don't keep up.
- *Coordinator*. A 'people process leader'. Concerned for the stability and development of the team over the long term and to enable team members to participate effectively. Invites contributions and involvement in decision making. Manner usually calm and confident, no ego issues. Communicates easily and listens well. Need not possess outstanding technical or strategic abilities, as other members of the team supply these.

- *Implementer*. The team's workhorse. Task oriented and practical, gets on with the job in an organized, disciplined manner. Happy with routine and structured work. Reliable, disciplined, predictable, tends to be conservative, sometimes overly so, may be inflexible and not open to ideas or change unless given clear reasons.

- *Teamworker*. Sensitive to the people issues in the group and accords them high priority. When positive, promotes team spirit and is able to support the Coordinator in gaining team members' involvement, commitment and cohesiveness. Intuitive, good listener, picks up information and 'vibes'. Can become so immersed in people issues as to lose task perspective and be indecisive.

- *Monitor Evaluator*. The quality control agent in the team, with a clear grasp of strategic direction and performance standards. Measures the team's progress and output against these. Coolly analytical, prudent, unemotional. Focuses on relevant issues, has clear judgement and is hard-headed. Others can find this person cold, uninspired and non-motivating.

- *Completer Finisher*. The person who makes sure that ideas and decisions are properly followed through and tasks are completed correctly. A stickler for deadlines and details. Painstaking and a perfectionist, this person likes to operate in an orderly way, gets anxious about cutting corners or leaving loose ends, and doesn't like moving on to new issues before current ones have been dealt with. Can get bogged down in minutiae.

- *Resource Investigator*. Interested in possibilities and exploring new ventures and opportunities. More involved with what's going on outside the team than within it, puts a great deal of energy into forming contacts. Extrovert and an active communicator, this person is essentially a fixer. An enthusiast: a bundle of energy when engaged, but can lack staying power and lose interest, and is likely to absent him/herself from the team.

- *Plant*. The team's chief source of ideas and creativity. This person contributes imagination, intellect and conceptual thinking, but may have little idea of, or interest in, implementation and practicalities. An abstract and original thinker, often unorthodox in outlook. Can be individualistic and prone to going off into a world of his or her own.

- *Specialist*. Someone who brings to bear expert knowledge and skill. May act as a resource for the team on a particular aspect of the brief, or gnaw away at a particular problem until a breakthrough is achieved. Usually contributes on a narrow front.

Working with team roles

To function effectively, the team needs to be structured so that there is someone to carry out each of the leadership, contributing, monitoring and boundary-spanning roles. It is seldom practical or necessary for each role to be assigned to a separate person – people can act in more than one team role – but it is important that each role is adequately represented in the group. On any given project, team members should know which people will be covering which team roles.

Any individual person will strongly feature the characteristics of one or more of the team roles, but not of all of them. By systematically identifying people's team role characteristics, it is possible to work out the best distribution of team responsibilities among a particular group of people. If a group lacks strength in certain team roles, it makes sense to recruit to the group someone who brings the missing characteristics. Realistically this is not always possible, so the team will need to design in some mechanism to make sure that the missing role gets covered. For example, if a team is weak on Completer Finishers, it is important to build a disciplined checking process into the team's programme of work.

From the descriptions given, it is noticeable that the positive qualities meaning that people suit particular team roles can be offset by tendencies that could be irritating to other team members or could, if not controlled, undermine productivity. That is the cost of reaping the benefits of bringing together people with complementary aptitudes. So there needs to be a clear enough team process to deal openly and quickly with the conflicts that will arise from time to time (Box 6.4).

Box 6.4 Practical example: Belbin team roles in a management group

In order to streamline operational input into strategic direction setting and the implementation of plans, the two directors of Isis Consulting set up a strategic management group. The company's consultants were already organized into two market sector teams, and a representative was chosen from each. The administration coordinator was the fifth member of the committee, which pulled together all the key functions and responsibilities in the firm.

The group started well. Market development goals were set for each consultant group and a broad plan of attack discussed. Problems with operating systems were diagnosed and remedies identified. There was a new sense of direction and momentum.

After three months, however, some goals had already been missed and the original action plans were constantly being rescheduled. The admin coordinator had managed to close off a database revision project, but no other decisions had been implemented. As the MD remarked, the group discussed issues thoroughly and took inclusive decisions, but fell apart on follow-through. The root of the problem was this: while general directions had been set for projects, specific goals for accomplishment had not; progress targets for projects had not been spelled out or checked, and the criteria for completion had not been identified. So project implementation could wander way off track, while those responsible thought they were doing well enough.

Analysis of team roles revealed that the group had no strong *Monitor Evaluator* to clarify key standards for the group and ensure they worked to them:

MD	Plant, Shaper, Implementer
Client Services Director	Coordinator, Resource Investigator, Specialist
Consultant Rep 1	Resource Investigator, Implementer, Plant
Consultant Rep 2	Teamworker, Implementer, (Monitor Evaluator)
Admin Coordinator	Implementer, Teamworker, Completer Finisher

The solution found was for the whole group to take a more disciplined approach to goal setting and progress evaluation. The client services director, who chaired meetings, and the consultant showing the highest Monitor Evaluator score worked together to enforce this.

Stages of team development

It is important for team leaders to be aware that groups that are newly put together need to go through a process of social development for the team to hit its stride and work to its full potential. Essentially what is required is for the differences between people to be recognized – it is after all the variety in the group that is its *raison d'être* – and for a way of working together to be established that enables people to contribute their full worth and interact freely. The stages of development are:

- *Forming* – the introductory stage of meeting and beginning to work with other members of the group. Usually characterized by politeness and reserve among the majority, while the bold (who are not necessarily the best suited) assume leadership. Properly, this stage should be used to explore the resources in the group: what skills, knowledge, aptitudes, interests and expectations people bring.
- *Storming* – discovering conflict. As the group starts to function, the differences among its members are likely to produce clashes as to priorities, what should be done, how and by whom. Struggles for dominance occur, while some members nurse silent dissent.
- *Norming* – as a response to disagreements, the group sets up its social 'norms' or code of practice: the way things are done in this group, the pattern of interaction that will prevail.
- *Performing* – getting on with the work of the group, without the problems of uncertainty and unresolved conflict that preceded the setting up of its code of practice.

A team that reaches the *performing* stage does not become free of conflict. Rather, it is able to bring conflict into the open and resolve it without undue loss of time or energy. The stages of *storming* and *norming* require attention and time to be given to people processes. Under time pressure, groups all too easily attempt to bypass these, usually with unfortunate results. Where conflict or differences are ignored, the pool of potential energy available to the group is siphoned off into inattention, creation of diversions, backbiting, minority reporting and splitting off. Or members stay politely at the forming stage, working around the differences between them rather than working through them.

Even without conscious attention, a set of *de facto* norms will emerge that will reflect the habits of the dominant forces in the group – either the majority, or the strongest personalities, or those with the best connections outside the group. These habits will become imposed by default. They are unlikely to reflect the best pattern for the group's members as a whole (Box 6.5).

Matching team processes to task and situation

All group members need to be clear on the goal, time availability and tasks to be accomplished to reach a given target. Beyond such basics, group processes need to be adapted to the particular purposes, tasks and circumstances with which the group is dealing at any one time.

In order to make the best use of resources, it is important to distinguish between requirements for people to *share in a task* – appropriate to exploring, pooling information, developing ideas, building consensus; and *executing defined tasks* while maintaining coordination.

For *exploratory or brainstorming work*, members need to work together. A *participative mode* of shared input and shared control among all members is often appropriate, where members can work with rotating leadership or appoint a Coordinator to facilitate the full use of resources and the drawing out of contributions from all members.

For *executing defined tasks* (such as carrying out a specific set of calculations, applying quality checks, analysing and classifying data), it is likely best to structure the group, identifying specific functions and a division of labour within a coordinating framework, probably with clear *task leadership*.

Team projects often consist of distinct stages of work, with the team's resources needing to be deployed differently at different stages. The team's leadership has the job of making the most effective use of team resources to achieve optimum task performance in the time available. It makes sense to employ a systematic model to allocate a time phase to each stage of work, using the most appropriate team formation at each stage.

The model in Figure 6.2 is designed to avoid the pitfall of rushing into action before people have a clear and unified understanding of what needs to be achieved and a plan of action to achieve it. Used explicitly with the team, this provides a basis for each member to know what should be happening and to make the appropriate contribution at each point. The four stages of work are *exploration*, *planning*, *action* and *review*.

- *Exploration*. At the start of a project there can be some uncertainty about what needs to happen; there is often a sense of inertia. Because this is uncomfortable, it is tempting to get beyond it by pushing forward into action – the 'shoot first, aim later' tendency. Instead, it is more sensible to acknowledge that you are not yet quite sure what you're doing and allocate a specific amount of time to exploring. This means getting some kind of rough overview of what the project entails, in order then to be able to set limits to it, define a goal and set up a plan of work. What is the *project aim* and how will the team know when it is achieving it (what performance standards and criteria will be applied)? If there are priority conflicts, how will these be settled? What *information* do you have to work with?, what is in the brief?, what else do you know?; what resources do you have?, and what will be needed?, do you need more information? Roughly *what has to be done* to accomplish the project?
- *Plan*. This calls for explicit decisions: defining goals, allocating time to stages of work, setting up processes to ensure that people contribute effectively and deciding who will do what. Importantly, the time plan needs to include *contingency time* for subsequent adjustments. It also needs to ensure adequate time left at the end for review.

Box 6.5 Practical example: Storming to team performance

The company had won its major customers through the founding directors' contacts. Its next phase of growth required a move into new markets and competitive tendering. It made sense to set up a multidisciplinary team to take on this remit, consisting of:

- Mick – major accounts sales manager
- Bob – operations coordinator
- Sarah – marketing manager
- Mark – technical development and research manager
- Roger – accountant (financial information and analysis)

Forming

Sarah expected the first meeting to be exploratory, leading to preparation of a plan. She prepared a market analysis and recommendations on which segments to prioritize. She was taken aback when Mick, with no preliminaries, announced that he had three hot prospects that needed tenders prepared straight away. Bob got very enthusiastic, and Roger was brought in to start work on price calculations. Sarah tried to question whether these were the right customers to go after, and Mark wondered whether the company would be able to deliver – but Mick and Roger sailed on.

This was how things continued. The team held regular weekly meetings. These were short and dominated by Mick. Once Mark raised his doubts about the suitability of the leads Mick was pursuing, but was firmly told by Mick that he had no commercial understanding. Mark began to miss meetings. Sarah could see that there were holes in the tenders being prepared, but was brushed aside when she said anything. Two tenders were put forward; neither even got shortlisted.

Storming

Mark rang Sarah. He had been looking into the third prospect and saw a way in which the company could offer a significant advantage, but it would be crucial not to price too low. Sarah could see how to pitch this tender, and outlined an approach.

'I've got some thoughts for the next tender,' she began at the next meeting.

'Oh, Bob and I have got that one sorted,' Mick cut in. 'We don't need to hang around on it any longer – there's two more prospects I've heard about ...'

Sarah stood up. 'I've had enough of sitting around while you two give mickey mouse presentations that don't hang together and shoddy documents that go straight in the client's bin. You think you're so dynamic, but we're just floundering around. *That's* what a proper presentation looks like.' She flung her papers in front of Mick.

'And I've had enough of you putting your oar in and boring on with your endless meaningless analysis,' he said between clenched teeth.

'You'd better look at her material. She's right, Mick. We got nowhere with the last tenders – they were in the wrong markets; you tried to push our stuff on to clients who can find suppliers much better matched to their needs. Frankly, this team has got to use the brain power available.' Mark said this with quiet determination. Bob looked sheepish.

Norming

Huffily, Mick agreed to let them do it their way. He would set up the client meeting, but Sarah would lead the presentation. This time they were shortlisted.

Mick admitted that they needed to operate in a way that used everyone's resources, instead of excluding half of them. However, he had felt let down when Sarah and Mark had responded negatively to his enthusiastic lead. A lot of their intellectual discussion was unnecessary in his view and slowed things down. He needed to be active.

Mark began to act as chairman in meetings. The full team met monthly to review progress and plan actions. People were tasked with specific responsibilities. In between, *ad hoc* sessions were held on specific agendas by those who needed to work together. Mark and Sarah drew up a market and development plan, consulting Mick where appropriate.

Performing

Pressure reduced. The team had its code of practice, so each member knew what they were expected to deliver. Less time was spent unproductively in meetings, but each person contributed. Mark and Sarah conducted their intellectual discussions in private and summarized them succinctly for the team. Each person came to respect the validity of others' viewpoints and capabilities. It became possible to laugh about the 'storm'. They won new business.

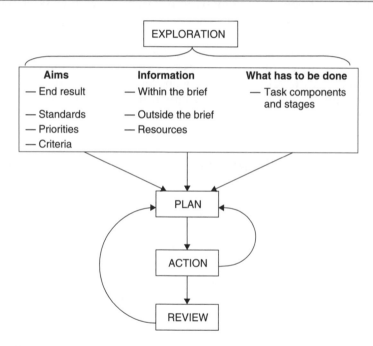

Figure 6.2: Systematic project management.

- *Action.* People now get on with implementing their planned contributions. However, once action begins, new *information* is acquired about what is possible and it may be necessary to revisit and revise the plan.
- *Review.* This stage should not be neglected. First, it is important to check the outcome from the team's effort against the aims and criteria originally set. Does the work measure up and, if not, how will any shortfall be managed? Secondly, this is an opportunity to evaluate the team's effectiveness, in order to improve future practice.

Finding the people for the team

The art of leadership lies in optimizing the performance of the people available to do the work, using skills of motivation, communication and coordination. That said, it makes sense to take steps to ensure that the people in your team are the best you can get for the purpose. A management team has to have people who measure up to what is expected of them, and who are able to work effectively in the kind of organization they are in. Two processes are crucial here: the company's internal *staff appraisal and development* practices, and *recruitment*.

When it comes to appointing responsible staff, the question arises of whether you should buy 'ready made' and try to recruit externally someone who has the expertise for the job, or 'grow your own' and promote internally. Importantly, the discipline of defining the role requirements first, and identifying a job holder to match second, should always be followed. It is tempting to use promotion tactically – to reward long service or to bribe the ambitious into loyalty. Nevertheless, if the person does not have the knowledge, skills and qualities for the job, they should not be appointed until they have acquired them.

Systematically appraising and developing the skills of all members of the firm helps ensure that, when the time comes to expand the organization, there are people on hand ready to respond to a new challenge. Not only this, by giving each person a direction to aim in, it can strengthen the integration of the company's overall team effort and enhance individual motivation.

Aligning people with purpose: Using performance appraisal effectively

The primary purpose of an appraisal system is to motivate individual job holders to achieve their own and the company's goals; thus, to enable each employee to develop their potential with the company and understand how their efforts will contribute most effectively to the achievement of company plans. Periodic, in-depth appraisal meetings between the individual employee and the person to whom they report are designed to take stock of job performance as a whole; plan how the individual can give their best to, and get the most out of, their work; and identify appropriate steps for development.

Appraisal should be mutually beneficial for both the individual employee and the company. When appraisals are well and consistently carried out, employees value the opportunity to regain a clear perspective on their role in the firm and how their performance shapes up, a perspective that frequently gets lost in coping with day-to-day demands. Putting time and effort into preparing and conducting a one- or two-hour meeting focused on a particular person can signal to that person that they, and their performance, matter to the firm. If management is seen to treat the process casually, the opposite message is all too easily conveyed.

Some ground rules for running appraisals are:

- The company should have one appraisal system used consistently by those conducting appraisals.
- The process should be treated as important by all members of the company. This requires appraisal meetings to be held with due regularity and properly prepared for and followed up.
- Since the appraisal process is designed to be of benefit to both the individual and the company, it needs to be participative and not merely something that is 'done to' the employee that has to be got through. Appraiser and employee both share the responsibility for ensuring that appraisal meetings are worthwhile and productive, which can best be done by discussing issues openly and straightforwardly.
- Having a set structure for appraisals means that both manager and employee can prepare and have clear expectations of the form that the appraisal meeting will take. Because there is a set format, people are free to concentrate on getting the best from the meeting.
- Appraisal meetings are not simply reviews of past performance as a prelude to salary review. Although looking back over past performance is part of it, the process is designed to be forward-looking and direction-setting.

Common misconceptions about appraisal include:

- *'People are only interested in their pay increase during an appraisal, so there's no point in discussing anything seriously.'* The mistake here is to muddle pay awards with performance appraisal. They are separate processes and it is much clearer and simpler to keep them that way. Pay awards are constrained by the company's business plan and by business performance as a whole. In most business structures, the pay award made to an individual is influenced by many factors beyond the quality of that individual's performance. So it makes sense to talk to an employee about their pay award in a meeting specific to that purpose. Make it clear that appraisal meetings are about job performance and direction setting.
- *'An informal chat will put the employee at ease and encourage them to participate better in the appraisal.'* All the indications are that informal approaches make the senior person feel more comfortable, but put the person with lower status at a disadvantage. Employees participate better when there is a clear, objective framework.
- *'Only very senior people can give appraisals.'* On the contrary, leaving appraisals solely in the hands of the directors all too often creates a bottleneck and leads to failure to hold them when they are due. The most appropriate person to conduct an appraisal is usually the person to whom the job holder reports on a day-to-day basis and who knows most about the work being done. If there is an effective system in place and people are properly coached to use it, valid appraisals can be run by junior managers.

A workable appraisal system

Taking into account the lack of time and scarcity of management resources in growing firms, an approach to performance appraisal should consider the following issues.

Who should conduct appraisals?

Each employee's appraisal should be held by someone senior to them who knows their work and with whom they work closely – usually, the person they report to on a day-to-day basis.

How often?

A full appraisal must be held every 12 months. There should be an interim appraisal (which can be briefer and less comprehensive) in between, at the six-month point. Everyone's annual appraisal *must* be held when it is due. It is not necessary for all appraisals in the company to happen at the same time – it can be more practical to spread them out through the year, by giving each individual their own appraisal date, on or close to their anniversary of joining the company.

Setting up

The actual time for the appraisal should be communicated and preparation forms issued at least two weeks in advance, to give adequate time for reflection and preparation.

Preparation

The job holder and the appraiser both prepare for the meeting by filling in an appraisal preparation form (Box 6.6). This is designed to serve as an *aide-mémoire* in the appraisal meeting, to ensure that each person covers the points they want to; there is no requirement to hand the form in. Additionally, the appraiser may ask some of the people with whom the employee works (this may include customers and suppliers, as well as colleagues) for feedback.

The appraisal meeting

The meeting is chaired by the appraiser, whose job it is to make sure that the agenda is worked through properly. A full appraisal meeting is likely to take between one and two hours, though an interim appraisal may take less time. The appraisal preparation form provides the framework for the meeting.

Box 6.6 Example of an appraisal preparation form

Preparation for full appraisal

Name: Date of this appraisal:
Job title: Date of last appraisal:
Appraiser: Date of next appraisal:

Review

1   What is the central purpose of this person's role? (Questions in this section are designed to make sure that there is a clear mutual understanding of the job holder's function in the company. Please consider what the current requirements of the person are, and whether there is any need to amend the job specification.)

2   Are there any points concerning the purpose of the job or the main job objectives, as specified in the job spec, that need to be clarified?

3   Goals set for achievement since the last appraisal. Have the goals been achieved? Write in the goals below, and indicate level of achievement for each, on a scale of 1–5 (5 = fully achieved; 3 = partially achieved; 1 = not achieved). Be prepared to comment on ratings.
    Goals set in last appraisal: Achievement rating/comment:

4   If longer-term goals have been set, comment on progress against them – is the person on track?
    Long-term goals: Comment on progress:

5   Performance standards of main tasks. (This section considers the quality of key aspects of job performance since the last appraisal. For each of the performance standards for the job, as given in the job spec or addendum to it, rate performance on a scale of 1–5 (5 = excellent; 3 = just meets the standard but room for improvement; 1 = seriously below standard).
    Performance standard: Performance rating:

6   Job strengths. What strengths are apparent? How have strengths contributed to job performance? How could they be built on?

7   Job weaknesses. What do you see as weaker areas? How have they affected job performance? How might they be improved?

8   Motivation. Please be ready to discuss issues of motivation, whether positive or negative. Do levels of challenge, enjoyment, satisfaction seem appropriate?

9   Do there appear to be motivational problems? Do you have ideas on how they might be dealt with?

10 Training and development review. What training/development support has been given in the last appraisal period? Is it being put to effective use?

Goal setting

11 Opportunities and direction. How might this person develop? Do you see opportunities to extend their contribution to the company?

12 What specific goals should be set for the coming appraisal period? Indicate how these would contribute to company goals.

Development support

13 What training or other development support might help this person achieve their goals?

14 Consider any further points on the person's ability to contribute to the company's plans; be prepared to discuss opportunities and problems.

Follow-up

After the meeting, the appraiser writes a brief note summarizing the goals set for the coming period and noting any key points arising in the meeting (Box 6.7). The contents of this note are confidential to the employee concerned, their appraiser and the appraiser's own senior management. The appraiser gives the employee a copy of this follow-up note within a week of the appraisal meeting. It is important for the employee to check the follow-up note and ensure that they understand and agree with it. This record serves as a reminder to the employee of their focus and priorities over the next period. It also provides the starting point for the next appraisal.

Box 6.7 Example of appraisal follow-up

Appraisal follow-up   **Confidential**

To:

From: Date:

This is a record of the key points arising out of our last appraisal meeting. Please keep and refer to it. Goals and points itemized will provide the starting point for the next appraisal meeting.

1   Goals set for achievement within the next six months:

2   Longer-term goals:

3   Overall focus and priorities during the next six months:

4   Key comments from performance review:

5   Training and development planned:

Conducting an appraisal meeting

The appraisal meeting presents an opportunity for a job holder to discuss openly their job performance, potential and future direction and the job holder needs to be as fully involved as possible. Within the basic framework set by the preparation form, a wide range of issues may have to be addressed, e.g. giving praise and recognition, confronting poor performance and helping someone talk about underlying problems. The appraiser has a dual role:

- To chair the meeting, guiding the agenda and keeping the process on track so as to give due weight to each section of the interview; ensure that appropriate issues are attended to; and ensure that discussion is relevant and clearly understood on both sides.
- To act as a participant in the meeting, giving input and responding appropriately to the appraisee, according to the stage of the interview and the nature of the issues to be tackled.

The appraiser is likely to have to vary their style of interaction as the interview proceeds, being prepared to use any of the following.

Consultation

Consultation is the key to running a successful appraisal meeting. Instead of telling the appraisee what you think, at each point ask for their own assessment first. In this way, you make it clear that they are responsible for their own performance and development. After all, it is their job and they know more about what they have and have not done than anyone else is likely to. Consulting does away with any embarrassing associations of being summoned to the head's study at school. The appraiser does not need to assume authority or talk down to the job holder, but simply sets in train a conversation between adults.

At the start of the meeting, it makes sense to set out the ground rules. Say clearly that this meeting is for the benefit of the job holder and will address two basic questions: 'How are you doing?' and 'Where do you go from here?' It is also designed to ensure that there is the best fit between the job holder's performance and development and the company's plans and goals. Then explicitly invite the job holder's participation in the meeting, explaining that on each question of the preparation form you will ask for their assessment and input.

The basis of consultation is simply to ask the appraisee to give their response on each issue: assessment of performance against objectives, diagnosis of strengths and weaknesses, problems and areas for development. Some constructive questions might be:

- How have you done in terms of the objectives set?
- That went well. What accounts for your success there?
- What do you think went wrong there?
- How have you rated yourself on that standard?
- How are your relationships with that group doing?
- Is there any feedback in particular that you'd like from me?

Listen to, and if necessary clarify, what is being said before disclosing your own assessment. This enables you to tune your feedback to the job holder's view of the matter. Often the job holder is more critical of their performance than is necessary, and your own feedback can be encouraging. Clarify the outcome of discussion, by giving clear praise and/or stating what change or improvement is required, then move to the next item. Encourage and coach the appraisee to put forward their own ideas about problem diagnosis, solutions, goals and plans.

Constructive feedback

Give praise and recognition and express appreciation. Make sure that any feedback you give is:

- Specific, using examples.
- Directed at actions and behaviour and not personality.
- Designed to help and improve.
- Balanced.

When you have to address faults and under-performance, it is important to establish what lies behind the failure to meet a standard or goal. Is the problem one of *learning* or *understanding*? Did the person not grasp what was expected of them or what they would need to put in to reach the goal? Is there a problem with aptitude? Do they lack knowledge or training? Having brought the problem into the open, you can explore what lies behind it and how it can be corrected.

Dealing with defensiveness

Most people respond positively to the opportunity to discuss their progress and prospects openly on an adult-to-adult basis. However, you may encounter difficult responses such as:

- Not wanting to participate or be involved.
- Non-committal.
- Negative.
- Defensive, appearing not to take anything on board, arguing, blaming others and the system.

Responses like these may arise because the appraisee is *unwilling* to be involved in sharing responsibility in the appraisal process; or because they feel *inadequate* to do so. In either case, if you remain steadily non-defensive yourself and make it clear that you would be interested in hearing what they have to say, it is possible to encourage participation:

- I'd really like to hear your view on this . . .
- In many ways it would be quicker and easier for me just to tell you, but we might both be missing out on something important . . .

- So you don't see this as your responsibility? There may be some misunderstanding here – what do see your part in this as being, then?

Confronting

Where there has been sustained under-performance or problem behaviour that has already been addressed using an exploratory/corrective approach, you need to confront the issue. A short, clear, direct statement is required:

- You are still not making out paperwork in the detail required by the system. We have discussed this twice before. There have since been three major problems caused by you, which have cost the company time, money and customer good will. You are not working to standard. I want to make it clear that this will not be discussed again. If you fail once more to complete paperwork, we will start disciplinary proceedings.

Be prepared for emotional responses to confrontation. You may need to repeat the message before it sinks in. Importantly, do not engage in argument; the time for discussion on this issue is past.

Goal setting

The key requirements here are:

- That the appraisee can see how achieving their personal goals will contribute to the ability of the company to meet targets.
- Gaining the appraisee's commitment to meeting goals.

Where possible, involving the appraisee in identifying the goals towards which they are to work is the most effective way to ensure commitment. With people who feel reluctant or unable to do this, showing them how their contribution will fit with what the company needs to be successful becomes particularly important.

The meeting finishes on a forward-looking note, with an evaluation of what the job holder needs to learn in order to progress towards goals and improve weaknesses, and outline planning of how that learning is to be provided.

Systematic development of competences

It should be apparent that appraisal provides the company with a systematic process for taking regular stock of the abilities available in the company, evaluating them against the competence demands of strategic plans and goals, and setting in train career development and training plans that can, as far as possible, prepare existing members of staff to grow with the company. At this point, it would be prudent to collate all staff training needs in a comprehensive training and development plan, with specific actions, dates and budgets.

Recruiting new people

Some positions will still need to be filled from outside the organization and an equally systematic approach to recruiting will be required. When we set out to hire a new person or consider an existing member of the firm for a job we need to fill, the basic task is assessing available candidates in the light of two questions:

- *Can they do the job?* Do they have the requisite knowledge and skills to accomplish the tasks involved?
- *Will they do the job?* Do they have the appropriate personal qualities and attitudes to make a success of this role in this company, with its particular culture? What motivates them, what are their career expectations?

Successful recruitment calls for a systematic process based on the following disciplines:

- Being specific about what you are looking for and defining *selection criteria*.
- Collecting *evidence* (rather than mere impressions) about candidates' past performance, capabilities and motivation.
- *Matching candidates to selection criteria* rather than comparing candidates with one another.

Specifying what you are looking for simply means drawing up a job specification and person specification (see Chapter 4). This process enables you to identify clear selection criteria, in the light of which candidates for the job can be systematically assessed. The specifications also provide the basis for targeting candidates, whether through agencies, contacts and word of mouth, or advertising.

Once candidates are located, the job of recruitment is to gather evidence about the candidates to be considered, and in each case to ask: How closely does this person match the criteria? The main source of evidence is the job interview. Properly conducted, this provides the most rounded opportunity to obtain the facts on a person's performance and achievements and to gain information about how they approach work and what matters to them. However, evidence comes from a number of other sources:

- For some jobs, aptitude and capability tests may be useful. These should always be done under appropriate conditions that do not introduce extraneous stress factors (such as being stared at by existing job holders).
- Samples of work can be vital for some jobs. Make sure that it is the candidate's own work – ask for practical detail on how and when the work was produced.
- References can be important, if only as an indication that this person can find someone to put in a good word for them. Taking up a reference gives an opportunity to check that the job content and responsibility that a candidate has claimed are not exaggerated.

Such additional sources of evidence can be used to back up and fill out the evidence we get from interviewing. We are trying to build up a prediction of how an individual will perform in a set of circumstances that they have not yet faced. All we can do is make an informed judgement about which of a series of candidates stands the best chance of meeting requirements. The best predictor we have is an accurate account of what they have done before, how they approach their work, and any patterns or themes emerging that reveal particular characteristics.

Selection interviewing

The aim is to get good evidence on what a candidate can do and how they conduct relationships. So a good interviewer allows candidates to show themselves as they really are, despite the artificial and potentially intimidating circumstances of a job interview. You want the candidate to drop any play acting: you want to get behind smoke screens and impressions, to allow the person to show who they are, how they set about things, what they've learned, what mistakes they've made, what they have to offer that is special.

Prerequisites for this are that the candidate and the interviewer are able to relax; and that the interviewer listens, using a questioning style that does not unwittingly contaminate the evidence.

Preparation

Allow enough time to review the application against the job and person specifications before you see the candidate. Which areas of the person's experience are likely to give you relevant information? Draw up a checklist of the areas you need to investigate. Plan how you will phrase an opening question for each area. Ensure that the interview is scheduled for a time and place that enable punctuality (on both sides), privacy and freedom from interruptions.

Interview format

The interview format will consist of four sections:

- *Welcome* – set up a relaxed atmosphere for the interview before you start. Settle the candidate in, outline the agenda, set the scene by running briefly over the job requirements and giving some context on the company.
- *Ask for information* – the main part of the interview, where you use exploratory questioning (see below) to draw out evidence.
- *Supply information* – the opportunity you give to the candidate to ask about the job and the company. Notice what they ask about.
- *Plan and part* – closing the interview by making clear what the next stages of recruitment will be and when the candidate can expect to hear from you. It is not appropriate at this point to indicate whether the candidate is likely to be successful.

Interviewing for evidence

Interviewing for evidence is a method designed to get candidates to reveal themselves and their work as they really are. The approach seems conversational: the interviewee is encouraged to talk freely and confidently, while the interviewer listens attentively and *follows up* on what is said. The interviewer periodically shifts the focus of question and answer so as systematically to cover all of the prepared areas of questioning. For each area you wish to explore, start with an open question:

- Tell me about your job as . . .

Listen and follow up with a question responding to what they have said:

- Which areas did you enjoy most?

Continue the process of listening and responding, then narrow down to specifics with more direct questions:

- What was it in particular that made that difficult for you?

Probe and ask for clarification to get information straight:

- Are you saying that the problem was lack of training?

Summarize briefly what you have heard:

- So you achieved a lot in that position, but you feel you were less efficient than you could have been with a better-trained team?

This process of opening up a topic and then narrowing it down to chunks of clearly examined information is known as the *interview funnel*. Once you have summarized at the end of a funnel, you are poised to open your next funnel, using your prepared list of topics to ensure that you cover all the areas planned. (In the series above, the interviewer could now move on to explore the candidate's approach to responsibility taking: did this person try to do anything to remedy having untrained staff?; if not, why not?)

When a job interview fails to produce an accurate assessment of a candidate's suitability, it is usually because the interviewer has accepted what they said at face value, without clarifying particulars. Often this is because the interviewer is mentally jumping ahead and thinking up their next question rather than paying attention to the candidate. Don't proceed so fast. You cannot think of a follow-up question until you have heard what the candidate has to say.

The direction of questioning all the time needs to be to get down to what this person actually did in a given situation, how they behaved, what shaped their thinking. Your job is to get beyond the vague generalizations that leave the interviewers making decisions on the basis of assumptions, not information:

- You say you were responsible for the day-to-day running of the department. What did those responsibilities consist of?

The answer needs to address what tasks the candidate undertook personally and what were delegated; who the staff were, whether they reported to the candidate, who hired them; who controlled the budget, how much discretion in decision making this person had. If it doesn't, the candidate is likely to be claiming higher status than they actually held. Check it out:

- Can you give me an example of the kind of decisions you had to deal with?

Evaluating the information

It is essential to note down the information you are collecting during the interview. As soon as possible after the interview, summarize your findings on an interview record form (Box 6.8), which is drawn up to match the categories on the person specification. When you have seen all the candidates, complete the ratings for each criterion, making a considered comparison of how each candidate rates relative to the standard. You should now be able to make your selection without too much difficulty and without over-reliance on subjective factors.

Box 6.8 Interview record form

Interview record

Candidate's name: Date:
Vacancy: Interviewer:

Category	Evidence	Rating
1 Knowledge		1 2 3 4 5
2 Skills		1 2 3 4 5
3 Personal qualities		1 2 3 4 5
4 Education and qualifications		1 2 3 4 5
5 Experience		1 2 3 4 5
6 Career expectations		1 2 3 4 5
7 Other		1 2 3 4 5

Avoiding recruitment pitfalls

Most mistakes in recruiting are made as a result of inventing the candidate, rather than seeing the actual person in front of us. This syndrome arises from a number of sources:

- Relying on impressions, especially first impressions, and interpreting everything in the light of them.
- Putting the candidate under pressure, in the mistaken belief that this will show whether they can do the job under pressure. (All it will show is how they cope with your interview technique.)
- Interviewer anxiety, so the interviewer focuses on what questions to ask rather than listening to the candidate.
- Interviewer hogs the conversation, talks more than listening.
- Interviewer completes candidates' answers for them, either out loud or mentally, by assuming that they have said what the interviewer expected them to.
- Over-reliance on apparently similar previous experience without checking out the content to find out what the candidate actually knows how to do. The same job title can encompass widely different duties in different company contexts.

Induction of new recruits

Once you have carried out a careful selection process, it makes sense to ensure that the new recruit gets off to a good start. The purpose of induction is to enable someone new to a job to become productive in it as easily and rapidly as possible, rather than leaving them to pick the job up haphazardly. The new person has to gain familiarity not just with new job content and performance standards, but with a new company, new surroundings, new people – and a new culture. This last can be the most difficult adjustment to make, since the person has to lose their sense of belonging to their last company and acquire the sense of belonging in this one.

The process of becoming competent in a new job and getting to feel at home in a new working environment takes several weeks, and often months. A good induction programme acknowledges this. There needs to be a systematic plan, distributed to everyone involved. In planning an induction, consider:

- What will this person need to learn to become technically proficient in this job?
- What information do they need (directly relevant to their role; and background on the company)?
- What systems and procedures will they have to follow, and of what others will they need a working knowledge?
- Which people do they need to get to know speedily?
- What can we tell the person about the way we do things around here?

Induction is not merely a ritual of shaking hands and listening to people talking about what they do – it needs to be based on the learning needs of the person concerned. Make sure that everyone involved understands what they should contribute, and that the new person is clear about what they are expected to gain from each part of the programme. With more senior appointments, also consult the new person on what they see as their induction needs.

It should be borne in mind that there is a limit to the amount of information that people can take in at one time, and that learning needs to be consolidated by practical application. Rather than devote a concentrated period to induction and then expect the person to retain all the information and signals given to them, it is more effective to intersperse induction sessions through the time that the person spends picking up and getting on with the job. As with any training process, it is important to review outcomes, to find out how much from the induction is clear and has been retained, and what may need to be gone over again.

Building and leading the team: The underlying skills

The essence of leadership is enabling: bringing together a combination of people, putting them in touch with a purpose, and acting in a way that appropriately promotes the ability of a particular set of people to meet that purpose. In this chapter, the underlying emphasis has been on leadership aimed at encouraging others to grow into leader roles, and on the delegation of responsibility. What skills should such a leader aim to possess?

The job combines strategic focus, and the ability to articulate this to others, with sensitivity to people and situations.

1 Strategic focus

- Focusing on the direction and purpose that are right for *this* team or company.
- Setting specific goals for accomplishment while holding a larger vision in view.
- Aligning the team or organization with the vision and purpose so as to pursue them effectively.

2 Managerial techniques

- Ability to reduce chunks of information to simple frameworks and essentials.
- Systematic and understandable decision processes.

3 People skills

- Varying leadership styles according to the needs of the people and the situation.
- Ability to set a climate of open, non-defensive communication, where people get the information they need, are able to express their point of view and are listened to.
- Setting clear boundaries and limits – ability to use tough skills.
- Encouraging learning and development – ability to use nurturing skills.
- Offering, and open to, helpful feedback.
- Teamworking, ability to move between functions and operate as a contributor and supporter as well as direction-giver.

- Ability to discern what prompts people to give of their best.
- Clarifying – ensuring that goals and expectations are explicit and clearly understood.

Notes

1 Hersey, P. and Blanchard, K. (1977) *Management of Organizational Behavior*, Prentice Hall, Englewood Cliffs, NJ.
2 Belbin, M. (1996) *Management Teams: Why They Succeed or Fail*, Butterworth-Heinemann, Oxford and www.belbin.com.

Further reading

1 Blanchard, K., Zigarmi, P. and Zigarmi, D. (1994) *Leadership and the One Minute Manager*, HarperCollins Business, London.
2 Handy, C. (1989) *The Age of Unreason*, Arrow Books, London.
3 Whitmore, J. (2002) *Coaching for Performance: Growing People, Performance and Purpose*, Nicholas Brealey Publishing, London.

Culture, Creativity and Change

CHAPTER 7

Key issues dealt with in this chapter are:

- What is meant by company culture?
- Is there a distinctive small-firm culture?
- Will formalizing the organization of the firm spoil its culture?
- Influencing culture positively: taking conscious steps to reinforce what is special.
- Embracing development: fostering learning and personal growth.

Culture and the growing organization

One of the concerns of people who have been present in the early stages of the formation of a business is that something special may get lost as the organization expands. If you ask people what the special quality might be, they talk about a 'can-do' atmosphere where people are ready to tackle anything; or a sense of resourcefulness, with opportunities being made and risen to; or freshness and creativity of approach; or a seamless camaraderie, where everyone pulls together; or a feeling of belonging to a family. What they are describing is their experience of the company culture during that phase of the firm's development where much of the organization is informal and unstructured.

If the firm is to grow, things will have to change. New people, who have not been 'baptized' in the same way as the original crew, will come in. New technology is likely to be acquired. Parts of the organization will have to be differentiated: people will no longer literally all be members of a single team as they could be in a single cell structure. The separate parts of the organization will need to be linked and coordinated by processes and systems that are clear to all those involved. This means that knowledge about how the organization works, which has probably been carried in people's heads, will need to be codified and written down so that it can be passed on uniformly to new entrants. There will need to be consistent policies and sanctions for dealing with any deviation from procedures and from standards of work and behaviour.

Is it possible to grow and develop the organization without losing the spirit of the venture? Can the original culture be preserved when the organization is enlarged and formalized?

Not exactly. A culture, by definition, is something that grows, so it is not possible to freeze it in a given state. All of the firm's members are, in some way, involved in it - culture cannot simply be manipulated to reflect what management thinks is best. Nevertheless, that is no reason to ignore it, for culture can deeply affect productivity and the impression that the firm creates on customers and other associates. While culture cannot be controlled, it is influenced by the management attitudes and behaviour that people see. So it makes sense for management to understand something about its workings, to maintain such awareness as they can of the state of their firm's culture, and to work within it for positive outcomes.

What is organizational culture?

It is interesting to watch a group of people who have not previously worked together collaborate on a task. Within a short space of time, certain assumptions will have developed about the way in which the members of the group go about things: what the group's purpose is, what matters they will give priority to, how closely they will stick to the brief, how they will treat one another in the group, who is more and who less important, whether the prevailing mood should be serious or light and so on. Some of these points may be made explicit: there might be a statement of the agreed purpose and specific roles might be assigned to individuals. However, it is likely that a number of the assumptions that shape the way people work together will remain unvoiced. The group will already have begun to form a culture. If all the members of the group come from the same employing organization, the culture in the group is likely to reflect aspects of the larger culture - but it will not necessarily replicate it entirely.

In Chapter 4, the culture of an organization was described as 'the way things are done around here', a set of shared assumptions and beliefs that accumulates when people come together in a group, through which they experience a sense of something to belong to. The beliefs are about what counts as important, the values, standards and expectations that people ought to subscribe to in their work and their behaviour towards one another. The scale of values embodies what people understand as *what really counts*. It may reflect official policy and company priorities - but it may equally reinterpret them or even subvert them.

To take a simple example, time keeping is often mediated through the firm's culture and deviates in practice from the hours officially stipulated - the norm may be to get in half an hour early in one firm, or ten minutes late in another. The 'long-hours culture' is not stipulated in people's contracts of employment, but results from their belief that visible devotion to work is a badge of valour and will be rewarded. In ways like this, expectations build up about what is normal and acceptable behaviour within the organization.

We can thus understand culture as an evolving set of beliefs and values that inform and channel people's behaviour in the firm. The culture derives from more than one source, comprising:

- Matters that are officially promulgated as important, such as the purpose, priorities, standards, values and ethics of the firm.
- How members of the firm experience and understand the official line.
- How members of the firm respond to the official organization and to one another – positively, neutrally or negatively.
- The values that people themselves bring to the mix.

Culture pervades the organization: it is carried in its structure and processes, which, consciously or not, embody values and transmit messages about what matters. Do you call people supervisors or use the more democratic-sounding term 'team leader'? Are staff appraisals carried out on schedule, or is there a habit of postponing them because something 'more important' takes priority? Culture is also carried by people – each person brings with them to the organization values and assumptions that they have developed elsewhere, which may or may not fit with what they meet in the work culture they join. And culture is carried in the physical and social environment – in the size, layout and décor of the workspace, in dress code, the way people address one another, whether and how they socialize and so on.

Understanding the organization's culture

The cultural brew is determined by what captures people's attention and has significance for them. It is passed between people, and develops, through various transmitters, which include *formal organizational processes* such as induction, appraisal and training, staff consultations, meetings and events; and which also include *informal means*, the language and jargon that prevail, jokes, gossip, stories and myths. All of these can bind people together in a community that gives them a shared history, as well as a shared value system. Culture develops in response to the *meanings* that people attach to actions and events. One of the issues that puts culture beyond the capability of managerial control is the way in which powerful people are regarded. The stories that are told about them, the way in which they are characterized and their motives interpreted, can contribute an important part of the cultural mix.

Although managers cannot control a culture, it makes sense for them to keep in touch with its development. The culture itself is expressed through a mixture of the official and the unofficial, so a mix of official and unofficial contacts and observations gives you the best chance of keeping in touch with and understanding it. Official processes of employee consultation, facilitating feedback from staff to their managers, inviting employee suggestions for improvements, engaging staff in SWOT analysis – all of these provide information on what holds significance for the members of the organization. However, there is likely to be a certain amount of holding back, with people revealing only what is felt to be prudent. So unofficial ways of staying in touch matter: walking the floor observantly, being a good listener over coffee or a drink, or on shared journeys.

Is there a small-business culture?

Each organization's culture is unique in some way, because it is produced by the particular set of people and circumstances that prevail in it. However, we can sense that certain types of organization may share cultural similarities – we can probably discern, say, an advertising culture or a banking culture. Is there such a thing as a typical small-business culture?

The question is worth asking because it comes up in recruiting: can a candidate whose experience is with larger organizations make the adjustment to a smaller one? In addition, the size of the firm, and whether staff see this in a positive, neutral or negative light, are often used as an explanation for the way things are. Working in a smaller, owner-managed business – whether as owner, manager or staff member – can prove a substantially different experience from employment in a large corporation. Key factors are likely to be:

- The involvement, visibility and accessibility of the owner.
- A smaller peer group – someone is more likely to be the only person in the firm doing that kind of work.
- Fewer opportunities to draw on the informal support of a group of colleagues.
- A comparative lack of established procedures and systems, so that people have to initiate these or cope without.
- A comparative lack of support services, so that people have to do more for themselves or cope without.
- Fewer role models for career advancement.
- Fewer opportunities for sideways career movement.

These factors, while not exclusive to smaller firms (local branches of many large employers will exhibit some of these), do condition the working climate in them and have an effect on culture. Employees in a small, growing business are likely to be looking at a situation where their chance to progress will depend on the firm's ability to grow; where they need to relate to people much senior themselves; where they have to make provision for themselves, rather than having things done for them; and where the trappings of corporate prestige are few. Some people will thrive, some will adapt readily with a little explanation and help. Others will find the distance between the working experience they are looking for and that on offer just too great for them.

This raises important issues for recruitment and induction. Taking stock of the working climate and the culture of the firm can help avoid the waste of time and resources that results from employing square pegs for round holes. As discussed in Chapter 6, before offering a candidate a job, assess how this person will *fit* with the climate and culture, and how they could *contribute* to it. On which aspects of their previous working environments does the candidate place value? What attitudes and beliefs underpin their approach to work? When a new person joins the firm, as part of their induction, check out what expectations they bring with them about the way things are done, and help them make adjustments to the norms that prevail here.

It is easy for the small employer to feel disadvantaged when assessing candidates with a big-company background and to slip into excusing or making apologies for the small-firm environment. Such an attitude can then have a knock-on effect on culture, being picked up as negativity and leading people to dwell on shortcomings in comparison with the supposed advantages of larger entities (Box 7.1). It is much more useful to stop and think: What is it that makes this a good place to work? What is special about the way we do things? What are the values that people subscribe to here? The answer may not lie in perks and marks of status, but it could lie in the opportunity to be part of a community where individuals can make a difference and see the outcomes of their work, and where people know that they contribute to the distinctiveness that has enabled the company to get started and grow.

Box 7.1 Unsuccessful employee, or mickey mouse employer?

Sandra had been with her new employer, a small, specialist financial services provider, for just under a year. Previously engaged in customer research in a large company in a similar field, she had been persuasive at interview about seeking the challenge of a new environment and her desire to return to selling.

Sandra was able to talk about contacting and developing customers, but there was little evidence of her actually doing it, and it was now clear that she would not meet her target and would miss her bonus. Her response to this was to find fault with the firm and its poor facilities, criticizing the work of the manager responsible for coordinating account planning and complaining that her section administrator, a non-graduate, was not up to her job. It was noticeable that wherever she was, Sandra slowed things down. At the weekly coordination meeting, as well as reporting lengthily on her own area she would prolong discussions with often irrelevant observations about her experience with other companies. At lunchtime, when people were keen to catch their customers, Sandra would draw colleagues into lengthy chats. Frequently she would interrupt someone during the day saying that she 'just needed a bit of support'. She would then complain about something that was wrong with management.

Sandra's criticisms were not without foundation: the firm's success was rooted in 'chutzpah', diligence and resourcefulness, and people often had to put in extra work to make up for shortcomings in the information systems. Nobody had been particularly conscious of this – they merely got on with it.

At first, Sandra's behaviour had little effect on this cohesive, get-on-with-it culture, but over time it began to divide the organization. As one camp became less tolerant of Sandra's moaning, the other took notice, starting to refer to the firm as a 'mickey mouse operation' and to excuse failures on grounds of the firm's lack of credibility.

Sandra had to go. She floundered in a situation where she needed to do her own groundwork without the support of a corporate structure. The firm improved its information systems, but also came out of this experience with more consciousness of the positive aspects of its 'just get on with it' culture.

The influence of founders and owners

Company founders and owners almost invariably have a high profile in their firms and are distinctively present and visible. As such, they influence the culture in important and interconnected ways: by the *symbolic power* attributed to them;

through the effects of their *personal motivation* on the direction and development of the firm; and when their relationship with the company and their management style tend towards *paternalism*. These three issues can arise around the leader of any organization, but when the leader is the owner of a small business, their influence on culture can be especially pronounced.

Symbolic power: The founder myth

The founder embodies the vision and set of values that got the company off the ground – he or she *is* the origin of the company and the living symbol of the company's history. The founder and/or owner is likely to be seen as the true leader of the firm, regardless of their official role on the organization chart. Special power grows up around such people, beyond their considerable actual power to take decisions affecting resources, through the build-up of stories and legend. It is often believed that they have a particular ability to win and keep customers, for instance, or that they can solve problems in some 'magic' or 'brilliant' way that lesser members of the organization cannot rival.

There may be a grain of truth in such suppositions. Customers are likely to be flattered by dealing with the real boss, and to make this preference known to others who try to approach them. The founder/owner is likely to carry a particularly keen sense of the firm's priorities and possibilities, a longer experience of dealing with its problems and greater confidence in using its resources than anyone else. Over-emphasis and over-reliance on capabilities like this will inhibit the empowerment of other members of the organization, holding back their competence to bear responsibility and represent the firm.

The myths that grow up around founders and owners are not always positive. They may be seen as capitalist exploiters (regardless of their actual financial gain, and ignoring the financial risk they have undertaken), or impractical visionaries who do not inhabit the real world (despite their proven ability to bring a business into existence). Attributions like these are, to some extent, made to all leaders. It is nevertheless as well to be aware of them, so as not to collude inadvertently with negative effects. A founder who has strong links with a key customer, for instance, may have to take deliberate steps to initiate a successor into handling that relationship and to reinforce confidence in their abilities (Box 7.2).

Founders' and owners' personal motivation

The personal motivation of the founders and owners is likely to carry exceptional weight in setting the direction for the firm and its development. This will influence culture in various ways, through the choices made about organizational structure and delegation practices at the official level, and through employees' perceptions of the factors that shape decisions. It is easy for employees to explain the reasons behind decisions and policies as 'what the boss wants'. That can feed into a strand of fatalism in the culture that goes against responsibility and initiative taking on the part of employees, if the idea becomes pervasive that 'it doesn't matter what we suggest, the boss will do what suits him/her'.

Box 7.2 Problems of the founder myth

The members of a small firm can often be seen to collude with a founding figure in according that person iconic power. In the past, the founder has been able to conjure up business, energize people, overcome problems and make things happen. He or she has done magic – and people like to believe that they still can.

In one firm, the myth of the magic founder was perpetuated by letting another senior person take on the duller aspects of running the company. The original founder and managing director concentrated on developing sales and seeking new markets, leaving another director to manage operations. Because of the opportunistic way in which the MD went about things, his field trips would result in urgent projects, leading to changes in priorities and moving goal posts back at base.

The second director was left with the problem of channelling staff efforts to meet shifting priorities. Staff became resentful at the frequent changes of schedule; nobody ever seemed to know what was going on. People who had been part of a 'can-do' culture in the company's early days lost motivation and started clock watching and complaining. Instead of taking responsibility for problems, they would simply dump them on the operations director. This person became the 'bad boss' who could not sort anything out. The founder was still regarded as the 'good boss'. He would breeze into the office, call in on people and say hello, call a meeting to announce his successes, change a couple of schedules and breeze out again.

The magical thinking that was going on here was damaging the organization. The 'founder myth' of the MD as a buccaneering hero uniquely capable of conjuring up business had something to it: he was a man with special standing in the industry, a nose for business and a gift for building relationships. His reputation attracted people to the firm and positively influenced motivation. However, it was wrong to imagine that only his way of doing things could bring in business, or that internal disorganization was the fault of the operations director.

In order for the company to grow, its members had to grow big enough to put the founder myth in perspective. First, the operations director had to challenge the MD's undisciplined approach. He insisted on a marketing plan and a simple procedure for checking the feasibility of orders before making promises to customers. Secondly, key members of the operations staff were empowered to take on management responsibilities, with the result that their chief source of motivation became pride in their section's performance, rather than sharing in the MD's reflected glory.

The founder's special qualities continue to be an asset to the company and to give it edge, and he is still able to inspire customers and staff – but as chairman, not MD. There is now a stable core management team running the business.

The founder's motivation can also complicate the development of structure and delegation. Not everyone who starts a business wants to manage an established company. The skill set and motivation that get a business off the ground emphasize opportunism and risk taking – there may be careful planning, but much will be done on a basis of 'promise first, deliver later', with a great deal of trial and error. Because the stock of knowledge in the business is low – everyone is still inexperienced in running this particular outfit – decision making can be quite free and priorities very clear. Within the company's delivery system there may be considerable muddle, but the job gets done and the team somehow wins through on enthusiasm, commitment and resourcefulness. It is like magic and the founder may feel – and appear – quite heroic, heading a band who are engaged in seizing an opportunity, a dream, and proving that it works. Company legends are made of this stuff!

A few years down the track, a company that has continued in business is qualitatively different from a fledgling and cannot rely on muddling through. However, it is not unknown for owner-managers to find difficulty in adapting to the differentiated role structure and disciplined processes of the developed organization. It can be tempting for the owner-manager – and some succumb – to ignore or override the rules of the organization. The way in which the owner is seen to treat the official organization, with respect or otherwise, will set up cultural messages affecting the image of the owner and of the company. If the owner is seen to flout the rules set for others, the messages will be negative. To avoid this, the owner may be better advised to step aside from the chief executive position, and to take a role better matched to their motivation profile and talents.

Paternalism

When someone has set up a business they identify strongly with it. It is their creation, they have taken risks to bring it into being and their life is entwined with it. Their conception of the firm and its employees often tends towards *paternalism*, a sense of parental responsibility on behalf of the staff. While this can feed into a very intimate and cosy culture, with high levels of loyalty, it leaves the owner saddled with unrealistic expectations of how staff should be treated. In a paternalistic culture, much is expected of the parent/leader, and little of the children/employees.

One big happy family: The cosy culture in the smaller firm

Related to paternalism is the idea of the firm as family. Family metaphors are often applied to work organizations. They have peculiar aptness for owner-managed and growing businesses, where the founder has indeed 'given birth' to the venture, and where the founder's partner in private life and other members of their real family may be present to complicate matters.

This idea of the business as family seems attractive: when people talk of their place of work as like a family, they are expressing approval and wanting to convey a sense of warmth and loyalty. Working here, they are implying, is about more than a cold contract of doing a job for money – it is about being involved and committed and being valued by a 'caring' employer.

The trouble with families, however, is that they can become dysfunctional. A family is a private entity that functions on affection, trust, morality and custom, and when any of these break down, it can produce the rawest and most wounding of emotional conflicts; not the sort of thing you want when you are trying to get your job done.

The idea of the business as family can all too easily hamper responsibility taking by employees accustomed to viewing founders and owners as powerful parents who are the source of everything – they hold the purse strings and take decisions, and only they can solve problems. Employees are viewed as smaller people who cannot be expected to contribute to grown-up processes but should work hard and eagerly, not causing trouble and abiding by the decisions of the adults.

Of course, this cannot be. Growth in the business will heap problems on a paternalistic management. It will expand the decision-making and problem-solving workload of senior management who do not delegate responsibility. Employees who stay grow older and their lifestyles and expectations change. Some may remain compliant, but others will become bored and frustrated.

Stepping out from the paternalistic culture

It is up to the boss to take the initiative in stepping out of paternalism, by consciously using a professional approach to leadership (see situational leadership in Chapter 6) and by inviting staff to contribute as adults.

A paternalistic culture is governed by one habit of mind: 'only the boss knows the answer'. The employee, faced with a problem or dilemma, does not want to make a mistake. Therefore, the problem has to be referred to the boss for a decision:

- To which client should I give priority out of these two?
- We're out of stock – what shall we do?

Loyal employees may also strongly wish to protect the boss against harm, and so they will give warnings of problems:

- I really don't think this supplier is reliable.
- There's a conflict brewing between those two people. I think you ought to know (and, by implication, do something about it).
- We're getting a bottleneck in order processing with two people on holiday.
- I've had six complaints from customers this week that they can't get through on the phone – this phone system is really not good enough.

From the outside, it is easy to see that the boss needs to start turning the questions and problems back to the person raising them, and saying: What do you propose? In leadership terms, this means shifting from a proactive style to a participative or a delegating style. However, what is also being invoked is a change in 'the way things are done around here' – a change in people's expectations and customs. It is best to make this explicit:

- You've brought me a problem to solve, but I'm not the right person to deal with issues like this. I think you should handle them, and I believe you are able to. From now on, instead of merely bringing me the problem, think about it first and try to bring me your suggestion for solving it. What would you recommend? Do you know what that would cost? Are there alternatives? Come back to me when you've looked into it.

When the boss stops giving the answers, staff can grow and contribute like adults. There need be no loss of control. The first step is to change a habit of mind – the employee has to recommend a solution instead of simply reporting an issue. The recommendation is then evaluated by the boss and accepted or rejected. The step after that is to expand the employee's area of discretion, to allow them to spend within an agreed budgetary framework or to decide client priorities within an agreed marketing and sales plan. The mechanism of control is shifted from the boss's exclusive power of decision to a set of plans, budgets and agreements. This looks like introducing more formality into proceedings, but that formality underpins a sharing of power that treats the employee as an adult capable of reaching a reasoned decision.

Structure, empowerment and the can-do culture

Is there any substance in the concern that formalizing the organization's structure will introduce bureaucracy, kill the buzz in a culture of contribution and inhibit initiative taking by staff? The question tends to be raised by those who are most comfortable with a loose and informal form of organization, which, as we have already seen, may well include the owner, for whom introducing structure may be a chore. However, it can also be prompted by a misconception about the way that structure and procedures affect people's ability to perform.

There is no automatic opposition between structure and procedures and people's motivation and willingness to contribute. Indeed, there are instances where a lack of structure inhibits motivation and contribution. A loose and informal organization suits people who are naturally confident and assertive and who identify and pursue their own goals. However, it disadvantages people who are less self-assured and self-directed – who may have a valuable contribution to make, but not be ready to push it forward. For people like this, clear differentiation of work roles, definition of standards and ordering of procedures are empowering – like the trellis that enables plants to climb. Whereas in an informal environment they are held back by uncertainty and overpowered by more confident players, supported by the right structure they understand expectations and priorities and can deliver their true worth.

The point is to use structure and procedures to clarify expectations and ease coordination, to support the firm's people in making their varied contributions – and to bring out potential strengths. Good structure and procedures enable people to play their part in the functioning of the organization in pursuit of strategic purpose, and keep them in touch with the results of their labours (Box 7.3). Bad ones tie people into the procedures themselves, so that serving the system becomes an end in itself. There is no need for that.

Influencing culture positively

While they cannot dictate the set of responses that constitutes the culture of the firm, management can do much to set its tone by the way in which they communicate and use the organization's processes.

If you do not wish to leave cultural development to chance, it is as well to have a clear idea of the *values that matter* and that you wish to endorse. Positive

Box 7.3 Scaling up the value of efficient administration in a creative business

Originally set up as a base for a trio of freelancers, the studio had over time developed into a firm employing 20 designers. The firm's understanding of the evolution of the retail environment and the quality of thought and execution of its creative solutions attracted customers and its reputation among designers was high. It was a good studio to have on your CV and vacancies were always easy to fill.

On the surface, this was a well-established business. However, profitability was a problem – too many jobs failed to make money, largely because they overran on time. Pre-presentation panics were a recurring event and stress levels ran high. The matter became serious when an important new client expressed alarm at what they saw as a lack of professionalism.

It was not that the studio lacked systems for managing resource allocation and expenditure. The problem was that people followed them in a perfunctory way and discrepancies only became apparent when it was too late to correct them.

The philosophy of the studio had always been that this was an association of designers, creative led. It was an article of faith to have no account handlers to come between the client and the designers whose expertise they were buying. So the lead designer on any job was supposed to act as project manager, controlling time and budget. In practice most designers took short cuts through the systems, and felt they were right to do so – after all, design values always had priority, that was the culture.

Attempts to convince senior designers of the need to put a higher value on efficient project administration were fruitless. In the end, the directors saw no alternative to appointing a non-designer as studio manager. They anticipated resistance and non-cooperation. In the event, the change to the organization was harmonious and produced almost immediate improvement. Senior designers, freed from their amateurish attempts at project management, respected the contribution of this professional administrator and approached their clients with renewed confidence.

values give people a reason to take pride in their work and the firm to which they belong. They can be centred on the firm's strategic competences – what is special about the product, expertise, standard of service to customers – as well as the standards of behaviour that prevail among people, ethics, the firm's contribution to the community, or shared passions or interests of the firm's members.

On an everyday basis, members of management influence culture through the *behaviour that people see*. What role models do they provide, what ways of behaving and responding to events seem to be preferred? What are the issues to which they are seen to pay attention? What do they watch, what is measured and controlled? What ways of going about things seem to bring recognition?

The interpretations placed on everyday behaviour are basic to the shaping of culture. This is why it is a good idea for managers to be transparent in communicating the thinking behind their priorities and actions – if no explanation is given, people will make one up for themselves.

Culture is transmitted through the *customs* that prevail in the company. These cover a whole spectrum, from official organization processes though semi-official events like the office party to matters such as celebrating birthdays.

The firm's *organizational processes and systems* embody its official customs for dealing with people. The way these are set up and carried out has an effect on shaping the community within the firm:

- Communication systems.
- Recruitment practices.
- Induction practices.
- Appraisal system.
- Training and development approach.
- Disciplinary system.
- Pay and benefits structure and its underlying approach.

Each of these can be conducted in a way that strengthens core values. This entails making sure that the way things are done has authenticity, that the approach used is suitable for the people involved, is understood and has relevance for them. Induction processes, for example, need to be planned with the learning and settling-in needs of the new person in mind rather than as a standard tour of introduction. Appraisal should be approached sincerely as an opportunity to focus the individual's contribution and renew their relationship to the company, rather than allowing that opportunity to be squandered by an appraiser who merely goes through the motions or appears to downgrade the process.

Managers have to be seen to believe in the ways of doing things that they prescribe, and these need to be viewed as fair, consistent and effective. There also has to be consistency between the values spoken about and those practised. If you say that teamwork is important but only give recognition and reward to individual achievement, you cannot expect people to put priority on helping one another – and the inconsistency will feed a belief that you cannot trust what management says (Box 7.4).

Management can also take a lead in ensuring that semi-official gatherings and customary events reinforce a sense of community between people. Employees do not choose their colleagues, by and large, but they do have to get along with them. Social events and customs that are not based around the work itself can build up common ground and ease relationships. They can be anything that strikes a chord with the firm's people, from the annual party, to raising money for charity, to outings, to simple things like remembering birthdays or everyone having lunch together. If the company is to fund an event, it is important to be clear what its purpose is. The Christmas party can be another embarrassing, empty ritual – or a thank-you present to the staff that they really enjoy.

Clearly, for events like these to stay in tune with the preferences of a developing staff body and continue to have value, there needs to be give-and-take between management and staff. Encourage consultation, let the right members of staff take charge of semi-official events, and ensure that they are allowed time and budget to do them justice.

> **Box 7.4 Attuning communication: The difference between empty ritual and inclusiveness**
>
> At the monthly company meeting, the managing director would show the month's performance figures and then each person would be asked to report on progress. For management this was an important company ritual, designed to promote a sense of involvement, to help people see the outcome of their contributions and to give recognition for achievements. However, it was noticeable that some people seemed not to treat the meeting seriously – they looked and sounded disengaged and said little.
>
> When staff were asked for their feedback it emerged that, instead of creating a bond, the meeting set up a division. The sales people responded positively, but administrative and production staff said that they felt the process was just an opportunity for sales people to boast. Sales people always talked about their targets and seemed to have something exciting to say, whereas admin and production were merely keeping going. In addition they were often confused by the figures shown, but feared that asking questions would show them to be ignorant. In any case, having everybody say something every time only dragged things out and made them boring.
>
> This ritual, which had begun when there was only a handful of staff, needed to be retuned to the growing organization. In its new form everyone still attended, but instead of each person reporting on their achievements, one representative from each section would give a report that the rest of their team had helped them prepare. Performance figures were shown in a simple summary chart of essentials only. A strict time allocation of 40 minutes was set, and instead of the MD assuming the chair each time, chairing was rotated between managers and team leaders. Feedback collected on the retuned meeting pronounced it worthwhile for keeping in touch and understanding how the company was doing.

Maintaining freshness: Encouraging better ways of doing things

What happens to the creative spark that brings a company into being as the company grows and its originator has to withdraw from day-to-day operations? Key figure though the founder is, if they are the only source of inspiration and ideas, the company is unlikely to develop into an entity that can exist independently of them. Building an organization is not simply a matter of making a delegation structure down which to offload work and responsibility, it also holds the opportunity to spark off new possibilities, through the development of people's potential and through the alchemy of people working together.

Creativity is an attribute that enables us to develop new ideas, look at things afresh, find new angles, solve or move clear of problems and respond resourcefully. While there are some people who are highly gifted with particular talent and carry a professional creative label, that does not preclude the rest of us from the need and ability to use our mind creatively, so as to improve ways of doing things and bring flexibility and variety into our routines.

A useful definition of the creative process is making new connections. New ideas start somewhere – and they are generated by taking an existing notion and putting it together with one you have not associated with it before. What would happen if you took a car engine and, instead of mounting it from front to back, you mounted it from side to side? Answer: you design the snub-nosed mini!

Making these connections requires us to move away from the constraint of an established pattern of thought, hence the expression 'thinking outside the box'. We need to move from thinking in straight lines (in Edward de Bono's term, thinking vertically) to thinking laterally. Much of the time at work we are engaged in thinking in straight lines: to prepare or analyse sets of figures, carry out calculations, answer questions, make out reports and so on. We dip into a set of existing pieces of knowledge and follow a logical sequence that we have used before, starting at the beginning and working through to the end. When the task is something familiar to us this method can serve us well – we can switch on the brain and we know what we are doing. Unless the mind wanders (stopping us getting on with the task in hand), we will not come up with fresh thinking.

It is when the mind goes off at tangents that we move into the lateral thinking that produces fresh ideas. Using the mind this way cannot be forced and does not rely on discipline and tidiness – it requires us to let go of preconceptions and think reflectively. Notice when ideas for solving problems strike you. Most of the time, it is probably not at your desk but in the car, or in the bath or the living room that the idea pops into your head.

We cannot 'switch on' creative thought in the way that we can switch on straight-line thinking, but we can encourage and stimulate it. Creative thinking needs to be allowed reasonable time and space. In coming up with fresh ideas, we are likely to make some false starts. Successful creative thought has these characteristics:

- Willingness to let go of existing frameworks and to tolerate uncertainty.
- Ability to ask the right questions.
- Mental mobility – finding new perspectives and challenging assumptions.
- Willingness to risk failure.
- Objectivity – testing ideas for strengths and weaknesses.

Growing the organization brings the opportunity to foster fresh thinking from staff, first by handing back to them the problems they bring us to solve; and secondly by encouraging the use of teamwork to bounce ideas around and stimulate lateral thinking. Holding brainstorming sessions, in which everyone is invited to contribute ideas and suggestions on a topic, with a rule that no evaluation takes place until the ideas cease to flow, can help people to practise and develop confidence in this way of using the mind.

Renewal through learning, contribution and growth

A healthy organization – like a healthy organism – is one that renews itself and is able to adapt to change in its environment. When you hire people for a firm, it is not for them to stagnate and grow stale but for them to make a contribution. Keeping the firm fresh, if you do not want to be continually hiring and firing people, means encouraging everyone in it to keep developing.

Creating a learning climate in the firm benefits both individual and organization. Learning and personal growth are important motivators and transmit positive cultural values. Many people acquire much of the knowledge and capability they possess as adults through their work, not merely through formal training or from direct acquisition of technical and task capability, but through exposure to different experiences, people and environments.

There is often a concern in smaller firms that they cannot offer employees with development potential a career structure comparable to that in a large organization – there can be no guaranteed progression through the ranks. However, that does not mean that employees will not grow in stature and capability, if the firm supports their development, and find new sources of satisfaction in their work as they expand their expertise.

Making the firm a learning organization means that those at the top demonstrate the value placed on learning by maintaining their own professional development. It means ensuring that attention and resources are given to systematic training of staff linked to job induction and performance appraisal (see Chapter 6). It also means recognizing and using a whole range of learning methods – not simply coaching and courses, but reading, tapes, distance-learning packages, job rotation, visits and secondments to customers or suppliers, learning on the job through projects or researching information, and encouraging people to find things out for themselves. To harness the benefits and channel them into practical outcomes, it is important to follow up on training with the questions: What have you learned? and How can

---

Box 7.5 What makes an organization a great place to work?

How might benefits derived from the firm's products, or from association with its clients or suppliers, be shared with the firm's people?

A seating-design company involved in the refurbishment of a theatre took advantage of a ticket offer for special previews before opening. Anyone interested was encouraged to participate, and the party included junior staff. A young project coordinator was thrilled by this experience, which took her into another world.

This young woman had been causing problems at work. Though technically proficient, she handled communication poorly. She had been offered a communications training course, which coincided with the trip to the theatre.

Up to this point, she had been undermotivated and when problems arose, instead of taking responsibility for solving them, she would blame others. Her attitude was that this was an insignificant company and they could stuff their job. That attitude changed overnight; the young woman realized that her small employer, with its unfashionable address and spartan premises, was a contributor to something exceptional. For her, the evening at the theatre constituted a rite of passage. Moreover, the training she was given not only helped her improve her communication skills and confidence, it also signalled that her employer valued and wanted to develop her contribution. She learned to treat problem solving as a challenge, and by widening her concept of her job gained a much greater sense of achievement from it.

you apply it? Moreover, a learning organization recognizes and rewards people's development – possibly with promotion, added responsibility and pay, but also with acknowledgement and praise.

Making provision for learning has special relevance to smaller firms, simply because there are fewer people around to ask when someone does not know how to do a task. Practical considerations apart, there is the sheer reward of seeing an employee develop capability and confidence, and grow into a valued contributor to the firm (Box 7.5).

Further reading

1 Hunt, J. (1992) *Managing People at Work*, McGraw-Hill, London.
2 Henry, J. (ed.) (1991) *Creative Management*, Sage, London.
3 Scase, R. and Goffee, R. (1987) *The Real World of the Small Business Owner*, Routledge, London.

Managing Business Performance through Financial Analysis

CHAPTER 8

Key issues dealt with in this chapter are:

- The importance of profit: profit and loss accounts explained.
- The meaning of adequate capital: building a sound balance sheet.
- The cash-flow statement.
- Analysing the financial statements to assist in business decision making.

The modern organization is most effective and efficient when all its employees understand the impact of their contribution to business strategy and the achievement of corporate objectives. For example, armed with information about which customers are the most profitable, employees should be able to work out for themselves what service levels to provide, how to prioritize their workload and when to set time aside for non-productive activities, e.g. training, appraisals, feedback. Even if non-managerial staff cannot easily grasp the complexity of financial performance, it should be possible to present the essentials in a form that can be easily assimilated by non-numerate people (Figure 8.1).

Directors and managers need a deeper understanding of financial performance information because their day-to-day and longer-term decisions should be framed with profitability (profit and loss account) and cash (balance sheet) in mind. Using a case study to illustrate key issues, in this chapter we will investigate and explain in detail the three main financial statements:

1 *Profit and loss account* – how the company has performed over the year in terms of profitability.
2 *Balance sheet* – how much the company is worth and whether its financial resources have been used effectively.

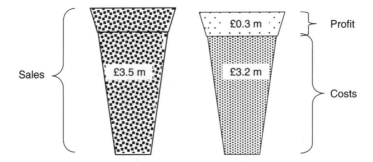

Figure 8.1: Profit: A diagrammatic illustration.

3   *Cash-flow (or funds-flow) statement* – provides valuable information about where the money has come from and what it has been spent on.

The financial statements

Financial statements (the accounts) must be prepared for the following reasons:

- First and foremost, the shareholders (owners) need to know how the business has performed and what it is worth at the end of the financial year. Profit performance and worth are related: profit can be reinvested in the business, which adds value and increases net worth.
- Producing the accounts is important not only when thinking of selling the business, but also for raising money. Investors and lenders alike will be interested in profit and worth. They will also be interested in the quality of business assets available as security for bank borrowing.
- All businesses (limited liability companies, sole traders and partnerships) in the UK are obliged to produce annual accounts for the Inland Revenue, to assess corporation or income tax due.
- Limited liability companies in the UK are required to file their accounts with the Registrar of Companies. Companies meeting the criteria for small and medium-sized status can file abbreviated accounts, as follows:
  - Small company: abbreviated balance sheet, special auditor's report.
  - Medium-sized company: abbreviated profit and loss account, full balance sheet, special auditor's report, directors' report, notes to the accounts.

A company is small or medium-sized if it meets two out of three of the conditions shown in Box 8.1.

Subject to certain exclusions, a small company in the UK need not have its annual accounts audited if it meets the following criteria:

- It qualifies as a small company in relation to that year in accordance with the Companies Act 1985.

Box 8.1 Definitions of small and medium-sized companies

Small company

1	Annual turnover	not more than £2.8m
2	Balance sheet total	not more than £1.4m
3	No. of employees	not more than 50

Medium-sized company

1	Annual turnover	not more than £11.2m
2	Balance sheet total	not more than £5.6m
3	No. of employees	not more than 250

Source: Companies House website, www.companies-house.co.uk, November 2002.

- Its turnover in the year is not more than £1 million.
- Its balance sheet total for the year is not more than £1.4 million.

The profit and loss account (P&L)

Annual income twenty pounds, annual expenditure nineteen nineteen and six, result happiness. Annual income twenty pounds, annual expenditure twenty pounds ought and six, result misery.

Mr Micawber in Charles Dickens' *David Copperfield*

The profit and loss account (P&L) is the 'history book' of the business. It shows how much profit or loss the business has made during a period (usually a month or year). It records the value of sales made during the year and the costs associated with these sales. It is quite simple: if sales are greater than costs, you have made a profit. If costs exceed sales, a loss has been made (like Mr Micawber).

The period for which the P&L is drawn up is called the 'accounting period'. This could be a full 12-month period (the financial year) or monthly (for the management accounts). Certain types of business, such as retailers, make up their P&L on a 52- or 53-week basis.

The balance sheet

The balance sheet is made up at a point in time and is like a photograph. It shows the things of value that the business owns or is owed (assets) together with money owed to creditors (liabilities). The balance sheet defines the worth of the company to the shareholders, represented by the excess of assets over liabilities. A number of other features are also shown, such as how the resources have been utilized and, in combination with the P&L account, how well managed, resourced and stable the business really is.

The money-measurement concept limits how much can really be understood about the business from the balance sheet, since the directors, managers and employees are not represented. People, who really are at the centre of all business success, cannot readily be valued. In owner-managed companies, the lack of a clear boundary between shareholders and managers means that the balance sheets of these companies are highly questionable, being made up largely with the interests of the owners in mind.

The cash-flow statement

The cash-flow (or funds-flow) statement shows all the monies received by the business and paid out by it during the year. It also shows the cash balance held by the business at the start and end of the year. (These figures also appear in the balance sheet.)

Accounting principles

There are a number of concepts and conventions associated with the financial statements, which are universally agreed by accountants as a way of maintaining consistency and comparability in accounting through the years:

1 *Realization concept.* Sales income is taken into the business at the time of invoicing and not when the goods are ordered or paid for. Thus invoiced sales are included when calculating profit, while payment received from customers is a question of cash flow.
2 *Accrual concept.* Costs accruing in a certain time period must be matched with revenues in the same period. Thus when compiling the P&L account, costs associated with sales income must be included for that period (and not for any other period). An example would be the auditor's fees, which are included as an expenditure item in the annual accounts although not billed until some months after the end of the accounting period.
3 *Money-measurement concept.* Only transactions that can be measured in monetary terms are included in the accounts.
4 *Business entity concept.* The business is treated as an entity for the purposes of drawing up accounts and is separate from its owners, employees or anyone else associated with it.
5 *Cost concept.* Entries in the accounts are taken in at historic cost – what was actually paid for the item – rather than the current value. In certain cases, however, items may be revalued (such as buildings) but normally only for a specific purpose (such as when the business is being sold).
6 *Going concern concept.* The business is valued as a going concern, rather than on the basis of being broken up for sale.
7 *Dual aspect* of the balance sheet. Entries show not only where money has come from but also what it is being used for. Thus for every transaction, whether involving cash going out or coming in, there must be a balancing transaction.

8 *Conservatism*. Profits are always understated rather than overstated. If there is any uncertainty about costs, they are always included at the higher level, whereas if sales are in doubt, they are always excluded.

9 *Materiality*. Small or inconsequential amounts are ignored or written off (if appropriate). For instance, a pencil sharpener should be written off immediately as if it were revenue expenditure, rather than being treated as an item of capital expenditure (with its appropriate rate of depreciation).

10 *Consistency*. Accounts are compiled on a consistent basis so that they can be compared over the course of time. If changes are to be introduced, for instance in the way an asset is valued or depreciated, then the basis of the change should be noted explicitly.

Exploring the profit and loss account

The profit and loss account (Box 8.2) starts with the company's sales and progressively deducts all relevant costs from it, arriving in linear fashion at *net profit before tax*. Tax and dividends (if any are paid) are deducted before arriving at the final *retained profit* figure (reinvested in the business – it goes into the balance sheet, as we shall see).

Box 8.2 Outline P&L

Item	Amount	Explanation
Sales	£1 000 000	Sales invoiced to customers in the period
Variable costs	£350 000	Costs of production or purchasing
Gross profit	£650 000	Available to cover overheads and profit
Direct fixed costs	£150 000	Costs relating directly to sales
Contribution	£500 000	To cover indirect overheads and profit
Indirect fixed costs	£400 000	Costs of running the business
Net profit before tax	£100 000	The most important line in your business!
Corporation tax	£20 000	Based on taxable profit
Dividends	0	The directors decide to reinvest for growth
Retained profit	£80 000	Reinvested in the reserves of the business

The example in Box 8.2 illustrates the linear arithmetic of a P&L. It is important to group costs in this way, as we shall see when analysing a full P&L. Conventionally, *variable costs* (often called 'cost of sales' or 'cost of goods sold') are deducted first. They include those costs that vary directly in proportion with the quantity of goods or services sold. For a retailer, variable costs would be the cost of buying merchandise for sale. For a manufacturer, they include the cost of raw materials and components plus the cost of labour directly involved in production. For service organizations, there could be no (or minimal) variable costs. The test of a variable cost is this: if sales units rise by x per cent, you would expect variable costs to rise by (roughly) *x* per cent. The profit figure arrived at after deducting variable costs is called *gross profit*.

Fixed costs (overheads) do not depend proportionally on the volume of sales, although there is clearly some kind of *direct* and *indirect* relationship with sales. Direct costs generally include most sales, product, marketing, distribution and customer service costs; indirect costs include the great mass of costs required to manage, accommodate, organize and finance the business and are grouped accordingly.

The profit figure after deducting overheads is net profit before tax – the so-called bottom line. While the Inland Revenue requires a share of it (corporation tax) and shareholders might receive a payout (dividends), the remainder is retained in the business.

In order to follow the financial statements in greater detail and consider the financial implications of management decisions, we can take another look at ABCO Systems, which we first encountered in Chapter 3 (Box 8.3).

Box 8.3 Case study: ABCO Systems Ltd

ABCO's main business focused on the banking and finance sectors in the City of London, with a small number of sales coming from other business sectors. It had developed a niche computer product that made back-office transactions highly efficient. The full service comprised a networked computer system including hardware, software, cabling, training, maintenance and support.

New leads were generated by developing contacts with decision makers, reached initially using mailshots and telemarketing. There was a small field sales force that regularly went out to do demonstrations.

ABCO had an office in London and consideration was being given to opening one in Paris. Software was designed in London and most hardware was sourced from local suppliers, except the memory boards, which were bought from a Californian company and assembled in the company's workshop. Delivery leadtimes from the USA were up to three months.

The bank manager had recently advanced a large loan to fund expansion.

After two years of profitable growth, however, the results to 31 March 1999 showed a substantial loss (see profit and loss accounts). The balance sheets showed further cause for concern.

The directors met to review the results and decide on their course of action.

What do the P&L figures tell us about what went wrong and what solutions should the directors consider to get the business back on plan? If the P&L truly is a history book, the set of three years' figures in Table 8.1 should tell a story about the success or failure of ABCO's management.

What happened to ABCO's profit between 1997 and 1999 and why? It is evident that the company was profitable in 1997 and 1998 (net profit before tax of £138 000 and £201 000 respectively), but made a loss in 1999 (£123 000).

Before moving on to discuss the causes of poor financial performance and the implications of the figures, an explanation of the terms used in the P&L might be helpful.

Table 8.1: ABCO Systems' P&L accounts, year ending 31 March (£'000)

	1997		1998		1999	
Sales		1562		1971		2019
Cost of sales						
Purchases	504		612		743	
Opening stock/WIP	52		69		84	
Closing stock/WIP	69		84		98	
	487		597		729	
Workshop engineers	42		57		58	
		529		654		787
Gross profit		1033		1317		1232
Sales/marketing expenses						
Travel and subsistence	38		55		76	
Motor running costs	51		71		62	
Telephones	43		70		86	
Print	73		85		102	
Salaries	75		125		154	
		280		406		480
Contribution		753		911		752
Establishment expenses						
Rent and rates	83		89		114	
Light and heat	7		8		12	
Insurance	5		6		9	
Repairs and maintenance	14		16		24	
		109		119		159
Administration expenses						
Employee training	21		16		20	
Post, stationery	20		25		31	
Audit and accountancy	15		21		30	
Salaries	368		417		481	
		424		479		562
Finance expenses						
Bank interest	26		33		44	
Provision for bad debt	12		15		35	
		38		48		79
Depreciation		44		64		75
NET PROFIT/(LOSS) BEFORE TAX		138		201		(123)
Taxation	38		56		0	
Dividends	0		60		0	
		38		116		0
To Reserves		100		85		(123)

1 Sales

Invoiced sales in the period (VAT excluded).

2 Cost of sales (or cost of goods sold)

Variable costs are costs that vary directly in proportion with changes in unit sales (or output). In other words, if you were to double unit sales, you would expect more or less to double variable costs. Examples are:

- Purchases of raw materials, components or merchandise for resale. Purchases are adjusted for *stock* and *work in progress*. Because the P&L is produced on an accrual basis (see the accounting principles listed earlier), we adjust for stock and work in progress by adding (bringing forward) opening stock and work in progress and subtracting (carrying forward) closing stock and work in progress. This produces an adjusted purchases figure. Stock can be in the form of raw materials, semi-processed goods or finished goods and is valued at cost. Work in progress is valued at cost of materials and labour plus a margin for overheads.
- *Direct labour* associated with the production process, including subcontracted labour or production and freelance people brought in to design, make or provide goods or services.
- Other variable costs of production, such as *carriage* (delivery) costs.

3 Gross profit

Profit remaining after deducting cost of sales. Because sales and purchasing/production are the primary components of all business organizations, the gross profit margin is arguably the most important measure of business success.

4 Fixed or overhead expenditure

For decision-making purposes, it makes sense to treat the fixed costs (or overheads) of running the business in a logical order. First come the direct fixed costs, such as marketing, selling and R&D costs, because they are typically closely related to sales activities, then the indirect fixed costs, such as rent, insurance, salaries, etc., which are not directly related to the level of sales.

5 Sales and marketing expenditure

Finding, getting and keeping customers, including the delivery of goods, e.g. advertising, promotion, exhibitions, publicity, public relations, printing of brochures and sales literature, postage and delivery, telephone calls related to sales, travel and subsistence, costs of employing sales and marketing staff, including salaries and motor vehicles, commissions paid, and any other costs directly associated with sales.

6   Establishment expenditure

Costs of premises, e.g. rent, rates, maintenance, etc.

7   Administration expenditure

The remaining running expenses, e.g. telephone, catering, stationery, salaries, directors' remuneration, professional fees, recruitment, training, etc.

8   Finance expenditure

The costs of financing the business, e.g. interest on bank loans, overdrafts and hire purchase, leasing and hire charges, bank charges. These costs are grouped separately because the profitability of companies, which are financed in different ways (combinations of equity, loans and off-balance-sheet finance), should be analysed independently of the financing method. Note that repayments of capital to a bank or to hire purchase companies are not an expense item and are not included in the P&L.

9   Provision for bad debts

The possibility of a customer not settling an outstanding debt (the reasons are numerous, e.g. a dispute about the amount, the customer is going bust) needs to be taken into account.

10   Depreciation

Does not involve a movement of cash and is an accounting concept to allow for the cost of using plant, equipment, machinery, motor vehicles and buildings over their useful lives. Note that it is not for replacing an asset, because you might decide never to replace it at all, e.g. some offices no longer have a fax machine. Depreciation is calculated using one of two methods:

- *Straight-line* method. If the asset is used up roughly in equal amounts each year, the cost of the asset should be apportioned in equal annual amounts over its useful life. For example, if a computer cost £900 excluding VAT and you determine that it has a useful life of three years in your business before replacement (when it will be worth practically nothing), the annual depreciation is £300.
- *Declining balance* method. A fixed percentage, e.g. 20 per cent, is applied to the balance at the end of each year (see Box 8.4). The percentage is related to the useful life concept and is often more realistic because it recognizes that assets such as a motor car decline in value more rapidly in the early years and normally have some residual value, particularly when serviced regularly. (Depreciation should not be confused with capital allowances, which are what the government is prepared to allow you to write off in lieu of depreciation on most capital equipment.)

Box 8.4 Example of declining balance depreciation

Cost of machine	£10 000
Annual depreciation	20%
Year 1:	
Machine	£10 000
Annual depreciation @ 20%	£2 000
Net book value at end of year 1	£8 000
Year 2:	
Machine	£8 000
Annual depreciation @ 20%	£1 600
Net book value at end of year 2	£6 400
Etc.	

---

11 Net profit

What remains after deducting all overheads from gross profit.

12 Corporation tax

This would normally be calculated at this point, based on taxable profit (adjusted net profit after adding back disallowable expenses, e.g. entertainment and depreciation and deducting capital allowances).

13 Dividends

Distributions of profit to shareholders.

14 Retained profit

Left over and transferred to reserves in the balance sheet.

Exploring the balance sheet

What do the balance sheet figures tell us about what went wrong and how do they corroborate what we found in the P&L? The balance sheet is a photograph, so the set of three years' figures in Table 8.2 should tell us how and why the picture has changed over a three-year period.

It is conventional to set out a balance sheet to show *net worth*, which is the outcome of what the business owns (*assets*) less what it owes (*liabilities*). Long-term *sources of finance* are normally divided into *equity* and *debt*, and short-term sources (*creditors, overdraft*) are grouped under current liabilities.

Net worth increased initially from £125 000 (1997) to £210 000 (1998), but then plummeted to £87 000 in 1999. What happened? Before an analysis can be attempted, here is an explanation of balance sheet terms.

Table 8.2: ABCO Systems' balance sheets, year ending 31 March (£'000)

	1997		1998		1999	
Fixed assets						
Equipment and vehicles	256				467	
Less: Depreciation	89		154		230	
		167		170		237
Current assets						
Stock and work in progress	69		84		98	
Debtors and prepayments	252		351		480	
Cash	14		112		2	
	335		547		580	
Current liabilities						
Trade creditors	206		236		270	
VAT and NI	48		60		60	
Corporation tax	38		56		0	
Dividends	0		60		0	
Overdraft	0		30		96	
	292		442		435	
Net current assets		43		105		145
Capital employed		210		275		382
Creditors due after 12 months						
Bank loan		85		65		295
NET ASSETS		125		210		87
Financed by:						
Share capital		10		10		10
Reserves (P&L Account)		115		200		77
SHAREHOLDERS' FUNDS		125		210		87

1 Fixed assets

Assets acquired to generate income and profits. They are divided into *tangible assets*, such as land and buildings, plant, equipment and machinery, motor vehicles and fixtures and fittings; *intangible assets*, such as licences, patents, good will, leases and major development costs; and *investments* in other companies. Fixed assets are recorded at historical cost and depreciated cumulatively over their useful life to show their *net book value* or *written-down amount*. Different rates of depreciation are applied to different assets, depending on their useful life, and an explanation of charges must be given in the accounts.

2 Current assets

These include in ascending order of liquidity *stock, work in progress, debtors, prepayments* and *cash*.

3 Current liabilities

Amounts owed by the business within the following 12 months. *Trade creditors* (owed to suppliers) include VAT, other creditors include money owed to the Inland Revenue (PAYE, income tax under Schedule D and corporation tax) and *VAT* to Customs and Excise, *prepayments* (by your customers), *hire purchase* and *bank loans* or *overdrafts* repayable within the next 12 months.

4 Net current assets (or liabilities)

Otherwise known as *working capital* (capital that changes on a day-to-day basis as stock is consumed, orders turn into work in progress, work turns into unpaid customer invoices and purchases turn into unpaid supplier invoices), current liabilities are deducted from current assets to give net current assets. The bottom half of the balance sheet identifies sources of long-term finance to support net current assets and fixed assets.

5 Creditors due after more than one year

Bank loans, hire purchase (only that which is outstanding for more than 12 months), directors' loans (generally repayable after 12 months) and deferred taxation.

6 Net assets (net worth)

This is what the business is worth (in book terms, not in the marketplace) after all creditors have been paid (with the exception of shareholders).

7 Share capital and reserves

Permanent or *share capital* is supplied by the shareholders. Included here could be paid-up share capital, share premium (where shares are sold for more than their nominal value), revaluation reserve (where assets are revalued but not sold) and accumulated profit or loss brought forward from successive P&Ls.

8 Balance

Share capital and *reserves* must equal *net worth*. This is the balance sheet equation and reflects one of the fundamental principles of accounting, which we encountered above.

Presentation of accounts for sole traders and partnerships

For tax purposes, the accounts of unincorporated *sole traders* and *partnerships* are presented somewhat differently. In the P&L, proprietors/partners take out *drawings* instead of salaries and these are not included in expenditure, but are treated as part of profit. In a partnership, net profit is apportioned to the partners in whatever proportion has been agreed by them.

In the balance sheet the presentation is very similar to that demonstrated above, except that drawings are shown now as a deduction against capital (which includes initial capital introduced and accumulated profits). In the case of a partnership, each partner's capital account is shown with drawings deducted.

Maintaining adequate capital

There is a very clear logic to business finance. Long-term finance is invested in business assets and other resources, which combine to create profits over time. They should logically be financed by instruments that earn a return over an equally long period of time. This would be efficient and equitable from a cost and repayment point of view. For example, a commercial mortgage over 25 years should be used to finance the purchase of a building with a life of (say) 25 years.

Conversely, short-term uses, such as buying stock and financing customers until they settle their bills, change within hours, days, weeks or months, so they should be financed over a short period of time. Short-term lines of credit, such as overdrafts or supplier credit, are more efficient for these purposes because they are less costly and easier to arrange. They are required for only a short time.

In practice, long-term sources often cover short-term uses, which is less efficient but more secure. In an uncertain world this security is worth having, even if it means paying a little more for it.

The worst possible case, however, is using short-term sources to pay for long-term uses, e.g. using an overdraft to pay for machinery or vehicles. Overdraft finance can be more expensive than long-term loans if used in this way; and most importantly, because a bank can withdraw an overdraft without notice, it is a very insecure method of financing business development or assets with long-term horizons.

The notion of adequate capital (see Box 8.5) describes the strategy of raising sufficient long-term funds (share capital, retained profits, long-term borrowings) to cover long-term needs (fixed assets, long-term cash outflows) and short-term funds (overdraft and supplier credit) to cover short-term needs (debtors, stock, short-term cash outflows). In particular, growing businesses should guard against the common problem of inadequate finance caused by:

1 Over-optimistic forecasts of sales and gross margins, especially when entering new markets.
2 Under-estimates of costs associated with marketing and product development.
3 Inadequate financial controls, particularly on working capital (credit control, purchasing control, stock control).

Cash-flow statement

As discussed briefly above, the cash-flow statement, also known as the funds-flow statement or sources and applications of funds, is the third of the financial statements and is used to clarify where finance comes from (sources) and what it is used for (applications). There is no legal requirement for smaller companies to prepare one, though it is required for large quoted companies.

Box 8.5 Checking financial strategy

Sources of finance	**Uses of finance**
Short term	*Short term*
1 Increase in trade creditors (by giving credit, suppliers effectively lend you money)	1 Increase in debtors (you effectively lend money to you customers until they pay you)
2 Increase in other creditors, such as Inland Revenue, Customs and Excise	2 Increase in stock and work in progress
3 Overdraft	3 Cash balances at the bank or on deposit
Long term	*Long term*
4 Shareholders through an issue of shares	4 Investing in fixed assets
5 Raising a loan, e.g. a mortgage, a bank loan	5 Acquiring new businesses
6 Reinvested profit (retained profit)	

The final balance (net cash flow) is the difference between the cash with which the business started the year and the amount shown in the balance sheet at the end of the year. Let's take a look at ABCO's cash flow over the period.

Table 8.3 shows ABCO Systems' cash-flow statements for two years. It will be seen that the company benefited from an increase in cash of £98 000 in 1998 but a severe outflow of £110 000 in 1999. The implications will be studied shortly. An explanation of the terms used is as follows:

Table 8.3: ABCO Systems' cash flow statements, year ending 31 March (£'000)

	1998		1999	
Cash flow from operations				
Operating profit	234		(79)	
Add back: Depreciation	65		76	
Stocks decrease/(increase)	(15)		(14)	
Debtors decrease/(increase)	(99)		(129)	
Creditors increase/(decrease)	30		43	
		215		(103)
Net cost of financing		(33)		(44)
Unpaid dividends		0		(60)
Unpaid taxation		(26)		(56)
Capital expenditure		(68)		(143)
Increase in borrowings		10		296
Net cash inflow/(outflow)		98		(110)

1 *Operating profit*. Profit before tax and interest, taken from the P&L.
2 *Depreciation*. A notional charge that does not involve a cash payment and must therefore be added back to the profit figure.
3 *Stocks decrease/(increase)*. If stocks decrease, cash has been released. If stocks increase, cash has been tied up.
4 *Debtors decrease/(increase)*. If debtors decrease, more customers have been paying their bills; if debtors increase, the opposite is the case.
5 *Creditors increase/(decrease)*. If creditors increase, cash is held in the bank account; if they decrease, more cash has been paid to suppliers.
6 *Net cost of financing*. The cost of interest payments net of any received.
7 *Dividends*. Unpaid at the end of the year.
8 *Tax*. Unpaid at the end of the year.
9 *Capital expenditure*. Cost of new fixed assets net of any disposals.
10 *Increase in financing*. Net increase in external borrowings. Could also include proceeds from share issues.
11 *Net cash inflow/(outflow)*. The balance of cash inflows and outflows. This should be the same as the difference between the cash figures in the balance sheets in successive years.

Why is profit not the same as cash?

The P&L and cash-flow statement both show income and outgoings for the business, but the profit for the year is not the same as the net cash inflow. In other words, profit and cash are not the same. The main reasons for this seeming anomaly are to be found in the accounting principles described earlier, in particular:

- *Realization*. In the P&L sales are accounted for when invoiced, not when payment is received (cash flow). Similarly, purchases are included when the transaction is made, not when the invoice is paid (cash flow).

Box 8.6 Profit vs cash

Profit	Cash flow
Depreciation deducted	Depreciation not taken into account (not a cash item)
Sales accounted for when invoiced to customers	Sales income accounted for when cash banked from customers
Purchases accounted for when invoice received from suppliers	Purchases accounted for when cash paid out to suppliers
Machinery, equipment and building purchases excluded	Cash purchases of all machinery, equipment and building included
VAT excluded (it belongs to the government)	VAT included (we collect it and pay it out)
No bank or other loans (only interest)	Loans included when received or paid back

Box 8.7 Common financial performance ratios (for unquoted businesses)

A Profitability

1 Net margin %

$$\frac{\text{Profit before tax}}{\text{Sales}} \times 100$$

Measures how much net profit is derived from each £ of sales. Should be the main financial objective. Its comparability over time and between companies in the same industry makes it an ideal yardstick for measuring performance.

2 Gross margin %

$$\frac{\text{Gross profit}}{\text{Sales}} \times 100$$

Measures the relationship between variable costs and sales. Vital as a measure of the intensity of competition, pricing policy, product mix, marketing strategy, production efficiency and purchasing efficiency.

3 Total overheads %

$$\frac{\text{Total overheads}}{\text{Sales}} \times 100$$

Measures the proportion of sales taken up by overheads (fixed costs). If this ratio is higher than the gross margin, the company is making a net loss.

4 Selling/marketing costs %

$$\frac{\text{Selling/marketing costs}}{\text{Sales}} \times 100$$

Helpful in controlling marketing costs and evaluating the success of different combinations of marketing expenditure.

5 Administration costs %

$$\frac{\text{Administration costs}}{\text{Sales}} \times 100$$

Similarly, this helps in assessing the impact on profitability of changes in administration expenses.

6 Payroll costs %

$$\frac{\text{Salaries and wages}}{\text{Sales}} \times 100$$

Helps in evaluating the impact of staffing changes on profits.

7 Return on shareholders' funds %

$$\frac{\text{Net profit after tax}}{\text{Share capital + reserves}} \times 100$$

A measure of whether the investment in the company is worthwhile in comparison with returns available on alternative investments where risk is similar.

8 Return on capital employed %

$$\frac{\text{Profit before interest and tax}}{\text{Capital employed}} \times 100$$

Measures the return on total investment, including borrowings and equity.

B Financial status

9 Current ratio

$$\frac{\text{Current assets}}{\text{Current liabilities}}$$

Measures the company's ability to meet its short-term creditors. Useful to creditors as an early warning of a possible cash crisis and should be above a value of 1.

10 Acid test

$$\frac{\text{Debtors + cash}}{\text{Current liabilities}}$$

Extends the measure of liquidity by excluding stock and work in progress from the calculation. They are considered to be relatively illiquid compared with debtors and cash.

11 Debt ratio (gearing) %

$$\frac{\text{Long-term loans}}{\text{Capital employed}} \times 100$$

Discloses how highly borrowed (geared) the company is. Its importance lies in determining whether the company is in a position to meet its longer-term financing needs, particularly if short-term needs are also growing.

C Efficiency

12 Fixed asset utilization £

$$\frac{\text{Sales}}{\text{Fixed assets (net)}}$$

Measures the level of sales generated by each £ spent on fixed assets, e.g. buildings, machinery and vehicles.

13 Stock days

$$\frac{\text{Stock and work in progress}}{\text{Purchases}} \times 365$$

Measures the number of days' worth of purchases the company is holding as stock and work in progress. The more money is tied up in stock, the greater are short-term financing needs.

14 Debtor days

$$\frac{\text{Debtors}}{\text{Sales}} \times 365$$

The average number of days taken by customers to pay their bills. A useful indicator of effective credit control.

15 Creditor days

$$\frac{\text{Trade creditors}}{\text{Purchases}} \times 365$$

The average number of days the company takes to pay its trade suppliers. A balance has to be struck between slow payments and maintaining good relationships with suppliers.

16 Sales per employee £'000

$$\frac{\text{Sales}}{\text{Employees}}$$

The amount of income generated on average by each member of the workforce. A useful measure of progress year to year and can be used as a measure of productivity in comparison with competitors.

17 Profit per employee £'000

$$\frac{\text{Profit before tax}}{\text{Employees}}$$

Measures the amount of net profit generated on average per employee.

18 Productivity £'000

$$\frac{\text{Value added}}{\text{Employees}} \text{ (Gross profit)}$$

Measures what each employee adds to cost of sales.

- *Accrual*. Costs need to be matched to sales in a period and must be accounted for in the same period as the sales with which they are associated, regardless of when they are paid.
- *Capital items (capital equipment, vehicles, buildings, loans)* are not included in the P&L, only the cost of using them (depreciation, interest). Depreciation is a purely notional amount and does not involve cash.

The main differences between profit and cash are summarized in Box 8.6.

Financial analysis

We can now use our understanding of the financial statements to analyse business performance. To do this effectively, we should be in a position to compare current performance against:

1 *Previous years' performance*. Is business performance better or worse than in preceding years?
2 *Plans, forecasts and budgets*. Have we achieved our objectives and targets?
3 *Competitors*. How do we compare against competitors or the industry average?

The primary tool for making valid comparisons over time is ratio analysis. We will confine our analysis to the most relevant ratios appropriate for small and medium-sized businesses. They are grouped into the following categories:

1 Profitability ratios.
2 Financial status ratios.
3 Resource usage and efficiency ratios.

Using ratio analysis to understand financial performance

Ratio analysis should be used to establish not only what went wrong but also what management decisions (or lack of them) could have caused the problems. The starting point in our case study is to take ABCO's P&Ls and balance sheets and calculate the 18 ratios described in Box 8.7. By using these ratios, as well as the original figures and some common sense, firm conclusions can be reached based on solid evidence, which can then form the basis for a plan to turn around the business.

The key question is: After performing relatively well in 1996/97 and 1997/98, why did ABCO lose £123 000 in 1998/99? And why did it have to borrow so much money in 1998/99 (£295 000)? The completed ratio analysis (Table 8.4) gives a clear indication that margins were erratic and costs out of control, and that monitoring and control systems were either missing or inexpertly implemented. From the point of view of financial management, a minor disaster!

Taking the P&L first:

1 Sales growth slowed from 26 per cent between 1996/97 and 1997/98 to just 2 per cent in 1998/99.
2 Gross margin declined from 67 to 61 per cent, knocking £120 000 off net profit.
3 Overheads increased rapidly, from 57 to 67 per cent of sales, reducing net profit by another £200 000.

A thorough examination of the ratios suggests a number of problems and associated underlying causes, which could explain the loss of £123 000 in 1998/99. Box 8.8 summarizes each key factor in turn.

Table 8.4: Completed financial ratios for ABCO Systems

	1996/97	**1997/98**	**1998/99**
A Profitability			
1 Net profit margin %	8.8	10.2	−6.1
2 Gross profit margin %	66.1	66.8	61.0
3 Total overheads %	57.3	56.6	67.1
4 Marketing/selling costs %	17.9	20.6	23.8
5 Administration costs %	27.1	24.3	27.8
6 Payroll costs %	31.0	30.4	34.3
7 Return on shareholders' funds %	80.0	69.0	(141.4)
8 Return on capital employed %	78.1	85.1	(20.7)
B Financial status			
9 Current ratio	1.1	1.2	1.3
10 Acid test	0.9	1.0	1.1
11 Debt ratio (gearing) %	40.5	23.6	77.2
C Efficiency			
12 Fixed asset utilization £	£9.35	£11.59	£8.52
13 Stock days	50	50	48
14 Debtor days	59	65	87
15 Creditor days	149	141	137
16 Sales per employee £k	£74	£82	£78
17 Profit per employee £k	£7	£8	(£5)
18 Productivity £k	£49	£55	£47

Maintaining and raising gross profit margin are the key to raising profitability (and protecting existing profit levels) in a small to medium-sized business, because the only alternative, selling large volumes at low margins, is not normally available. So the analysis must start with gross margin, where there are only six possible reasons for a change (Box 8.8 Part A).

1 Pricing decisions

The obvious one and the area for immediate action, because of its instant impact on profitability. ABCO was probably guilty of discounting to secure more business, ending up without higher volumes; or the marketing director might have miscalculated gross margins in new markets (or both). The latter is always a distinct risk when entering a new market because customer price sensitivity is largely unknown.

Action	1 Review pricing policy and practices, including discounting rules.
	2 Check gross margins by market segment.
	3 Review strategy (choice of markets/products).

Box 8.8 Summary of symptoms and causes: P&L

Symptom	Possible causes
A Decline in gross profit margin [67% > 61%]	
1 Purchases rising faster than sales	Unprofessional buying policies and practices
	Change in strategy (see 5 and 6)
2 Disproportionate growth in direct labour (production)	Inefficient production methods and/or production management
3 Stock and work in progress write-offs	Inadequate stock and work-in-progress controls
	Change in strategy (see 5 and 6)
4 Underpricing and/or discounting	Absence of clear pricing policies and practices
	Absence of effective costing
	Inadequate management information
	Price-sensitive customers – change in strategy (see 5 and 6)
5 Change in customer/market mix (price-sensitive customers)	Lack of a coherent strategy and a strategic business plan
	Inadequate management information
6 Change in product mix (lower-margin products/services)	Wrong customers/market segments – change in strategy
	Inadequate management information
B Disproportionate rise in overheads [57% > 67%]	
7 Disproportionate growth in most overheads	Lack of budgetary control
8 Disproportionate growth in marketing costs [18% > 24%]	Unplanned changes in marketing methods (travel, telephone, printing)
	Change in strategy
	No plans, budgets or controls
9 Uncontrolled growth in certain administration costs, e.g. audit	Cost structure not adjusted for lower sales growth
	Change in strategy
	No plans, budgets or controls
10 Excessive growth in finance costs, e.g. interest, bad debts	Rise in borrowing and/or loans on unfavourable terms; excessive gearing
	Lack of credit control

2 Purchasing decisions

Lack of controls on purchasing, particularly on supplier selection and prices negotiated with suppliers. This could also be the result of being in the wrong market and making the wrong purchasing decisions.

Action	4	Review purchasing policy and practices.
	5	Improve purchase order system.
	6	Review strategy.

3   Production decisions

Inefficient production (including workshop assembly) could result in higher costs through e.g. unplanned overtime, inefficient layout and workflow, using the wrong resources, lack of quality control.

Action	7	Review production efficiency and management.

4   Stock and work-in-progress decisions

Keeping too much stock could affect profitability because of the overhead involved. But as a variable cost this cannot be a factor because surplus stock/work in progress is deducted and carried forward to the next period (an accounting principle described earlier in this chapter). However, stock might deteriorate over time or might become obsolete, and therefore might have to be scrapped or written down. Work-in-progress controls would include proper monitoring and recording of costs.

Action	8	Review stock controls and management.
	9	Review work-in-progress controls.

5   Target market decisions

Crucially important are the choices of market segments (customer groups, see Chapter 2) and the profitability and risk information available about the options. Different markets have different margins and the objective should be to maintain or raise average margins, which usually requires aiming at higher margin segments. This places a premium on the quality of management and market information available to key decision makers.

Action	10	Review strategic marketing options.
	11	Review availability of strategic information (gross margin information).

6   Product/service mix decisions

These typically accompany target market decisions and the availability of information about customer needs, preferred products and services and areas of satisfaction and dissatisfaction is crucial to product mix decisions.

Action	12	Review product/service mix.
	13	Review product/service margins.

In the light of the foregoing analysis, consider this proposition: managing a small to medium-sized growing business is all about managing gross profit margins. Managing gross margins entails effective customer and market segmentation, knowledge of customer behaviour, profit information for each segment and purchasing and production skills. This is where new ideas should be flowing and where creative competences should be strongest, e.g. imaginative new ways to improve services to existing customers, expeditionary marketing to find new customers, new products and services, innovation and invention to stay ahead of competitors, revolutionizing production technology and revitalizing purchasing practices.

The main action points arising from the analysis in Box 8.8 Part B are as follows:

1   Total overheads

Increased from 56 per cent of sales to 67 per cent, indicating an inability to align capacity (costs) with sales in both the short and long term. In an era of rapid change, organizations need to retain their essential flexibility in the face of catastrophic collapse of markets or the simple fickleness of customers themselves confronted with so much choice. The ability to act quickly in response to changes in demand depends largely on the quality of external market data and internal operations' flexibility.

Action	1	Improve budgetary control.
	2	Improve customer and market data.

2   Marketing/selling overheads

Increased from 18 per cent of sales to 24 per cent without a commensurate improvement in sales volumes or margins. Market and customer information probably needs to be improved and practical marketing activities are clearly not focused on achieving realistic goals and are in need of a comprehensive overhaul.

Action	3	Review market research activities.
	4	Review marketing activities and produce a marketing plan.
	5	Improve marketing budgets and monitoring/controls.

3   Payroll increases

Most areas have raised their payroll costs disproportionately, suggesting over-zealous recruitment and ambitious salary increases during a period of growth, without keeping in view the risks associated with building up inflexible capacity.

Action	6	Review recruitment decision making.
	7	Investigate more flexible capacity options, e.g. outsourcing, use of associates.

4 Increases in finance costs

Certain finance costs have risen considerably, e.g. interest, bad debts.

Action	8	Review financing options.
	9	Improve credit controls.

Controlling overheads, particularly indirect costs, is important, but the skills and capabilities needed are different from those for managing gross margins. Here the hard, thankless task of setting up appropriate information and control systems, monitoring procedures and reporting pays dividends. It is an indispensable part of managing a growing profitable business, but is typically the area that can be safely delegated to appropriately qualified people.

Moving on to the balance sheet, we can observe two key changes:

1 A decline in net worth from £210 000 in 1997/98 to £87 000 (1998/99).
2 An increase in bank borrowing to £295 000 in 1998/99.

The ratios suggest further problems and underlying causes. Box 8.9 examines each key factor in turn.

Box 8.9 Summary of symptoms and causes: Balance Sheet

Symptom	Possible causes
1 High debt levels (gearing up from 24% to 77%)	Financial strategy dependent on loans, not equity
	Absence of long-term planning
2 Cash outflow of £176 000 (net cash of £82 000 to net overdraft of £94 000)	Ineffective cash-flow forecasting
	No effective business planning
3 Overinvestment in capacity (fixed asset ratio fell from £11.60 to £8.50)	Capacity not adjusted to lower sales
	Lack of capital budgets and controls
4 Debtor days rose from 59 to 87 days	No credit control
5 Long creditor days (137)	Lack of purchasing controls

The balance sheet analysis continues to highlight serious flaws in the financial management of ABCO, some of which are a consequence of neglecting profitability while others are a symptom of serious financial instability.

1 High gearing

The effect of high gearing (the relative contribution of borrowed money) is to create a high level of debt servicing in subsequent years, a severe drain on cash flow. With negative or low profitability already, this could be the body blow that kills off the business.

Action	1	Review options to reduce gearing (sale of assets, new equity, moratorium on repayments).

2 Cash drain

The business has clearly been haemorrhaging cash and the directors need to take immediate action to reverse the outflow.

Action	2	Identify outgoings that can be deferred or eliminated.
	3	Produce weekly cash-flow forecasts for the next three months.

3 Excess capacity

There has been mystifying over-investment in fixed assets (fancy cars, possibly?), which has drained the business of much-needed cash. Where possible, some of these wasteful assets should be sold to release cash (though in a forced sale they would not be expected to realize their market value).

Action	4	Sell unnecessary assets to raise cash.

4 High and rising debtors

Debtor days have gone up from two to three months (87 days), which indicates a lack of credit control. There is a large amount of cash tied up in debtors, which must be released urgently.

Action	5	Identify due debts from customers and collect urgently.
	6	Improve credit controls.

5 Extended supplier credit

The company has been taking a long time to settle its suppliers' bills. While additional credit can be helpful, in a situation where suppliers might be alerted to ABCO's financial instability extended credit might be withdrawn, leading to some creditors seeking winding-up orders.

| **Action** | 7 | Identify key suppliers in the event of supplier action to recover outstanding debts. |
| | 8 | Introduce purchasing procedures to reduce creditor days over the long term. |

Ratio analysis on its own would not produce a definitive conclusion about ABCO's performance. Combined with a strong infusion of common sense and an understanding of how consistent profits are made over time, however, a clear pattern of mismanagement emerges from the analysis. The essential facts are that the company performed well enough for at least two years (growth in net profit margin from 8.8 to over 10 per cent; growth in net worth to £210 000 with £112 000 in the bank), then inexplicably changed direction and failed to deal with emerging problems in existing markets, which led to a loss of £123 000 and borrowings of £295 000 to shore up the balance sheet.

By putting the P&L together with the balance sheet (supported by a cash-flow statement), a dire picture of crisis proportions emerges. Clearly it would take time, probably a full year, to turn around the business from loss to profit (and another full year at least to achieve former levels of profitability). However, does the business have adequate capital to fund cash flow over this period, bearing in mind current borrowings, gearing levels and poor financial controls? For instance, payments (capital and interest) to the bank of around £100 000 will be needed in 1999/2000.

An action plan needs to take into account not merely profitability, an elusive objective in the short term, but also the availability of cash to pay immediate bills and people's salaries. The danger of the bank manager calling in the overdraft is ever present.

The earlier analysis of P&Ls and balance sheets should lead the directors to produce an action plan for both the short and longer terms, dealing with profit and cash (Box 8.10). This crisis action plan can form the basis of a more formal business plan.

It is evident from Box 8.10 that very little can be done in the short term to improve profitability significantly, though it should be possible to raise sufficient cash to permit a long-term recovery plan to be formulated and implemented. The implication is clear: you should endeavour to keep a very close watch on profitability and cash flow on a weekly (preferably) or monthly basis – quarterly accounts are too late! Changes to opportunities and threats happen so rapidly these days that no serious business can afford to be without basic financial controls and monitoring procedures (see Chapter 9), of which weekly or monthly reporting forms an important part.

In the final analysis, the lack of plans, information and controls could hamper the company's rapid return to profitability, because effective planning and information systems are difficult to initiate if there is no culture of planning and analysing information. The lesson is to get started in the good times when people typically have more time to experiment with new ways of doing things.

Box 8.10 Action plan for dealing with ABCO's crisis

	Short-term actions	Long-term actions
Profitability	1 Eliminate unnecessary expenditure	1 Redundancies (to reduce capacity)
	2 Swingeing salary cuts (including directors)	2 Review pricing policy and practices
	3 Eliminate unnecessary marketing activities	3 Review purchasing policy and practices
	4 Raise prices	4 Review production efficiency
		5 Produce marketing plan
		6 Introduce effective budgetary control
		7 Improve job costing
		8 Improve management information systems (MIS)
		9 Review strategy and produce strategic plan
Cash	1 Sell unnecessary assets (e.g. expensive cars)	1 Review gearing, raise more equity (owners') capital
	2 Collect outstanding debts	2 Improve credit controls
	3 Raise loans from directors	3 Improve purchasing controls
	4 Draw up business plan and visit bank manager to raise or secure overdraft	4 Improve cash-flow forecasting and cash management

You have seen how using ratio analysis can assist the process of uncovering the root causes of financial under-performance. It is now your turn to analyse your own accounts and work out ways to improve overall profitability and cash flow by managing gross margins, controlling overheads and maintaining rigorous financial controls.

Further reading

1 Oldcorn, R. (1996) *Company Accounts*, Palgrave, London.
2 O'Gill, J. (1991) *How to Understand Financial Statements*, Kogan Page, London.
3 Smith, S. (1996) *Accounting for Growth*, Random House, London.

Management Information Systems and Financial Controls

CHAPTER 9

Key issues dealt with in this chapter are:

- Characteristics of an effective management information system.
- The effects of a well-controlled business.
- Management information to plan, monitor and control profit margins and finance.
- Principal monitoring procedures and financial control systems.

There are several important characteristics of an effective management information system:

1 *Accuracy*. Since business plans and management decisions to implement them will be formulated on the basis of information gathered from internal records and external sources, their accuracy could have a significant effect on business performance. For example, if you do not establish accurately where you make profits and why your customers buy from you, any attempt to focus scarce resources on developing core competences could be wide of the mark and a great deal of effort could be wasted.

2 *Comprehensiveness and completeness*. Partial and incomplete information could suffer from undue bias (particularly in the event of abnormal circumstances affecting the source of the information) and point to the wrong conclusions.

3 *Relevance*. To ward off information overflow, the information should be checked for relevance, because unnecessary information tends to cloud the issue, which either slows up decision making or results in errors of judgement.

4 *Currency*. Out-of-date information can be misleading, e.g. using costs from last year's profit and loss accounts for costing purposes. Basing mark-ups on these

costs could easily lead to underpricing and lower profit margins than would be the case if costings were based on forward projections.

5   *Cost-effectiveness*. Gathering, storing, analysing, retrieving and using information should be cost-effective. The costs of gathering usable information must be recouped from somewhere and if there is no obvious market or product to attach them to, there is some doubt that the information is worth gathering.

6   *Usability*. It must be possible to present the information in a usable form. If the information is too complex to present in a practical way, it is unlikely to be understood by the user and therefore will be of little value.

7   *Systemic*. Information should be the product of a system and generated and used systematically. While there will always be a role for *ad hoc* information, most long-term and day-to-day business decisions require drawing on a constant throughput of information.

An effective management information system should be designed with the specific needs of the business in mind, following three stages.

Stage 1

Undertake a review and analysis of business decisions to identify their nature, frequency and timing. What information is required? For instance, pricing policy requires information about the type of products being sold to a particular market segment, the contributions demanded from each product line, the buying habits of customers in that market and the frequency and timing of their buying decisions. To supply this information in a timely fashion, an information system needs to draw systematically on internal and external sources.

Stage 2

Analyse and record the information requirements at each decision point, identifying what information is available, where the gaps are and whether they can be filled from internal and/or external sources.

Stage 3

Having established how the information is to be used and what types of information are required, you are now in a position to design an information system to produce the information. There are three elements at this stage:

1   Information must be collected, collated and stored in an appropriate way. Much information already exists but needs to be organized. Some of the best information is collected by people who are constantly out in the marketplace talking to customers and competitors, keeping their ears close to the ground and their eyes peeled for signs of opportunity and change. How can all this valuable data be collected and stored?

2   Once stored, the raw information has to be retrieved and processed. Database design requires that the end use of the data should be specified very accurately.

3   Finally, information has to be presented and used effectively. Clear and concise presentation, particularly if other people are involved in the decision making,

will help get the right decisions made as quickly as possible. Most information is used for decision making in the areas of business planning, plan implementation (in all business functions), monitoring key indicators of performance and controlling profit and cash.

Controlling profit and cash

There are two principal areas for financial control: profit and cash. Generating the level of profit called for in the business plan with appropriate monitoring procedures while simultaneously keeping a firm grip on the uses of cash, allocating it in the right quantities to fixed and working capital, should ensure long-term financial stability.

But how does an effective system ensure that profit and cash objectives are met? The following example using ABCO Systems (discussed in Chapters 3 and 8) demonstrates the consequences for profit and cash of a controlled versus uncontrolled business. In the profit and loss accounts and balance sheets shown in Tables 9.1 and 9.2 respectively, we see the 1998/99 actual figures in the left-hand columns together with financial ratios, and in the right another set of 1998/99 figures together with ratios, but this time a hypothetical 'controlled' situation based on applying a range of financial controls. The final column, headed 'notes', explains the controls in each case.

What would have happened to ABCO under a regime of effective financial controls and a more focused strategy? The evidence is clear (refer to the notes column in Table 9.1):

1   Marketing and sales planning to identify target markets and set out sales targets and profit margins (though here assumed to be too late to matter).
2   Pricing policy to agree price levels and discounts and costings to confirm profit margins.
3   Improved purchasing controls and ordering procedures produce cost savings on materials and lower order volumes closely matched to sales.
4   Lower stock levels result from tighter stock control; lower work in progress results from improved invoicing procedures.
5   Effective workshop management results in lower labour costs.

The overall effect so far is to raise gross profit by £41 000 (up 2.1 per cent).

6   Travel to overseas destinations (unprofitable) is reduced after a detailed marketing plan and strategy review.
7   Motor running costs increase because of the focus on local markets.
8   Telephone costs reduce as marketing plan focuses on key accounts.
9   Print costs likewise reduce.
10 New appointments are reduced by one because of improved use of people.

A total of £91 000 is saved on marketing and selling costs, which, in combination with a higher gross margin, raises contribution by 6.6 per cent. So far, so good.

11 There is no change to premises costs on the assumption that they are inflexible.
12 Post reduces because marketing costs are better controlled.

Table 9.1: The results of effective financial controls on profit

ABCO Systems Ltd, profit and loss accounts, year ending 31/3

| | 1998/99 (£000) | | 1998/99 (£000) | | |
	Actual	Ratio%	Controlled	Ratio%	Notes
SALES	2019	100.0	2019	100.0	1, 2
COST OF SALES					
Purchases	743	36.8	660	32.7	3
Opening stock + WIP	84	4.2	84	4.2	
Closing stock + WIP	98	4.9	50	2.5	4
	729	36.1	694	34.3	
Labour (workshop)	58	2.9	52	2.6	5
	787	39.0	746	36.9	
GROSS PROFIT	1232	61.0	1273	63.1	
DIRECT OVERHEADS					
Marketing/selling expenses					
Travel and subsistence	76	3.8	50	2.5	6
Motor running expenses	62	3.1	70	3.5	7
Telephones	86	4.3	70	3.5	8
Print	102	5.1	75	3.7	9
Salaries	154	7.6	124	6.1	10
	480	23.8	389	19.3	
Contribution	752	37.2	884	43.8	
INDIRECT OVERHEADS					
Establishment expenses					
Rent and rates	114	5.6	114	5.6	
Light and heat	12	0.6	12	0.6	
Insurance	9	0.4	9	0.4	
Repairs and maintenance	24	1.2	24	1.2	
	159	7.9	159	7.9	11
Administration expenses					
Employee training	20	1.0	20	1.0	
Post, stationery	31	1.5	25	1.2	12
Audit and accountancy	30	1.5	20	1.0	13
Salaries	481	23.8	420	20.8	14
	562	27.8	485	24.0	
Finance expenses					
Bank interest	44	2.2	24	1.2	15
Provision for bad debts	35	1.7	20	1.0	16
	79	3.9	44	2.2	
Depreciation	75	3.7	60	3.0	17
Total indirect overheads	875	43.3	748	37.0	
Total overheads	1355	67.1	1137	56.3	
NET PROFIT/(LOSS) BEFORE TAX	(123)	−6.1	136	6.7	
Taxation	0	0.0	25	1.2	
Dividends	0	0.0	0	0.0	
RETAINED PROFIT/(LOSS)	(123)	−6.1	111	5.5	

Table 9.2: The results of effective financial controls on cash

ABCO Systems Ltd, balance sheet, year ending 31/3

| | 1998/99 (£000) | | 1998/99 (£000) | | |
	Actual	**Ratio**	**Controlled**	**Ratio**	**Notes**
Fixed assets					
Equipment, vehicles	467	£ 4.32	400	£ 5.05	1
Depreciation	230	£ 8.78	214	£ 9.43	2
	237	£ 8.52	186	£ 10.85	
Current assets					
Stock + work in progress	98	46 days	50	25 days	3
Debtors and prepayments	480	87 days	249	45 days	4
Cash	2		0		5
	580		299		
Less: Current liabilities					
Trade creditors	279	137 days	163	90 days	6
VAT and IR	60	3.0%	60		
Corporation tax	0		25		
Dividends	0		0		
Overdraft	96		0		7
	435		248		
Net Current Assets	145		51		
Capital Employed	382		237		
Bank loans	295	gearing 77%	84	gearing 35%	7
NET ASSETS	87		321		
Financed by:					
Share capital	10		10		
Profit and Loss Account	77		311		
SHAREHOLDERS' FUNDS	87		321		

13 Audit and accountancy charges reduce because of better purchasing practices.
14 Salaries reduce by £61 000 because fewer people are needed in back-office roles as a result of reorganization and a more productive workforce.
15 Lower interest payments are the result of eliminating the overdraft and not having to borrow so heavily from the bank (see the balance sheet in Table 9.2).
16 There are fewer bad debts because of improved marketing (selling to higher-quality customers) and tighter credit control.
17 There is lower depreciation because of planned purchasing of fixed assets and effective policies on care of company assets.

The overall effect is to eliminate the loss of £123 000 and generate a small profit before tax of £111 000 (5.5 per cent).

It is evident that effective financial controls, combined with a more focused strategy and a realistic marketing plan, can:

- Raise gross profit margin by a few percentage points.
- Reduce overheads considerably.
- Raise the net profit margin to an acceptable level (though not as high as the previous year).

A summary of P&L planning, information and control systems is as follows:

- Marketing and sales plan to identify target markets and sales and gross profit required from each segment.
- Pricing and costing controls.
- Work-in-progress control.
- Monthly sales and profit reports (by customer, segment, project/product/ service).
- Purchase control.
- Stock control.
- Production control (management).
- Budgetary control (whole business).
- Credit control.
- Cash management.
- Fixed assets control.

The balance sheet also needs to be more effectively controlled, as Table 9.2 illustrates.

The main improvements brought about by effective plans, information and controls are as follows (refer to the notes column in Table 9.2):

1 Taking better care of fixed assets (regular maintenance) eliminates the need for new equipment; improved planning and budgeting will do likewise.
2 Accumulated depreciation is lower as a result.
3 Stock and work-in-progress controls were mentioned earlier.
4 Credit control was mentioned earlier.
5 Cash management was mentioned earlier. Effective cash-flow forecasting will predict cash demands and reduce interest payments.
6 Purchase control was mentioned earlier.
7 Increasing retained profit and tightening up financial controls releases cash, eliminates the need for an overdraft and reduces the need for a large bank loan (the loan could, of course, be in the form of an overdraft).

The end result is that the business is financially stable with higher profitability and reduced gearing, an outcome of small improvements in key areas to control its fixed and working capital needs. In summary, controls on the balance sheet are as follows:

- Fixed asset control.
- Stock control.
- Work-in-progress control.

- Credit control.
- Cash management.
- Purchase control.

Controlling profit: The P&L account

There are essentially two parts to profitability: gross profit and overheads (see Chapter 8). Gross profit arguably constitutes the most important part of the business, because it is made up of the sales and purchasing/production functions. Consider the business decisions in these critical areas:

- Choice of target markets.
- Choice of products/services.
- Pricing decisions.
- Purchasing decisions.
- Stock decisions.
- Production decisions (make or buy).

Much of the decision making at the gross profit level is of a strategic nature – the choices of markets, products and technology are long term – and even the others (pricing, stock, purchasing, production) require effective forward planning and efficient organization to ensure that costs are controlled and margins achieved. This is where clear strategic thinking, entrepreneurial drive and creative juices are put to the test.

The rest of the business – the overheads – follows strategy. The overhead functions are a matter of effective and efficient organization and human resource management competences; this is where planning, monitoring, feedback and control should come into their own. However, they generally do not call for innovation and 'thinking out of the box', as gross profit activities clearly do.

Consider first, therefore, the information needed to plan, monitor and control the business so that it achieves objectives for a) aggregate gross profit margins and b) gross profit margins by customer, market segment, product and project. These objectives need to be specified in the strategic business plan (Chapter 10).

Managing strategy through gross profit margin

The choices of markets and products, which we have defined as marketing strategy (Chapter 2), are determined by expected profitability and financing needs in each area of opportunity. This means understanding gross profit margin. Box 9.1 illustrates the differential effects on gross profit of discounting (Options A1–A4) and strategic change (Options B5–B7).

The strategic and tactical options are as follows:

- *Option 1* – current pricing arrangement. Unit sales = 10, contribution 100p.
- *Option 2* – discount of 5p (±17 per cent) per can. No contribution after extra marketing costs (100p per day), even with sales doubling to 20 cans per day. This option would be foolish!

Box 9.1 Gross margins and strategy

Take the case of a shop buying and selling baked beans at a steady 10 cans per day:

Selling price per can = 30 p
Cost price per can = 20 p

The shopkeeper wants to make more money from baked beans. He is faced with several options, set out below.

Option	Price per unit	Cost per unit	Gross margin per unit	GPM %	Units sold	Total gross margin	Extra marketing cost	Contribution to overheads
A	**Options to generate more profit per day through discounting:**							
A1	30p	20p	10p	33%	10	100p	0p	100p
A2	25p	20p	5p	20%	20	100p	100p	0p
A3	25p	20p	5p	20%	40	200p	100p	100p
A4	25p	15p	10p	40%	20	200p	100p	100p
B	**Options to generate more profit per day through higher margins:**							
B5	40p	25p	15p	37.5%	7	105p	0p	105p
B6	80p	30p	50p	62.5%	6	300p	150p	150p
B7	100p	25p	75p	75%	20	1500p	200p	1300p

- *Option 3* – discount of 5p (±17 per cent) per can. To produce the same total contribution as before, the shopkeeper would have to sell 40 cans per day. Also a foolish option!
- *Option 4* – same discount, but negotiate a cost reduction with the supplier to 15p per can, so gross margin up to 40 per cent. However, sales must be more than twice the current volume to produce a higher contribution, after marketing costs. Is it worth it? Probably not, considering the risk.

So far it seems that cutting prices will not work unless a significant increase in volume sales can be achieved. What other options are there?

- *Option 5* – change the product to fancy-grade beans and raise price (40p) and margin (15p = 37.5 per cent). This can be done by refocusing the target market on customers who prefer better quality beans. Now only seven cans need to be sold to match the current contribution. This is possible under certain conditions, e.g. customers rushing home late after work with nothing in the pantry.
- *Option 6* – introduce new products with higher gross margins (62.5 per cent), e.g. range of sandwiches, aimed at existing customers. Contribution now shoots up. Looks promising!
- *Option 7* – introduce fresh pasta and sauces aimed at yuppies,[1] dinkies[2] and lombards[3] going home late at night. An example of a new strategy, changing

both customers (attracting higher-income professionals) and products (still higher gross margin). Doubtless changes will have to be made to the shop to accommodate the new strategy.

While selling baked beans might seem a frivolous example, it does demonstrate that strategic decision making requires a thorough understanding of the differential effects of strategic and pricing decisions on gross profit margins. The following sources of information are required to provide effective control of gross profit margins.

Sales records

Records need to indicate sufficient information about customers, products and aspects of buying behaviour to inform the key strategic (which markets? what products?) and tactical (what mix of marketing Ps?) marketing decisions. The design of a sales information system should reflect the particular needs of the business and information should be recorded by customer, market segment, product and project, to include:

- Customer profile (see Chapter 3) and market segment.
- Sales by volume and value.
- Gross profit.
- Products purchased.
- Prices paid and discounts given.
- Source of sales leads.
- How customers heard about the business.
- Reaction to promotional and sales literature.
- Any additional information for analysing response and conversion rates.

Purchases and production records

A proper record of materials purchases, direct labour and other variable costs is required to enable accurate costings to be calculated and contribution rates to be assessed on each product and market segment. The matching of actual to budgeted costs for projects is an important monitoring procedure and can only be effective if the discipline of keeping time and job sheets is strictly observed. Frequent reviews of standard costs should be undertaken to ensure that costings are based on the latest available information. Contribution rates by product group and market segment should be calculated and stored in costing records for use in later pricing decisions.

Competitors

Moving outside the business, financial and marketing information about competitors will help business planning (see SWOT analysis in Chapter 10). Monitoring the activities of competitors and possible new entrants to your market should be supplemented with records of competitors' products, prices and marketing effort to assist in decision making about your own marketing activities.

Environment

Information having a bearing on financial and marketing decisions, such as domestic inflation, currency exchange rates and macro-economic forecasts, should be gathered and stored on a regular basis. This type of record, invaluable for planning purposes, could consist of newspaper cuttings or government statistical publications.

Budgetary control

Using budgets as a means of control is the most effective method of monitoring profit performance on a regular basis and identifying potential problem areas. Budgetary (or variance) analysis provides a ready picture of detailed income, expenditure and margins on a monthly as well as year-to-date basis, comparing actual figures with budgets in all areas of the business. Variances (expressed as $+/-$ against budget) provide an 'at a glance' picture of business performance. But budgetary analysis can only identify the problem areas; it cannot reveal the causes on its own. The management information system should include some of the detailed profitability reports and records described above, but even then a good deal of additional investigation and analysis is often warranted.

The effectiveness of control through budgets lies in two areas: budgets must be properly constructed, and the control system must be applied proactively. Many growth businesses make the mistake of reporting variances religiously every month, but find that once the information is in the accounting system, it is too late to take effective action (other than cut costs). Budgets should be constructed rigorously following the business planning process described in Chapter 10 and should be monitored by departmental managers regularly to prevent actual expenditure exceeding budget limits (and to take early action on underperforming sales). In other words, regular monitoring of departmental business plans and budgets should permit action to be taken long before budgets are exceeded or sales targets missed. To get to potential problem areas in good time, there should be 'lead' indicators of performance, e.g. sales lead generation, lead/order conversion rates, reports on key account activities, production delays and bottlenecks, etc. (see Chapter 10 for the most common performance indicators).

At times, however, budgets can be restrictive and some flexibility should be permitted, with sufficient discretion for managers to exceed them if good reason can be given. Flexible budgeting is a practical response to the ever-changing business environment, particularly for fast-growth firms. A budget set before the start of the year could be significantly out of date six months later, particularly if plans change at short notice. Budgets should not be cast in stone; if a change in plans is forced on the business, then new budgets should be prepared based on the new plan.

Costing and pricing reviews

When customers' needs and market conditions change rapidly, periodic reviews of pricing and costings will ensure that prices are pitched at a level that produces planned profit margins. In order to set prices on the basis of total costs per unit of output plus a satisfactory profit margin, the information in Box 9.2 is required.

Box 9.2 Costing information

variable cost per unit
+ fixed cost per unit
= total cost per unit
+ net profit per unit
= price per unit

For a single-product business where the production process is uniform, a simple costing procedure can be devised and applied with accuracy. However, in more complex growing businesses, the costing process requires considerable attention. A worked example is provided in Appendix 4. The main steps in costing for a simple business are as follows:

Step 1

Calculate variable costs per batch/project:

- Total costs of materials and subcontractors.
- Add carriage costs.
- Add direct labour costs (calculate direct hourly rate for each category of worker by dividing and remuneration plus relevant on-costs, e.g. pensions, overtime, employers' taxes), by productive hours.[4]
- Add other variable costs (only those costs incurred for the sale).

Step 2

Calculate variable costs per unit:

- Divide variable costs by number of units (allow for wastage).

Step 3

Calculate overhead recovery costs per batch/project:

- Calculate full production capacity per annum in terms of productive (chargeable) hours when operating normally (add each worker's productive capacity to produce a grand total for the business).
- Calculate total overhead costs for the year (or period) ahead.
- Convert total overhead costs into an hourly recovery rate by dividing costs by total number of productive hours. This rate is very sensitive to changes in the

two variables (total hours and total overheads) and regular reviews of both are desirable.

- Multiply hourly overhead recovery rate by number of worker hours on the job.

Step 4

Calculate total cost per batch/project and per unit:

- Add variable costs to overhead recovery for the batch/project.
- Divide by number of units to produce unit total cost.

Step 5

Consider pricing options:

- Use planned net profit margin for this customer/market/product line/project to calculate ideal pricing option from total cost calculation, e.g. if your planned net profit margin is 10 per cent, then total costs must be 90 per cent of price, so price = total costs ÷ 0.9.
- Run sensitivity analyses on key assumptions, i.e. following steps 1 to 5, calculate and evaluate alternative pricing options assuming shorter productive hours, lower recovery rates, higher variable costs, lower gross profit margins, etc.

While costing is largely a financial issue, pricing is a marketing one and in the final analysis your customers will pay what they consider to be a fair price, given their preference for a combination of price, delivery, quality and service. Knowing what price to charge should reflect on the comprehensiveness of your customer information system; knowing how low to go either to break even or to make a desired level of profit would be greatly helped by adopting a logical approach to costing.

The problems of costing are multiplied for a more complex business, one selling many products/services to several market segments. Different production and delivery processes warrant different rates of overhead allocation (unlike the uniform rate assumed above), because a) direct overheads, e.g. marketing and selling, can be directly related to a particular sale; and b) indirect overheads, e.g. rent and rates, although they cannot easily be related in the same way, should nevertheless be allocated using an appropriate factor. To calculate the net profitability of every activity or sale (unit/project/batch), all costs should be allocated on a defensible basis to ensure that the profitability of individual jobs is not distorted, and that jobs losing money (because they do not recover their true overheads) do not lead to a misallocation of resources. Indirect overheads can be allocated to individual sales, market segments or projects using one of the following factors:

- Proportion of staff numbers working in specific areas, e.g. focused on specific market segments or on specific products.
- Proportion of staff payroll working in specific areas.
- Proportion of productive hours worked in specific areas.
- Proportion of sales floor or display area devoted to specific products (appropriate for retailing).

- Proportion of total floor area devoted to specific areas.
- Proportion of sales revenues in specific areas.

It is up to managers to develop the best costing methods for their business. So taking our earlier step-by-step approach, a more complex business would deviate at step 3 as follows.

Step 3

Calculate direct overheads per activity – unit/batch/project:

- Identify direct overheads associated with each unit/batch/project.
- Allocate directly to unit/batch/project on a total or pro rata basis.
- Divide by number of units.

Step 4

Calculate indirect overheads per activity – unit/batch/project:

- Identify indirect overheads.
- Choose one or more allocating factors (see above).
- Apply factors to indirect overheads either as a total or by overhead type, e.g. premises costs allocated on basis of proportion of square footage, administration costs allocated on basis of proportion of sales turnover.
- Adjust allocations as necessary.

Step 5

Calculate total cost per activity – unit/batch/project:

- Add variable costs to overhead allocation for the unit/batch/project.

Step 6

Consider pricing options:

- Use planned net profit margin for this customer/product line to calculate ideal pricing option from total cost calculation.
- Run sensitivity analyses on key assumptions, e.g. allocation basis, variable costs, competitor reaction, customer reaction, and consider alternative pricing options.

The effects of applying fully allocated direct and indirect costs to each activity, market segment, product, product line or project, on an accurate and defensible basis – e.g. for costs projected over the coming period, rather than those incurred over past periods – are that the net profitability of each activity can be measured with confidence. Ultimately, strategic and tactical decision making should be easier, and so should the propensity to delegate to key managers, who will be able to allocate team resources efficiently to the highest-profit customers, market segments, products and projects.

Controlling cash: The balance sheet

Balance sheet controls are designed to minimize financing requirements, although there are incidental consequences for profitability. Any action that results in lower costs or higher revenues will affect profit as well as cash. We are principally interested in cash in this section, but will note in passing the impact of controls on profit.

Controls on fixed assets

There are three primary ways to control the growth of fixed assets and the capital they consume: take care of existing fixed assets so that they do not have to be replaced before their useful life expires; plan the purchase of fixed assets closely aligned with need; and take possession of and use assets required in the business without purchasing them, or finance them without having to pay the full purchase price immediately.

1 Care of fixed assets

The rate of depreciation of fixed assets, which is normally based on their useful life, should reflect business policy on care and maintenance of assets. Longer life means a lower rate of depreciation and therefore higher profitability. Since conservatism is a guiding principle in the preparation of accounts, it is normal to depreciate assets at a higher rate than reality might dictate, but this should not obscure the fact that the business will gain by not replacing assets until it becomes necessary.

There are several actions that can be taken to ensure that assets are replaced at the right time: you need to have a policy on the care and maintenance of equipment, tools, machinery, buildings and motor vehicles and the attention of all employees should be drawn to this policy; it is prudent to designate someone to ensure that the policy is implemented; employees can have a clause in their contracts of employment obligating them to look after company assets; drivers of company vehicles should sign a vehicle care document; users of specific items of equipment (such as computers) should have their attention drawn to correct operating and maintenance procedures; equipment and vehicles should be stored correctly when not in use; and maintenance of equipment and regular servicing of vehicles should be fully costed into budgets.

2 Acquisition of fixed assets

Plan and budget for the purchase of capital items – buildings, plant, equipment, machinery and vehicles – just as with revenue expenditure items. These purchases must conform to general purchasing policies and practices, e.g. quotations must be sought from several potential suppliers and the best deals struck to minimize initial capital outlays, payments over the life of the assets and annual depreciation charges.

3   Use and ownership of fixed assets

A fundamental question is whether the business should own the assets (and therefore have to finance them) or simply have the use of them (and therefore not have to finance them). Ownership of certain assets is inevitable because it is not realistic to hire or lease them. But many others can be hired on a short-term basis (no finance required), bought with hire-purchase over a period of time (finance spread over the period), leased (no capital outlay required) or contract rented (mainly for vehicles where no finance is required). In a growing business, there is a sound argument for having and using the asset but not necessarily owning it: without certain knowledge about future needs, it could be risky to tie the business to a particular asset, such as commercial premises, in the interests of 'building the balance sheet'. Such an action would reduce operational flexibility and therefore could damage profits as well as needlessly tie up finance that might be deployed more productively elsewhere.

The value of fixed assets can be monitored using an 'asset utilization' ratio, which relates the written-down value of assets to sales value (see Chapter 8 for a description of key financial ratios), and by monitoring actual capital assets expenditure against budget for the period.

Controls on working capital

The control of working capital has proved to be an enduring obstacle to successful growth of the smaller business. The reasons are not as arcane as they at first seem: working capital, unlike fixed capital, cannot be 'observed', it changes daily as new items are added or subtracted. It is a financial phenomenon that many owner-managers find daunting. In the hurly-burly of managing the growing business, working capital is often ignored or inadequately supervised, giving rise to severe cash-flow problems. The right monitoring procedures and controls on working capital will ensure that potential problems are quickly identified and nipped in the bud. We will discuss these procedures and controls in logical balance sheet order: stock control, work-in-progress control, credit control, cash management and purchasing control.

Stock control

Controls on the level of stock held in the business are designed to achieve two things simultaneously: to reduce the costs of holding and managing stock, and to reduce the amount of finance tied up in stock. There are several types of cost of holding stock: the financing of stock attracts interest charges; there are costs of storage, both in terms of physical space (rent, rates, insurance) and people to manage it (salaries); there are administration costs (salaries, data handling); there are risks associated with merchandise where stock value could erode rapidly; and there is the possibility of damage to and pilferage of stock (shrinkage).

The object of stock control is to carry a level and range of stock that match requirements for filling orders, while having sufficient buffer stock until new deliveries arrive. Information needed to decide on the right stock level and to design an appropriate control system is as follows:

- Current stock level in units.
- Expected sales in units in the period ahead.
- Minimum stock level required.
- Reorder lead times and minimum quantities.
- Stock-holding capacity.

The principles of stock management form an integral part of stock control procedures and embrace the following: order only what the business needs and do not be deflected by 'special offers', no matter how tempting (stockrooms all over the world are full of special offers for which there is no demand); keep stock to a minimum, in line with sales and delivery lead times; store stock on or in appropriate storage systems and use it in strict rotation, drawing older before recently delivered stock (this is called 'FIFO', or first in, first out); clearly label and price stock from the most recent price lists; count stock at regular intervals to check computerized records and calculate 'shrinkage' – the amount of stock lost through damage, theft or error; and enforce a strict code of practice when deliveries are received, checking quantities and condition before signing for them.

Stock levels are normally monitored by setting 'stock days' or 'stock turn' ratios for the various types of stock, relating stock value to either purchases or sales values, or by monitoring the value of stock against projected sales or purchases (projected for the period ahead that the stock holding is designed to cover).

Work-in-progress control

Like stock mismanagement, a great deal of finance can be tied up in work in progress as the business grows. This problem affects growing manufacturing and service businesses disproportionately because both can suffer from uncontrolled value of uninvoiced work, e.g. the accumulation of uninvoiced project time in professional service firms, and uninvoiced time and materials in manufacturing, particularly with new product development or complex production processes. The answer is to arrange the terms of trade with customers to ensure advance and periodic payments to finance work in progress (where possible); and to invoice promptly once projects are completed.

Work-in-progress values can be monitored against projected sales (projected for the period ahead in which the work in progress will be invoiced).

Credit control

The uncontrolled growth of credit to customers is potentially very destructive. Businesses frequently grant credit facilities without asking any questions and are then surprised when their customers cannot pay. There are two potential problems with debtors: the more serious is when customers make a purchase and never pay for it, either because they go out of business leaving no assets to cover outstanding liabilities, or because there is a dispute about the sale that is never settled; the less potentially damaging is the length of time that customers can take to pay their bills, often because there is no incentive to pay on time. So how can monitoring and control systems be used to reduce and eliminate debtor problems?

Debtors should be monitored by keeping under surveillance a comprehensive list of outstanding debts and reviewing it weekly, while at the end of every month, when the regular monthly management accounts are prepared, a list of aged debtors should also be prepared and the potential problem payers identified for action. The most important control is to telephone debtors (if not all, certainly the larger ones) before an invoice becomes payable to confirm that it a) has been received; b) is correct and has been passed for payment; and c) is due for payment on a certain date, i.e. it is in the cheque run.

Other controls include the following procedures.

Making the right strategic and customer choices

Creditworthiness is an important criterion in choosing to target new market segments or customers. Certain types of businesses are bound to have more problems paying their bills than others, e.g. small retailers and those whose own customers take many months to pay them.

Taking trade references

It is standard practice to ask for at least two trade references from new customers. It is up to the supplier to contact these references and make enquiries about the customer's creditworthiness, including the amount of credit given, the customer's record in paying their bills on time and any problems that have arisen. Nevertheless, it would be unwise to place too much reliance on this credit check alone.

Using credit reference agencies

Checking your customer's creditworthiness with a credit reference agency will inform you about any history of defaults and the credit rating of the customer. The weakness of using an agency is that the most untrustworthy businesses are either too small or too elusive to be included in its records. Since the agency charges for this service, the costs must be related to the amount of potential debt being incurred – normally credit reports are only worthwhile for large amounts or regular custom.

Taking a bank reference

There is very little a bank reference can achieve except to verify the customer's business name, establish that a bank account exists and that an agreed amount of credit per month could be met. This itself might be sufficient, however, and would help generally establish a customer's credibility.

Agreeing credit limits

Before agreeing to supply a new customer, agree a monthly credit limit. If there are no reliable references (particularly if the company is new or very small), it is wise to extend only a small amount of credit or preferably, if the customer agrees, to request cash with order until a relationship of trust can be built up. By monitoring each customer's account very carefully, there will be ample warning of any imminent over-running of the agreed credit limit.

Agreeing trading terms

Often a dispute arises because the terms and conditions of the sale are not made clear before the sale is closed. Minimum terms should be established and agreed in writing between the parties so that there is clarity on both sides. Commercial law provides a framework to which commercial transactions must conform (such as the Sale of Goods Act) and the purchaser will have certain rights. To avoid expensive litigation, however, minimize the possibility of disputes arising by getting the customer to agree to certain basic conditions: an agreed maximum credit period by which payment should be received in full, the amount of discounts and under what conditions they may be taken, late payment penalties (it is unlikely that the courts will enforce these unless they are expressly agreed to before the sale is concluded), when the transfer of ownership is effected between the seller to the buyer (the so-called Romalpa clause whereby beneficial ownership does not pass until full payment is received), what form arbitration should take in the event of a dispute arising and other more specific conditions suited to certain industries. These and other terms should be set out clearly in advance of the sale (and signed by both parties) and noted on the invoice for the customer's benefit.

Invoicing procedures

A sequence of sending delivery notes (if relevant), invoices and statements should be adhered to strictly in order to simplify the presentation of bills for payment and ensure that all amounts sold and delivered are actually charged to the customer. If there are frequent deliveries of goods, a delivery note is essential to confirm that delivery has taken place and that the customer has received the consignment in good condition. A statement of account is required when there are several invoices in a period to ensure that the customer pays all due invoices on time.

Insuring bad debts

Another method of minimizing the financial cost of bad debts is to insure invoiced sales against the debt going bad. Bad debt insurance can be quite expensive, but could be used selectively for larger or more risky sales, such as those to foreign customers, where a comprehensive package of financial and other trading assistance should be sought.

Chasing doubtful and slow debts

There are as many methods of tackling slow payers as there are slow payers themselves and everyone will have their favourite. Having ensured that no disputes can arise about the goods delivered by implementing all the controls mentioned above, in the event of a debt showing no signs of being paid, the following are generally accepted approaches to collecting debts. The first question to settle is whether there is a dispute or not and, indeed, whether the customer actually received the invoice. The use of heavy legal or other threats at this stage is bound to prolong payment and the best approach is to give the customer the benefit of the doubt with an enquiring telephone call to establish whether there is a problem. If this is not the case and no satisfactory explanation is forthcoming, it could be worthwhile offering to call immediately to collect a cheque. This direct approach often works well; otherwise you should set a time limit for payment.

Taking legal action

If all reasonable attempts to recover the debt fail and there is no prospect of collecting it without legal action, you will have to decide whether the reward is worth the likely costs, bearing in mind that there is no certainty that you will have the costs of the action awarded against the defendant, should you win. The larger the customer, the more likely it is that you will end up paying out more to pursue your rights than you would wish and the more damaging this could be financially. To avoid this, design a procedure that comes into effect when a bill is late for payment, starting with a telephone call, following through with a strong letter and ending with a threat to take the customer to court. If you adopt this procedure, you must be prepared to carry out your threat, which can be time-consuming and there is no guarantee that, even if judgment is entered against the defendant, you will ever be paid. Another option is to use professional debt collectors who work on a commission basis; a final option is to pass the responsibility of collecting debts to a factoring company, which will manage your sales ledger and collect any slow or doubtful debts on your behalf.

In the end, you will have to consider whether the bad feeling engendered by continual badgering of slow payers is worth the potential reward. At some point you will decide that it is not worth having customers who pay late and cause you endless grief. The costs of chasing them up could start to affect other parts of the business. At this point it would be prudent to 'bite the bullet' and write off the worst cases.

Cash flow control and treasury management

The treasury function is to manage the balance between cash surpluses and deficits and to place surpluses in interest-earning investments. Efficient cash management should minimize interest payments on overdrafts and bank loans and maximize interest received when monies are on deposit. This is achieved through two actions: diligent cash-flow forecasting on a regular basis (daily or weekly), which allows borrowing to be planned in advance of new finance being needed; and monitoring of cash balances on current accounts. (See cash-flow forecasting in Chapter 10.)

Purchasing control

The monitoring and control of creditors form the final area for increasing profit and containing the amount of finance needed in the short term. Creditors (suppliers) are a valuable source of short-term finance through the credit negotiated with them. It is in your interest to maximize the amount of credit you can get, within reason, since you have a reciprocal relationship with your suppliers; taking undue credit is likely to disturb any good relationship that exists. Other supplier measures should be considered.

Supplier selection

When selecting new suppliers, particularly when the selection is a strategically important one, it is advisable to 'shop around' for availability, credit and delivery terms and prices. Negotiating favourable terms can bring considerable additional benefits and suppliers are often prepared to offer quite substantial discounts or special credit and delivery terms to win new business. In recent times businesses have resorted to single sourcing to secure the best possible terms and to ensure that suppliers provide high levels of service.

Order procedures

Instituting appropriate ordering procedures should be a priority as the business grows and the founders are no longer able to exercise close personal supervision of purchasing. Purchase orders should form the backbone of creditor control, together with the signature of the person authorized to approve purchases. Once the delivery is received, the delivery note should be filed with the purchase order, matched with the invoice when received and finally checked against the monthly statement. This procedure ensures that only those goods and services ordered and delivered are actually paid for, and at the right price.

Once this system is in operation, payment procedures are quite straightforward. Every statement or invoice should have a matching purchase order and delivery note, thus nothing is paid in error. Exceptions can be made for payments where a purchase order is superfluous, i.e. for regular payments such as leasing or bank charges.

We have explored the management information systems needed for effective decision making and for monitoring and control systems to produce the required level of profit within available financial resources. You should now review your own systems and procedures, starting with the key question: What information is needed for strategic and tactical decision making and for monitoring and control purposes?

Notes

1   Young urban professionals.
2   Households with double incomes and no kids.
3   Describes wealthy young people working in finance and banking in the City of London.
4   Productive hours should be based on total annual hours less annual leave, statutory holidays, sick days and training days. Then apply a productivity rate, e.g. 85 per cent, based on the worker's (or team's) productivity (which should be measured from time to time).

Further reading

1   Kaplan, R. and Norton, D. (1996) *The Balanced Scorecard*, Harvard Business School Press, Boston, MA.
2   Drury, C. (2000) *Management and Cost Accounting*, Thomson Learning, London.
3   Attrill, P. and McLaney, E. (2002) *Management Accounting for Non-Specialists*, FT Prentice Hall, Harlow.

Planning for the Future

CHAPTER 10

Key issues dealt with in this chapter are:

- Why planning ahead matters.
- Planning and flexibility: mutually exclusive or a condition for successful growth?
- Business planning as a whole-company concept.
- The techniques of strategic business planning.
- Making business plans work in practice.
- Forecasting the financial statements.

Types of business plans

We all plan informally to some extent, even if only by keeping a diary of sales meetings or producing cash flows for the bank manager. There is much to be said for a greater degree of formal business planning, however, particularly with rapid change forcing more flexibility in business decision making.

There are several types of business plans, each produced for a particular purpose. The main ones are:

1 *Strategic (corporate) business plan*. Its purpose is to identify target markets and products, organizational actions and financial outcomes to enable the company to compete effectively. The strategic plan answers the questions:

- Where are you now? (current position).
- Where do you want to go? (objectives).
- How will you get there? (strategy).
- How much will it cost? (finance).

2 *Financing plan*. Its purpose is to identify how much finance is needed to pursue a particular business plan (used to raise finance from external sources).
3 *Marketing and sales plan*. Its purpose is to set targets, identify sales and marketing activities and produce budgets.
4 *Production/operations plan*. Its purpose is to identify production schedules, needs and resources.

5   *Staffing/organization plan*. Its purpose is to identify human and other physical resources needed in the business.
6   *Project plans*. Devoted to setting up and developing specific projects.

This chapter focuses on strategic business plans, operational business plans (such as a marketing plan) and project plans, since they are the most common and most useful for managing a growing business.

The strategic business plan

By focusing on profitable activities (and cutting out unprofitable ones), well-managed organizations are implicitly putting into practice the process of strategic planning. The concept is quite simple: match your current strengths to market opportunities to produce maximum profits, continuously develop these strengths, overcome internal weaknesses and counter threats.

Strategic planning is carried out by directors and key managers, but ideally embraces all employees in the organization. There is considerable value in involving more than only the directors because of the knowledge gained in the process of trying to understand what makes the business succeed and how profit arises. This also allows key managers to communicate the plan's fundamentals to their teams and achieve a whole-organization understanding of how profits are made.

Why produce a strategic business plan?

1   To assess competitiveness and identify, evaluate and select options for future development.
2   To integrate all parts of the business (divisions and functions) into a strategic and coherent whole through an analysis of each component.
3   To identify resources required to implement the strategy, particularly physical and human resources.
4   To assess financing needs and sources of finance.
5   To identify potential problems/constraints and actions required to resolve them.
6   To act as a control device by measuring outcomes against plans and forecasts.

Stages of strategic planning

The process of strategic planning is divided into six main stages, as follows:

- *Stage 1*. Where is the business now? Where has it come from? A review of the existing business to establish sources of profits, competitive advantage and opportunities for growth and development.
- *Stage 2*. Where do you want the business to be in *x* years' time? Set out a vision statement and business objectives.
- *Stage 3*. How will it get there? Choose a strategy to achieve the objectives.
- *Stage 4*. Is the strategy viable and how much finance will be needed? Produce a set of financial forecasts.
- *Stage 5*. How will it be implemented? Produce a set of operating plans.

- *Stage 6.* How will you keep the business on course? Set up monitoring and review arrangements.

Preparation

Box 10.1 Strategic planning stages: Preparation

Strategic planning stages	You are here
1 Preparation for strategic planning	⟸
2 Undertake a business review	
3 Undertake customer/market research	
4 Set corporate objectives	
5 Evaluate options and set corporate strategy	
6 Calculate forecasts	
7 Review and revise objectives and strategy	
8 Produce operational action plans, budgets and set goals	
9 Set performance indicators	
10 Agree monitoring and review procedures	

Strategic planning takes up a good deal of time yet only works well when everyone has a clear idea of what to expect, what contribution they are expected to make and there is a clear route to follow. The checklist in Box 10.2 clarifies how the process works.

Box 10.2 Strategic planning checklist

Action	Completed
1 Appoint and brief planning team	
2 Produce planning schedule and agree responsibilities	
3 Brief whole company	
4 Identify sources of profit by market segments/product groups	
5 Identify distinctive competence	
6 Identify core competences	
7 SWOT analysis	
8 Undertake customer and market research	
9 Set objectives	
10 Produce mission/vision statement	
11 Set out strategic options	
12 Undertake evaluation of strategic options	
13 Choose corporate strategy and communicate to whole company	
14 Forecast profit and loss accounts, balance sheets, cash flows	
15 Check strategy is viable, adjust and confirm figures	
16 Department managers produce operational plans and budgets	
17 Produce performance indicators to monitor strategy	
18 Set up plan monitoring and review meetings	

The planning team

The modern view of business planning is that all employees have the potential to contribute to business plans and help to achieve corporate objectives. This is common sense, because everyone must be an entrepreneur if the organization is to give its customers high and rising standards of service. Involvement in the strategic planning process helps employees gain an unparalleled understanding of the business and how it meets customer needs.

It is important that the team of people charged with producing a strategic plan gets on well with one another and, in particular, with the person leading or facilitating the planning process. So choose your planning team carefully from shareholders, directors, key managers and specialist personnel.

Consider these criteria for including people in the planning team:

- Significant shareholders and owner-managers.
- People who are charged with making choices about markets and products (strategic marketing choices).
- People who have close working relationships with and knowledge of the market/customers.
- People who have close working relationships with and knowledge of suppliers.
- People who have in-depth knowledge of the industry (including competitors).
- People with knowledge of internal information (especially financial and operating information, including sources of profits).
- People with previous experience of the planning process.

When you have selected your planning team, brief them comprehensively about:

- The planning process and benefits to your company.
- Their specific role in creating the plan, communicating it to the whole company and making it work successfully.
- The importance of involving everyone in the creation of the plan.
- The importance of effective and efficient teamwork at a senior level in creating and implementing the plan.
- The timescale for producing the plan and the amount of time the team can expect to spend on the process.
- The importance of preparation for each session.

You are now in a position to brief the entire organization about the strategic planning process. In a small organization, it is normally quite easy to get the entire staff together for about 30 minutes to explain the reason for and process of strategic planning, in particular what is expected of each person (this will be explained later) and how their contribution can make a difference.

Box 10.3 Tips: Strategic plan briefing

1   Make sure senior people are properly briefed themselves and are committed to the idea that involvement of their own staff is a good thing. Anything less will dilute your own efforts in implementing a truly devolved planning process.
2   Provide handouts and presentation slides to allow your senior people to communicate effectively and uniformly with their teams, and ensure that the language and style of presentation are appropriate for the type of person being briefed (e.g. avoid jargon).
3   Keep the messages simple to allow focus on key issues.
4   Do not expect a comprehensive contribution from everybody. Rather, brief them to contribute only in their areas of expertise and knowledge.
5   Allow sufficient time for the briefings to be completed before starting the strategic planning process.
6   Always suggest to people how much time they will have to devote to the activity and over what period of time.
7   Always consider people's motivation (try answering the question 'why should they help me?'). Do as much as possible to boost their motivation by giving them incentives as well as eliminating or reducing disincentives, because if there is something in it for them, they will be generally willing to get involved for their own self-interest.

Planning period

What period should a strategic business plan cover? The answer will vary according to the type of market segments you operate in and the external factors affecting development. For example, in today's rapidly changing markets there is little point in planning ahead for more than two or three years for most businesses. If it takes three years to enter a new market successfully or build up a competitive position in an existing one, then your plan should cover a three-year period. So, when considering your planning horizon, weigh up how long it will take to:

- Introduce new products profitably into your existing markets.
- Enter new markets profitably.
- Make continuous improvements to the existing organization.
- Implement major changes to the existing organization.
- Implement major technological changes.
- Raise large amounts of finance.

Err on the side of caution by planning over longer periods when introducing major changes. This is because it always takes longer than you think to get changes embedded and working smoothly.

With all the preparation firmly in place, it is now time to draw up a planning schedule and to secure the approval and agreement of colleagues. The schedule (see example in Box 10.4) should show:

1 Main phases in the planning process on a session-by-session basis.
2 Who is involved and who might provide back-up support.
3 How long you propose to spend on each phase.
4 When you are scheduled to meet.
5 Planning assignments for completion by the next phase, with who is responsible for carrying them out.

Box 10.4 Example: Strategic planning schedule

Session No.		Activity	Who attends	Date and Time
1	1	Outline sessions, explain planning process, agree schedule of work, assign responsibilities	Team	30/4 2pm
	2	Identify sources of profit and loss		
	3	Establish distinctive competence		
	4	Establish core competences		
	5	Introduce SWOT analysis		
		Assignment: Confirm profits, distinctive and core competences; SWOT and data collection		
2	6	SWOT analysis: Discussion	Team	7/5 2pm
		Assignment: Finalize SWOT		
3	7	Competitor response: assess competitor strengths and weaknesses	Team, market research exec	14/5 2pm
	8	Discuss marketing strategy: options for growth in existing and new markets/products		
	9	Choosing the right options		
	10	Agree actions for plan including market research		
		Assignment: Produce sales forecasts, market research (selected survey)		
4	11	Agree corporate objectives and mission	Team, account managers	21/5 2pm
	12	Agree sales and margin forecasts		
	13	Capacity to meet sales: organization and operational requirements of chosen strategy		
		Assignment: Confirm revenues and costs; adjust and confirm forecasts		
5	14	Discussion of marketing and sales plan	Team	28/5 2pm
	15	Confirm forecasts and budgets for marketing and sales plan		
	16	Adjust business plan		
		Assignment: Review marketing/sales plan, budgets, forecasts and draft plan		
6	17	Profit and loss and balance sheet forecasts: discussion of assumptions and sensitivities	Team, accountant, HR manager	4/6 2pm

	18	Review of organizational structure, roles, people, processes: major changes proposed		
	19	Discussion of operational/development plans		
	20	Confirm forecasts and budgets for operations and development plans		
	21	Adjust business plan		
		Assignment: Review operations/development plan, budgets, forecasts and draft plan		
7	22	Review and adjust business plan, action plans	Team	11/6 2pm
		Assignment: Review forecasts and draft plan		
8	23	Discuss final plan	Team	18/6 2pm
	24	Agree plan review meetings		

Business review

Box 10.5 Strategic planning stages: Business review

Strategic planning stages   **You are here**

1 Preparation for strategic planning
2 Undertake a business review   ⟸
3 Undertake customer/market research   ⟸
4 Set corporate objectives
5 Evaluate options and set corporate strategy
6 Calculate forecasts
7 Review and revise objectives and strategy
8 Produce operational action plans, budgets and set goals
9 Set performance indicators
10 Agree monitoring and review procedures

Sources of profits

The right strategy is the one that achieves your corporate objectives. Since profitability is usually the number one objective, you must know where the business makes and loses money; in other words, which markets and products are the most and least profitable. To establish sources of profits, your management information system (MIS) should collect and allocate sales, variable costs and overhead to each market segment and product/service type. This will allow you to investigate and analyse market and customer information with a focus on profitability and not only on sales values. (See Chapter 2 for detailed coverage of sources of profits.)

Can you produce clear, accurate and up-to-date information about your existing markets and individual customers, particularly about profitability? Most business information systems can produce such data by product or product group, but customer and market data is generally harder to obtain. What is yours like? (Refer to Chapter 9 for details of an effective management information system.)

Distinctiveness

The strategic plan should identify distinctiveness and the core competences that underpin it, spelling out in detail the skills, knowledge and technologies needed to enable you to plan a course of action to develop existing competences, or build new ones. (See Chapter 2 for a detailed explanation of distinctive and core competences.)

SWOT analysis

The SWOT analysis – strengths, weaknesses, opportunities and threats – remains one of the most widely used strategic planning methods. We discussed SWOT in detail in Chapter 2; please follow the guidelines given there. SWOT is the most time-consuming part of the planning process because it requires a comprehensive internal review of the organization (the planning team will not necessarily agree on all points) and a survey of external factors affecting sales, profits and competitiveness in existing and new markets. To adhere to the suggested planning schedule (which should allow between a half and a full day), the activity needs to be deftly managed if it is not to be reduced to a shambles (see Box 10.6).

Box 10.6 SWOT tips

1 Prepare a single sheet with strengths and weaknesses columns and a checklist of headings for each. This will facilitate the merging of contributions and cut down your time enormously (see the checklist below).
2 Produce a set of rules or guidelines for contributors as well as for your planning team.
3 Discourage contributions longer than a single sheet of paper. Use the slogan 'less equals more'.
4 Give deadlines and stick to them.
5 Use your management team to distribute the SWOT sheets to their teams through team leaders.
6 Remind contributors that they should write down only items that can be actioned. The basic criterion for acceptability is that items should be actionable.
7 Be prepared for the process to go off track at this point as people either struggle to grasp the relevance of the various phases and activities or find that their contributions require endless discussion before agreement can be reached. Enforce a five-minute discussion limit for each point raised.
8 In spite of doing your best to control the process, you might have to schedule extra time for discussion.

At the end of these deliberations, you should have a completed SWOT analysis, cleaned up (eliminating trivial points and improbable outcomes) and agreed by the planning team, though there are bound to be outstanding points giving rise to the need for new market research or customer feedback. These might delay publication of the plan, although a better option is to delegate their completion to the marketing team (or other key personnel) for finalization in the near future.

Customer feedback and market research

Comprehensive, accurate and up-to-date customer and market information lies at the heart of effective strategic planning. The main external sources are systematic feedback from existing customers and market research conducted into existing and new markets. Internally, there should be a large amount of data available on customers and markets. The main sources are:

1 *Internal information system for sources of profits and sales history.* In order to make effective choices about which markets to target and what products to sell to these markets, you need to know where you currently make sales and your profits.
2 *Distinctive competence.* You need to relate your sources of profit information to the reasons your customers buy from your business.
3 *SWOT.* Everyone will have opinions about SWOT, but what do your customers, suppliers and other influencers say about your organization and its external environment?
4 *Existing market data.* What factual market information do you have about market size, trends, your share of the market segments in which you operate, your competitors and prices?
5 *New market data.* What information do you have about new markets identified in your SWOT analysis?

Please refer to the detailed discussion of feedback and market research in Chapter 3. The collection of customer and market data should not hold up the planning process, which by this time should have achieved a positive momentum. Fact-finding teams should be appointed and tasked with collecting relevant data as quickly as possible.

Setting objectives

Establishing a clear, final destination for the business requires shareholders, directors and senior managers to decide on the financial, organizational, operational, marketing and other objectives that they want to achieve over the planning period.
Corporate objectives should be *SMART*:

1 *Specific* (relating to a single, particular result, e.g. pre-tax profit, customer service).
2 *Measurable* (permitting some kind of numerical measure, e.g. net profit margin percentage).

Box 10.7 Strategic planning stages: Setting objectives

Strategic planning stages   **You are here**

1   Preparation for strategic planning
2   Undertake a business review
3   Undertake customer/market research
4   Set corporate objectives   ⇐
5   Evaluate options and set corporate strategy
6   Calculate forecasts
7   Review and revise objectives and strategy
8   Produce operational action plans, budgets and set goals
9   Set performance indicators
10 Agree monitoring and review procedures

---

3   *Achievable* (in terms of previous achievements and current or future trends, e.g. historical performance, expected growth in demand).
4   *Relevant* (taking account of the different stakeholders' needs, e.g. profitability for the shareholders, employment conditions for employees).
5   *Time bound* (relating to an agreed time period, e.g. for each year of a three-year strategic plan).

The concept of the stakeholder evolved to take account of the needs of a wider group of people with an interest in the organization than merely the narrowly defined interests of shareholders, whose short-term financial interests the business organization has traditionally served. The most common stakeholders and their objectives are as follows:

1   *Shareholders* are interested in profits and the market value of their investment. From the former they derive dividend income, from the latter they derive capital growth.
2   *Employees* have an interest in remuneration, job satisfaction and job security.
3   *Customers* are interested principally in quality product, competitive prices, assured supply and service levels.
4   *Suppliers* are interested in assured sales, prompt payment and new product ideas.
5   *The community* wants good jobs, ethical and safe local employers and contributors to community projects.
6   *Strategic partners* and joint venturers want market penetration, R&D, sales income and profit.
7   *Financiers* want repayments of capital and interest, dividend income and capital growth.

By first identifying the stakeholders and their interests, you will be in a position to set objectives to reflect their needs. By so doing, you should improve company motivation by increasing the commitment of all stakeholders to your corporate endeavours.

Typical business planning objectives are as follows.

Financial

- Net profit margin (net profit before tax as a percentage of sales).
- Return on investment (net profit before tax as a percentage of shareholders' capital).
- Gross profit margin (gross profit as a percentage of sales).
- Net worth growth (net assets growth as a percentage on the previous year).

Marketing

- Sales growth (sales growth as a percentage on the previous period).
- Market share (sales as a percentage of total market sales).
- Customer retention (current customers less customers gained in the period as a percentage of customers at start of the period).
- New business (new customers gained in the period as a percentage of customers at the start of the period).
- Marketing spend (marketing expenditure as a percentage of sales).
- Lead generation (marketing spend divided by number of leads generated).
- Lead conversion (number of sales converted to orders divided by number of leads generated).

Operations

- Production efficiency (cost of sales as a percentage of sales).
- Productivity (number of productive hours as a percentage of total hours).
- Value added (total value added to materials as a percentage of materials costs).
- Overtime (number of overtime hours as a percentage of total hours).
- Machine efficiency (machine downtime as a percentage of total machine time).
- Quality control (number of defective returns as a percentage of total output).

People

- Efficiency (sales divided by number of employees).
- Profit per employee (net profit before tax divided by number of employees).
- Payroll burden (payroll as a percentage of sales).
- Staff turnover (number of staff leaving in a period divided by total number at the start of the period).
- Training index (number of training days as a percentage of total days in a period).
- Staff development index (number of employees with qualifications as a percentage of total number of employees).

The personal objectives of owner-managers should be taken into account. Some common personal objectives are the desired growth rate (consolidation rather than growth is very much a personal matter), reduction of hours spent in the office (always a thorny issue for owners), raising directors' salary levels (the owners may feel that they have been subsidizing the business for long enough), introduction of family or other partners into ownership and management positions (the question of succession could arise), and sale of the whole or part of the business (the owners might want to retire).

Vision/mission statement

You are now in a position to set out your vision or mission for the organization. The vision/mission should have meaning for your shareholders, employees and customers and should attempt to convey the essence of your distinctiveness, while trying to avoid clichés. Examples of corporate vision/mission statements are given in Box 10.8. These statements have different emphases and some attempt

---

Box 10.8 Corporate vision/mission statements

Morgan Motor Company

Our mission is to maintain our traditions of coach building and craftsmanship ... while continually developing our people and processes which will enable us to make more cars and delight more customers by making them Morgan owners.

The Body Shop

To tirelessly work to narrow the gap between principle and practice, whilst making fun, passion and care part of our daily lives.

To creatively balance the financial and human needs of our stakeholders: employees, customers, franchisees, suppliers and shareholders.

To courageously ensure that our business is ecologically sustainable: meeting the needs of the present without compromising the future.

To meaningfully contribute to local, national and international communities in which we trade, by adopting a code of conduct which ensures care, honesty, fairness and respect.

To passionately campaign for the protection of the environment, human and civil rights, and against animal testing, within the cosmetics and toiletries industry.

Ford Motor Company

Our Vision. To become the world's leading consumer company for automotive products and services.

Our Mission. We are a global, diverse family with a proud heritage passionately committed to providing outstanding products and services that improve people's lives.

Our Values. The customer is number one. We do the right thing for our people, our environment and our society. By improving everything we do, we provide superior returns to our shareholders.

M&S

- Vision. To be the standard against which all others are measured.
- Mission. To make aspirational quality accessible to all.
- Values. Quality, value, service, innovation and trust.

to recognize the needs of several groups of stakeholders, not merely shareholders and employees. The practical value of a vision or mission statement, however, has been questioned in recent years, mainly because organizations have found it hard to adhere rigorously to their statements in times of rapid and turbulent change.

Setting corporate strategy

Box 10.9 Strategic planning stages: Evaluation

Strategic planning stages	You are here
1 Preparation for strategic planning	
2 Undertake a business review	
3 Undertake customer/market research	
4 Set corporate objectives	
5 Evaluate options and set corporate strategy	⇐
6 Calculate forecasts	
7 Review and revise objectives and strategy	
8 Produce operational action plans, budgets and set goals	
9 Set performance indicators	
10 Agree monitoring and review procedures	

With most of the data-collection and analysis stage and the hard thinking work completed, you should be able to reach a conclusion on the corporate strategy that will achieve your stated objectives. The four components of corporate strategy are as follows.

Marketing strategy

The first two questions pertain to the setting of marketing strategy: Which market segments to target? What products or services to sell to them? You should have considered every combination of existing and new markets, with existing and new products/services, taking into account the many shades of grey around the meaning of 'new'. Your final choice of strategy depends on your assessment of:

- The probable profit potential associated with each option.
- The amount of cash needed to finance each option.

Depending on the outcome of the SWOT analysis, your optimism and the objectives set earlier in the planning process, you should be in a position to decide on growth: will you go for rapid growth, modest growth, consolidation and improvement, or 'downsizing' and swingeing internal improvements? The options should be set out clearly and evaluated thoroughly before confirming your chosen direction. (Refer to the fundamental choices and techniques discussed in detail in Chapter 2.)

Organization strategy

The third question is: What kind of organization is needed to deliver the strategy? Here you should set out a plan to align the whole organization with the chosen strategy. If all physical and human resources are acting with a sense of purpose in pursuit of business objectives, the task of implementing the strategy should be that much easier. This is achieved by fully understanding customer needs and diagnosing and reshaping the organization to meet these needs more effectively.

Strategic planners need a good understanding of organizational diagnosis and design. What makes an organization work effectively and efficiently? What are the building blocks of effective organizational development? They are the structure, people, processes and systems. When they are all working well, the organization is said to be in alignment with its markets. If your plan proposes changes to markets and products, changes to organization will undoubtedly be needed:

1 What are the options for changing the organization's structure, people, processes and systems to relieve any problems encountered in the diagnosis in relation to the new strategy?
2 Which of these options would most successfully preserve the positive (distinctive) factors in the organization's functioning and eliminate or neutralize negative factors, particularly as the new strategy takes effect?

You are now in a position to propose what organizational changes are required to implement the new strategy successfully, having debated the merits and implications of the changes and costed their consequences. (Refer to the details in Chapter 4.)

Financial adequacy

Box 10.10 Strategic planning stages: Forecasting

Strategic planning stages   **You are here**
  1   Preparation for strategic planning
  2   Undertake a business review
  3   Undertake customer/market research
  4   Set corporate objectives
  5   Evaluate options and set corporate strategy
  6   Calculate forecasts   ⇐
  7   Review and revise objectives and strategy
  8   Produce operational action plans, budgets and set goals
  9   Set performance indicators
10   Agree monitoring and review procedures

Now turn to the final question: Is the strategy financially sound? In other words, is there adequate finance available to pursue the strategy and achieve the stated objectives? To settle this question, a set of profit and cash forecasts must be completed, showing that the chosen strategy:

1   Is viable (it will achieve profit objectives).
2   Can be adequately financed (there is sufficient short- and long-term finance to make it work).

Managers need to know that they will be able to put their plans into action with adequate financial backing. The purpose of forecasts is to calculate how much finance will be required to implement the strategy and whether external sources of finance will have to be tapped. This means producing the following:

1   Projected annual P&L accounts to confirm the level of pre-tax and retained profit resulting from the chosen strategy. Reliable forecasts of the P&L necessarily require detailed sales and contribution forecasts.
2   Projected annual balance sheets to confirm financial adequacy (that the right magnitudes and types of short-, medium- and long-term finance are in place).
3   Monthly cash-flow forecasts to confirm that adequate short-term cash is available.

Forecasts give a general picture for a period of several years ahead, rather than providing specific detail. They differ from budgets in this respect. Budgets are generally for a shorter period (typically 12 months) and provide details of sales revenues and associated expenditure. They relate very closely to working plans and are also used as a basis for monitoring actual sales revenue and expenditure.

Forecasts start with a clear set of financial objectives and an explicit strategy. After that, the forecasting process should follow the steps below (see Chapter 8 to review the essentials of financial accounts).

1   Prepare historical accounts

Assemble current and previous years' profit and loss accounts and balance sheets (in times of rapid change, one or two previous years should be enough). Since you will be preparing forecasts before the end of the financial year (planning can start in month 11 in a small to medium-sized organization), use management accounts for the year to date plus budgeted figures for the remainder of the current year.

2   Calculate financial ratios

The purpose of these historical accounts is to observe trends in your sales, expenditure and balance sheet figures by calculating financial ratios. (See Chapter 8 for details of these key ratios.)

3   Agree forecasting assumptions and business policies

Decide on forecasting assumptions and financial policies to be used as guidelines throughout the forecasting process, as follows:

●   Consider running spreadsheet forecasts on the basis of a *'best guess' scenario*, reflecting extrapolations of past performance suitably adjusted for current trends, internal constraints and resource availability, market opportunities and threats, other environmental factors and the personal aspirations and needs of shareholders and directors.

- Add a *pessimistic scenario*, reflecting a zero growth or even breakeven outcome, in order to demonstrate that the business can survive even under the most trying conditions.
- *Business policies* to be adopted over the planning period, covering production, marketing, finance and employment. The main business policy changes that could affect forecasting include changes in production arrangements (such as whether production should be contracted out or brought in-house), changes in marketing (such as pricing policies, use of external sales channels and agency agreements), changes in financial arrangements (such as the financing of assets on an 'off-balance-sheet' basis) and changes in recruitment and employment policies (such as whether to recruit experienced people or train them from scratch).
- Further *sensitivity analyses* should be run, asking 'what if?' on key variables. You should forecast prudently using modest assumptions about growth in sales and gross profit margins, and realistic to cautious assumptions about increases in costs. This does not prevent the company from setting more ambitious sales and profit targets, which serve a different purpose.

4   Agree net profit margin

This will be your main financial objective in the strategic plan and should be agreed for each year of your planning period. It sets the bottom line of the profit and loss account.

5   Agree gross profit margin

This will be a key financial or marketing objective in the strategic plan. Gross profit is the outcome of strategic choices (the selection of specific target markets and products/services to sell into these markets). It sets the vitally important gross profit line in the profit and loss account.

6   Forecast sales income

Use one of the methods described below to set the top line of the profit and loss account. You can view a completed sales forecast in the marketing plan in Appendix 2.

7   Calculate net profit and gross profit

Using the margins in steps 4 and 5 above, apply them to the sales forecast to calculate gross profit and net profit.

8   Forecast direct overheads

Apply key ratios (suitably adjusted to reflect changes in business policy) to the sales figures for each year to calculate direct overhead expenditure for marketing, sales, warehousing and R&D and any other direct activity that you might have. For example, assume marketing expenditure has been historically overspent at 16 per cent of sales and you are determined to produce a plan to tighten up costs over the next three years. Apply 15, 14 and 13 per cent to the next three years' sales to produce ideal marketing expenditure.

NB: It is important to understand that this forecasting process is iterative and that once you have examined your marketing plans in detail, you might have to review this forecast. All the forecast says at this stage is that to make a certain level of profit, marketing expenditure should be no more than a given percentage of sales determined by senior management.

9   Forecast indirect overheads

In exactly the same way, apply key ratios adjusted for new business policies to indirect expenditure categories, e.g. premises, administration and finance.

10   Complete the forecast of profit and loss accounts

The next step is to put sales, gross profit and overhead expenditure categories together to produce an outline profit and loss account, so demonstrating that profit objectives can be achieved over the planning period. Adjustments will almost certainly need to be made before the forecasts are finalized. View a worked example of projected profit and loss accounts in Appendix 1.

11   Forecast balance sheets

Balance sheets should be projected in order to show what the business will be worth and how much finance will be needed each year. See a worked example of projected balance sheets in Appendix 1. The steps in balance sheet forecasting are as follows:

- *Assemble ratios.* Just as with the profit and loss accounts, calculate and assemble key balance sheet ratios.
- *Decide on key balance sheet policies.* Typically, this means making decisions about investing in new assets, changes to stock management, work-in-progress control, credit control, cash management, creditor control, gearing and liquidity preferences.
- *Apply ratios and policies/strategy to balance sheet items.* Calculate a new set of balance sheets using ratios and bringing forward reserves from your projected profit and loss accounts.

12   Determine financing gap

The new set of figures should leave a *financing gap* – either a surplus or a deficit, depending on the ratios and policies that you have applied. This gap indicates either surplus cash balances, or deficits that have to be financed by equity or loan finance.

13   Forecast cash-flow requirements

The cash-flow forecast reveals the projected monthly cash position at the bank over the next 12 months (discussed below).

Detailed forecasts of P&Ls and balance sheets are provided in Appendix 1, following the step-by-step approach described here. You should refer to these forecasts at this point, as well as to the ratio analysis for ABCO in Chapter 8, for a more in-depth illustration of how such forecasts are compiled.

Cash-flow forecasting

Cash-flow forecasting is a widely used financial management tool. The purpose of a cash-flow forecast is to identify how much cash the business will need over the coming 12 months (or longer) and therefore when additional bank facilities will be needed. This is achieved by forecasting cash banked each month and subtracting cash paid out each month.

The process operates as follows:

Money paid into the bank in the period (receipts from sales + loans)
less
Money paid out in the period (payments to suppliers, employees, petty cash, etc.)
=
Net cash flow in the period

or

Bank balance at the start of the period
add
Money banked in the period
less
Money paid out in the period
=
Bank balance at end of the period

This flow of cash into and out of the bank account takes place hourly, daily, weekly and monthly, but it is conventional to forecast cash flow on a monthly basis (although at certain times there might be a need to forecast cash more frequently).

There is always some confusion between *cash flow* and *profit*. The essence of profit and loss accounts, which show income and expenditure for a period, is that they are produced on an invoiced basis. So income is recorded for the period in which it is invoiced (the realization concept) and expenditure relating to that income is also taken in on an invoiced basis, after adjusting for accruals and prepayments (the accrual concept).

Cash flow treats income and expenditure not on an invoiced basis, but solely on a cash paid basis. There are many instances where cash is paid that do not give rise to an entry in the profit and loss account e.g. VAT. We receive VAT from customers and pay it to suppliers, with the balance to Customs and Excise, so it is a matter of cash flow, but it does not appear in the profit and loss account.

Before starting the cash-flow forecast, there are a few preparatory steps:

1 Prepare budgeted monthly profit and loss accounts.
2 Have available records of money owed to suppliers and other creditors (such as VAT, PAYE and tax) at the start of the year and money owed by customers (debtors).
3 Decide on policies about payment periods both from customers and to suppliers. You will need to translate invoiced amounts from the profit and loss account into payments in the cash-flow forecast.
4 Review purchases of plant, equipment and vehicles for inclusion in the cash-flow forecast and methods of financing them.

Set out your cash-flow forecast in a spreadsheet as follows.

Cash in

1 Cash from sales. Take sales income figures from the monthly sales forecast and enter these amounts into the cash-flow forecast in the months in which you anticipate they will be paid by your customers. Be realistic.
2 Output VAT at $17\frac{1}{2}$ per cent (current UK standard rate) will be received from each sale and should be itemized separately in the cash-flow forecast.
3 Other amounts such as loans or other forms of income should be entered in those months in which they will be banked.
4 Cash brought forward from the previous year should be entered in the first month.
5 Total of CASH IN is calculated by adding up the 'in' items each month.

Cash out

1 Payments for purchases of materials/consumables/subcontractors are forecast on the basis of your suppliers' credit terms, e.g. if you get 30 days' credit, enter the payments in the month following the invoice.
2 Direct labour will be paid at the end of each month and therefore the amounts should be transferred from the profit and loss account in the same month.
3 Overheads are entered when they actually fall due for payment, e.g. monthly accounts, quarterly, etc.
4 Equipment purchases should be entered when items will be paid for, or when finance payments will be made. Hire purchase payments will include interest and capital.
5 Loan repayments should be entered when due (quarterly or monthly) and should include interest and capital.
6 Input VAT at $17\frac{1}{2}$ per cent will be paid out on purchases that incur VAT and should be itemized separately in the cash-flow forecast.
7 VAT to Customs and Excise should be entered in the payment month.
8 Total of CASH OUT is arrived at by adding up the items for each month.

Cash flow

Cash flow is calculated by subtracting cash out each month from cash in. Forecasting the bank balance, the object of the exercise, is calculated by bringing forward the positive or negative balance from the previous month to the current month's cash flow. Table 10.1 illustrates the detail.

Principles of cash-flow forecasting

- Accuracy and realism should be observed when calculating large amounts because they will materially affect the outcomes, but small sums should not unduly occupy the forecaster's time. Equally, since forecasts are never 100 per cent accurate, forecast in £000 or £m, depending on the size of your business.
- Check for accuracy. Errors in the cash-flow forecast will prevent the balancing of projected balance sheets.
- Caution rather than optimism should be a guiding principle. While the general rule is that amounts in the cash flows should be entered in the months in which they are actually to be paid out or banked, if there is any doubt about when amounts fall due, then it is preferable to err on the side of caution. For example, if your customers tend to ignore agreed terms (say 30 days) because they pay their bills at a certain time in the month, the receipts from sales should be entered on the assumption that they will be paid in 60 days, not 30. On the expenditure side the reverse should always apply: if there is any doubt about a payment to a supplier, then assume that it should be paid as soon as possible.
- Most cash-flow forecasting is over-optimistic. This will result in an under-assessment of short-term financing needs, which in turn will lead to a shortage of funds. While sales receipts suffer from the problem of late payment, payments suffer in three areas: costs tend to be higher than expected, there tend to be more cost categories than were originally assumed and costs have a habit of happening sooner than anticipated.
- Changes will always be needed before the forecast can be accepted because it rarely works out perfectly the first time. Forecasting is an iterative, experiential process and should not be treated as a science.

Preparing a sales forecast

An annual sales forecast sets out the anticipated annual sales volume (units) and revenue (£) to each market segment and for each product or group of products over the planning period. It is further broken down into monthly forecasts.

There are a number of methods of sales forecasting, depending on corporate objectives, market maturity and sales history.

Forecasting by volume and value

This method covers situations where there is sufficient historical information on record about customers, products, sales volumes and values to complete a set of forecasts for the 'known' part of the market. Sales to individual customers and market segments can be projected by volume and value: sales income is calculated by multiplying volume of sales, i.e. the number of products or services sold, by unit

---

Box 10.11 Sales forecasting stages

How much can the business sell?
↓
Is this enough to create a profitable business?
↓   ↓
YES   NO →→→→→ How can more be sold?
↓
Will customers buy this much?
↓   ↓
YES   NO →→→→→ How much will they buy?
↓
Does research confirm this?
↓   ↓
YES   NO →→→→→ Back to drawing board!
↓
Complete the forecast

---

price. Forecasting by volume and value therefore requires you to know a great deal about customer business plans and buying behaviour, which necessarily involves close key account relationships and reliable customer feedback.

However, most sales forecasts involve sales to new customers in addition to existing ones, and possibly even to new markets, so the forecast is more than merely a matter of adding up projected sales to existing customers. The gap should be identified between the sales forecast called for in the strategic plan and the level of 'known' sales, largely from existing customers. This gap – sales to new customers and to new markets – requires a different treatment.

Steps in building a forecast are:

1   Decide on a suitable time period for the business. A detailed monthly sales forecast will be required for 12 months, and aggregate annual forecasts for the remainder of the planning period should be produced.
2   Identify the unit of sale. If sales vary from customer to customer, use these units for large-value customers, but typical or average sales units will be appropriate for small ones.
3   Estimate the number of unit sales in each time period to produce a sales pattern, using information gleaned either from customers' plans or from historical data. Start from a realistic base and build up sales volumes slowly if the activity is new, since sales are usually hard to make in new markets when products are not widely known.
4   Multiply the volume for each type of unit by the price for that unit to obtain the sales value. Add these values together to produce monthly and annual sales revenues.
5   Identify the sales gap by subtracting these sales values from sales required to achieve business objectives. Examine the gap and allocate sales values to target market segments (new customers in existing markets, and in new

Table 10.1: Cash-flow forecast

Monthly cash flow	Apr	May	Jun	Jul	Aug	Sep	Oct	Nov	Dec	Jan	Feb	Mar	Total
CASH IN													
Sales	240 000	200 000	60 000	150 000	155 000	204 000	179 200	130 000	112 000	132 900	201 700	190 300	1 955 100
Output VAT	42 000	35 000	10 500	26 250	27 125	35 700	31 360	22 750	19 600	23 258	35 298	33 303	342 143
Total	282 000	235 000	70 500	176 250	182 125	239 700	210 560	152 750	131 600	156 158	236 998	223 603	2 297 243
CASH OUT													
Suppliers	123 000	87 000	90 600	53 100	54 750	70 140	65 736	44 100	38 160	46 857	67 941	65 799	807 183
Advertising	0	2 500	2 500	2 500	2 500	2 500	2 500	2 500	2 500	2 500	2 500	2 500	27 500
Seminars	0	2 000	2 000	2 000	2 000	0	2 000	4 000	2 000	2 000	2 000	2 000	22 000
PR and publicity	0	833	833	833	833	833	833	833	833	833	833	833	9 167
Telephone marketing	12 000	2 500	2 500	2 500	2 500	0	5 000	2 500	2 500	0	5 000	2 500	39 500
Postage (mailing)	3 300	2 000	2 000	2 000	2 000	0	2 000	2 000	2 000	0	2 000	2 000	21 300
Print (mailing)	2 300	2 500	2 500	2 500	2 500	0	5 000	2 500	2 500	0	5 000	2 500	29 800
Market research	0	0	0	8 000	0	0	0	0	8 000	0	0	0	16 000
Marketing salaries	5 000	5 000	5 000	5 000	5 000	5 000	5 000	5 000	5 000	5 000	5 000	5 000	60 000
Travel and subsistence	2 500	2 500	2 500	2 500	500	3 500	3 500	2 500	2 500	2 500	2 500	2 500	30 000
Motor expenses	4 167	4 167	4 167	4 167	1 000	4 167	5 200	4 267	2 000	5 200	5 500	6 000	50 000
Hospitality	417	417	417	417	417	417	417	417	417	417	417	417	5 000
Sales support	417	417	417	417	417	417	417	417	417	417	417	417	5 000
Sales salaries	7 500	7 500	7 500	7 500	7 500	7 500	7 500	7 500	7 500	7 500	7 500	7 500	90 000

	M1	M2	M3	M4	M5	M6	M7	M8	M9	M10	M11	M12	Total
Rent	6 000	6 000	6 000	6 000	6 000	6 000	6 000	6 000	6 000	6 000	6 000	6 000	72 000
Rates	4 000	4 000	4 000	4 000	4 000	4 000	4 000	4 000	4 000	4 000	4 000	4 000	48 000
Insurance	9 000												9 000
Repairs	1 500	1 500	1 500	1 500	1 500	1 500	1 500	1 500	1 500	1 500	1 500	1 500	18 000
Training	1 500	1 500	1 500	1 500	1 500	1 500	1 500	1 500	1 500	1 500	1 500	1 500	18 000
Post and stationery	2 000	2 000	2 000	2 000	2 000	2 000	2 000	2 000	2 000	2 000	2 000	2 000	24 000
Accountancy		24 000											24 000
Salaries	35 000	35 000	35 000	35 000	35 000	35 000	35 000	35 000	35 000	35 000	35 000	35 000	420 000
Bank interest			5 000			5 000			5 000			5 000	20 000
Bank repayments			10 000			10 000			10 000			10 000	40 000
Equipment	10 000	10 000											20 000
Input VAT	26 005	20 533	19 413	18 451	14 335	14 258	16 118	11 643	11 257	10 714	16 556	15 394	194 679
VAT to C&E	27 600			21 548			42 031			34 691			125 871
Corporation tax													0
Total	273 205	199 867	207 347	207 433	156 252	173 731	213 252	140 177	152 584	173 164	168 629	180 360	2 245 999
In – Out	8 795	35 133	-136 847	-31 183	25 873	65 969	-2 692	12 573	-20 984	-12 472	63 833	43 243	
Opening balance	-94 000												
Bank balance	-85 205	-50 072	-186 918	-218 101	-192 228	-126 259	-128 951	-116 378	-137 362	-149 833	-86 000	-42 757	

markets) according to opportunities and threats identified in the earlier SWOT discussion. Break down the values into average sales orders and target numbers of customers, bearing in mind conversion rates (leads to orders). Allocate these figures to the marketing and sales plan – the part that deals with new business development.

Forecasting by extrapolating from past trends

The second method suits situations where there is a sales history but it is not practicable to break down sales volumes and values by product group and customer segment because individual purchases are too small or individual customers are not easily identifiable, e.g. in retailing. Forecasting must rely on extrapolations of past trends, taking into account expected future trends and internal considerations. An analysis of sales growth over a period of three years is required to produce a sales trend, which can then be applied to future sales, adjusted appropriately for changes in internal and external conditions. This is known as *extrapolation*. Using these extrapolations, you can devise a monthly forecast by applying a *weighting factor* to the monthly average.

Forecasting with the breakeven (gross profit margin) formula

The third method relates to new business situations where there is no history at all, e.g. a start-up or developing a new market, or no reliable history, e.g. loss making situations, volatile or unforeseen sales patterns. It can also be used where the previous track record is not regarded as desirable or where a turnaround is required. The immediate objective is usually to reach a breakeven level of sales in the first year, moving into profit thereafter. Fixed costs and gross profit margin are the two components of the breakeven formula (Box 10.12).

Box 10.12 Breakeven formula

$$\text{Breakeven sales in £} = \frac{\text{Fixed costs}}{\text{Gross profit margin}}$$

$$\text{Breakeven sales in units} = \frac{\text{Fixed costs}}{\text{Gross profit}}$$

$$\text{Where gross profit} = \text{Sales} - \text{Cost of sales}$$

Gross profit margins for the year ahead may not be known, particularly if some combination of new products, new markets, new production processes and new sources of supply is being introduced, all of which could change existing gross profit margins. So calculating the breakeven will involve making estimates of:

- Selling price of a basic or standard sales unit. If selling prices are not known at this point, it is useful to refer to prices being charged by competitors.

- Variable costs (cost of sales) of the basic unit that could be built up from costings or estimated on the basis of comparable products.
- Gross profit, or 'contribution', of the unit can now be calculated:
    selling price − variable costs = gross profit
- The fixed costs of running the business or project for a year.

Having calculated breakeven sales, you are now in a position to work out if the resulting figure is realistic by converting gross sales revenue to number of customers required to breakeven, which should then be researched in order to confirm its probability. The example in Box 10.13 illustrates how the breakeven works.

Box 10.13 Example of forecasting with the breakeven formula

In this family-run restaurant business, the owners have produced a business plan to turn around a loss-making year into breakeven in year 1, then profit of £50 000 in year 2.

		Breakeven year 1	Net profit £50 000 year 2
Direct fixed costs	Waiting staff	£123 000	£135 000
	Marketing	£65 000	£87 000
Indirect fixed costs	Premises	£146 000	£146 000
	Administration	£187 000	£187 000
	Finance	£32 000	£32 000
	Depreciation	£18 000	£18 000
Total fixed costs		£571 000	£605 000
Net profit required		£0	£50 000
Total fixed costs + profit		£571 000	£655 000
Gross margin		68%	68%
Breakeven formula		Fixed costs Gross margin	Fixed costs Gross margin
Sales		£839 706	£963 235
Av customer bill (ex VAT)		£45.50	£45.50
Customers p.a.		18 455	21 170
Customers p.w.		355	407

Box 10.13 demonstrates how the breakeven formula can be used to forecast sales with different levels of profitability. The final figures are readily researchable (the owners would anyway know the probabilities from experience) and adjustments can be made to the fixed costs and gross margins until a realistic outcome is reached. It should be clear that there are only two ways to lower the breakeven and thus improve the chances of a profitable outcome: lower fixed costs (always difficult in a tightly run small business) and higher gross margin (often an under-exploited route to higher profits).

In this way, sales forecasting is taken out of the realm of uncertainty and replaced by a proactive planning ethos. So the question becomes: What sales level do we need to achieve to generate profits of £50 000? followed by a plan to make the sales happen, rather than the more quixotic: What sales level do we think we can achieve? (See Appendix 2 for a detailed sales forecast.)

Reviewing and revising the strategic plan

Box 10.14 Strategic planning stages: Plan review

Strategic planning stages	You are here
1 Preparation for strategic planning	
2 Undertake a business review	
3 Undertake customer/market research	
4 Set corporate objectives	
5 Evaluate options and set corporate strategy	
6 Calculate forecasts	
7 Review and revise objectives and strategy	⟸
8 Produce operational action plans, budgets and set goals	
9 Set performance indicators	
10 Agree monitoring and review procedures	

You have now reached the point where a careful review of objectives, strategy and forecasts is desirable before going on to complete the planning process by specifying the actions that need to be taken to implement the plan – the operational plans and budgets. This makes strategic planning an iterative process.

The most urgent reason for a review would be that the forecasts demonstrate that a large injection of external finance is needed to make the plan workable. Raising such large sums might be difficult (given your track record) or undesirable (you just don't want to go through the stress). Other reasons might include the implausibility of the assumptions that underlie the forecasts, the lack of objective data on market opportunities, erroneous beliefs in your key strengths (which no one was able to justify), recent competitor responses that make your moves very risky, etc. Ultimately a growing business has to take a view on the quality of its management resources and their propensity for implementing a business plan successfully. How successful have they been in the past? Can they be relied on to lead and drive their functions in the right direction? How effective are you, the owner-manager, at implementing a detailed business plan?

The planning team needs to ask these questions:

1 Are the choices mutually compatible? Will the product range suit the chosen market and can sales be delivered with available capacity?
2 Are the choices consistent with corporate strengths and weaknesses? A strategy should exploit strengths, not weaknesses.

3 Are the choices compatible with corporate objectives? Given the choices made, can the business achieve its stated objectives in the period?
4 Is there internal harmony and is efficiency maintained? The choices must not be allowed to disrupt (for long) the smooth working of existing activities.
5 Is there compatibility between products and markets? Research will need to show that new customer segments have demonstrated a need for the proposed product range. In particular, check your assumptions and calculations used to evaluate strategic options. Have you accounted for all the costs of changing strategy and have you been sufficiently restrained in your sales forecasts?
6 Can the choices be accommodated within the existing resource base? What other resources will be needed? Can these be acquired on the right terms?
7 Is there sufficient cash to fund short-term needs? Is longer-term profitability assured? It is surprising how many businesses proceed with a course of action without knowing whether it will be profitable.

Having asked these questions, it is possible that changes will need to be made to the forecasts. The key areas for adjustment are as follows.

To raise gross profit margins

Review and change your strategy

By modifying target markets and products/services that comprise your marketing strategy, you should be able to raise gross margins. For example, cutting out low-margin business will not only raise average gross margins, but also eliminate wasteful overhead dedicated to looking after it.

Review and adjust pricing

A selective or across-the-board price rise will provide an instantaneous increase in gross profit margin and make the objective of generating higher net profit more realizable. You might lose price-sensitive customers, but then their loss might be welcome!

Reduce cost of sales (variable costs)

A few well-targeted improvements to buying practices, production management, productivity levels or production technology could help to reduce unit variable costs and raise gross margins.

To reduce direct overheads

Review and adjust marketing, sales, R&D, customer services or other direct expenditure

By improving the planning and budgeting process and focusing marketing expenditure on higher-margin activities, you could reduce direct overhead expenditure considerably. It might also be possible to eliminate wastage and reduce buying prices by improving buying practices.

To reduce indirect overheads

Review and adjust premises, administration, finance and other fixed overheads

More efficient use of space, elimination of unnecessary duplication of administration activities, controlling fixed asset purchases (depreciation) and other related cost-control improvements could all contribute to lower fixed overheads. An important by-product of this review process is the tightening up of financial controls and monitoring procedures, e.g. budgetary control.

To reduce assets

Fixed assets

Postpone purchases of new equipment and vehicles, seek better prices, make more efficient use of existing assets and sell unnecessary assets.

Reduce working capital
- *Stock and work in progress.* Improve stock control practices to eliminate high stock levels and wastage and reduce stock levels in line with sales; also consider introducing just-in-time purchasing.
- *Debtors.* Improve credit control to reduce debtor days; chase up long-overdue accounts.
- *Creditors.* Negotiate more credit from suppliers and don't pay your bills early.

To reduce gearing

Reduce gearing and interest charges on the profit and loss account by raising more equity capital and tightening up internal controls to release more cash.

Having made all your strategy, policy and planning changes to improve overall profitability, again stand back and take a bird's-eye view. If the figures now seem more realistic, then the strategic plan can be given the seal of approval. The process of communicating the essentials to the whole organization can begin.

Operational action plans

With your organization's long-term objectives and strategic plan in place, you are now in a position to produce operational (departmental) action plans with their own objectives, as well as team and individual goals, since these can now be linked firmly to organization-wide objectives. The link between corporate strategic planning and goal setting at the individual employee level is illustrated in Box 10.16.

Box 10.15 Strategic planning stages: Operational plans

Strategic planning stages   **You are here**

1   Preparation for strategic planning
2   Undertake a business review
3   Undertake customer/market research
4   Set corporate objectives
5   Evaluate options and set corporate strategy
6   Calculate forecasts
7   Review and revise objectives and strategy
8   Produce operational action plans, budgets and set goals   ⟸
9   Set performance indicators
10 Agree monitoring and review procedures

Box 10.16 Cascaded business planning

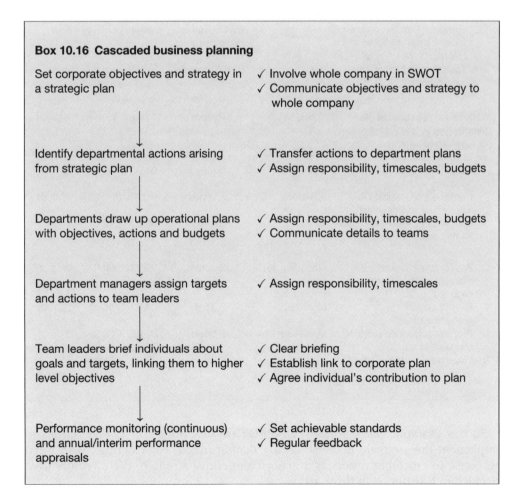

Set corporate objectives and strategy in a strategic plan	✓ Involve whole company in SWOT ✓ Communicate objectives and strategy to whole company
Identify departmental actions arising from strategic plan	✓ Transfer actions to department plans ✓ Assign responsibility, timescales, budgets
Departments draw up operational plans with objectives, actions and budgets	✓ Assign responsibility, timescales, budgets ✓ Communicate details to teams
Department managers assign targets and actions to team leaders	✓ Assign responsibility, timescales
Team leaders brief individuals about goals and targets, linking them to higher level objectives	✓ Clear briefing ✓ Establish link to corporate plan ✓ Agree individual's contribution to plan
Performance monitoring (continuous) and annual/interim performance appraisals	✓ Set achievable standards ✓ Regular feedback

In a fully delegated management structure, directors and key managers involved in the strategic planning team should agree the essential components of the strategic plan and the task of drawing up departmental operational plans would fall to heads of departments and their team leaders. Where an experienced management team does not exist or where key managers do not have the necessary skills to draw up their departmental plans, directors should assist in the process.

The central purpose of an operational plan is to implement the strategic plan. It should contain specific practical actions (see the marketing plan in Appendix 2), each of which should be linked to the strategic plan, as the example in Box 10.17 illustrates for a plant and tool-hire business (extracts from the company's plans).

Box 10.17 Example of links between strategic and operational plans

Factors identified in strategic plan	Where identified
1 Lack of key account management skills	SWOT analysis – serious weakness
2 Rapid response to customer orders	SWOT analysis – major strength (possibly distinctive competence)
3 Growth in building contracts for renovation of social housing	SWOT analysis – major opportunity (new market segment)
4 Tougher competition from local outlets	SWOT analysis – threat in existing markets

↓

Actions for operational plans (numbering below refers to numbering above)	Function	Responsible person	Start	Finish	Budget
1 Train key account managers	Sales	J Irving	06/02	08/02	£5 000
Recruit manager for key accounts	Sales	S Simms	04/02	07/02	£8 000
Continue team training in sales office and despatch	Sales + Despatch	A Jones	04/02	On-going	£1 000
Recruit sales order processor	Sales	J Ames	09/02	12/02	£500
Review sales and despatch procedures	Sales + Despatch	A Jones	01/03	03/03	0
2 Project team to produce marketing plan for new segment	Marketing + Sales + Purchasing	S Joren	08/02	09/02	0
3 Review market communications	Marketing	S Joren	04/02	06/02	£10 000
Proposals to widen product range	Marketing + Purchasing	F Dobb	06/02	08/02	0
Investigate customer loyalty incentives	Marketing	S Joren	09/02	10/02	0

In this example, the link between SWOT (as described above) and actions to implement the strategic plan are clearly demonstrated. For example, with rapid response to customer orders as a major competitive strength, the directors have decided to take action in three areas:

1 Reinforce and develop this further through team training.
2 Further recruitment.
3 Review of procedures to cut out unnecessary stages in the ordering and despatch process. Notice that this also deals with the fourth threat.

This example implies that the organization has a delegated management structure with departmental heads (sales, marketing, despatch, purchasing) responsible for producing their individual operations plans. If your organization is not as developed as this one, you or your key managers should produce these operational plans, majoring on marketing/sales and operations/production.

Budgets

Each function requires a budget and the origin of the budget is the operational plan for that department. Budgets cannot be produced with much reliability without a business plan. There is no rational basis for taking last year's actuals and adding or subtracting a percentage to reach a budget for this year.

Budgeting is the process of representing in financial terms all the necessary actions to achieve agreed objectives and targets on a monthly basis for a 12-month period. A budget could include sales and gross profits (such as in a sales and marketing budget), though for non-sales departments it would cover expenditure only.

Budgets are used as a basis for monitoring expenditure and are an important component of effective delegation. Once managers have agreed plans and budgets, they should be able to get on with the job of managing performance to achieve agreed outcomes, without constant interference from higher authority.

Follow the steps below methodically to produce a budget.

1 Prepare actual expenditure figures

Use actual figures for the year to date and add budgeted figures for the remainder of the year to produce a full year's set of figures.

2 Calculate expenditure ratios

Calculate financial ratios for these figures (express expenditure for each item as a percentage of sales) to provide a relative measure against which to judge your new budget.

3 Check your strategic business plan

Check the strategic business plan for changes in strategy and operational changes that have implications for your budget. Note any actions and expenditure in the plan affecting your department. Forecasts in the strategic business plan should set upper limits to your departmental budget.

4 Produce a departmental operational plan

Undertake a full review of your department's operations, including a SWOT and competence analysis to produce an action plan for the next 12 months. (Follow the same process for business planning discussed earlier, including involving all your people.)

5 Produce a departmental budget

- Budget for new activities. Identify new actions from your departmental plan and from the strategic plan, and any budgeted amounts that have been set in these plans, allocating them to their budget headings in your spreadsheet. Enter them monthly over the next 12 months.
- Budget for on-going activities. Having checked for relevant information in the strategic plan and financial limits in the forecasts (or having received your budget guidelines from your manager), produce a budget for your on-going operations for each expenditure item. Check the realism of these figures by applying the expenditure ratios calculated above. For example, if in previous years expenditure on motor and travel has consistently been at 2 per cent of sales (your ratio analysis will tell you this), then over the next year a similar percentage should obtain, suitably adjusted for changes you are proposing in the action plan.
- After producing your annual budget, allocate expenditures realistically to each month of the year, based on your departmental action plan. (Do not simply divide the total into 12 equal amounts.)

6 Review budgets

Because forecasting and budgeting are an iterative process, you should make further adjustments at this point in order to bring the budget into line with budgets from other departments, and with the overall business plan for the year. A detailed marketing budget is illustrated in Appendix 2.

Project plans

Because project work is quite normal in certain types of businesses, such as construction, consultancy and media businesses, planning and budgeting can easily be done on a project basis following the above procedures. Ideas for new activities, e.g. introducing new products/services, new areas of business, e.g. entering new markets, or improvements in organizing functional activities, e.g. production, marketing, operations, HR, also constitute projects that need evaluation and planning. The evaluation process should go through several stages of information gathering and analysis. At the end of each stage, the question should be asked: Is it worth going on to the next stage? The stages are as follows:

1   Is the idea technically feasible?

Examine technical, legal, ethical, political, social or other obstacles in the way of implementation.

2   Is there a strategic fit with the rest of your business?

Examine fit with existing markets and products/services (use product/market matrix).

3   Is the idea viable?

- What sales are needed to a) break even and b) make an acceptable profit (forecast profit and loss accounts)?
- Are these sales achievable?
- At what cost?

4   What are the financial implications?

How much finance will be needed (forecast balance sheets and cash flows)?

5   What could go wrong?

Check main sensitivities (what if?).

6   Business plan

- Produce a project business plan.
- Integrate project plan with overall business plan.

Monitoring the strategic plan

Box 10.18 Strategic planning stages: Monitoring and review

Strategic planning stages	**You are here**
1 Preparation for strategic planning	
2 Undertake a business review	
3 Undertake customer/market research	
4 Set corporate objectives	
5 Evaluate options and set corporate strategy	
6 Calculate forecasts	
7 Review and revise objectives and strategy	
8 Produce operational action plans, budgets and set goals	
9 Set performance indicators	⇐
10 Agree monitoring and review procedures	⇐

Business plans are there to guide managers through turbulent times. They seldom work out in the way that you want, so they have to be monitored, reviewed and changed where necessary.

Business plans do not necessarily fail because they are too ambitious, but because changing customer needs and the actions of rivals generally overtake the plan. You should meet every three months to monitor and review the strategic plan to ensure that changes can be implemented in good time if external conditions change. The example in Box 10.19 illustrates the point.

Box 10.19 Example of monitoring deficiencies

Smiths, a food-distribution business, took orders from customers on the basis of 48-hour delivery. Customers needed a more rapid service and they frequently pressed the sales department for faster turnaround.

Then a new competitor began offering next-day delivery. Smiths was caught off guard and within a month had lost three major customers to the newcomer. More were soon to defect.

An urgent directors' review followed these defections. They found that no one was listening. If managers had had their fingers on the pulse of the market and had listened to their sales staff, they would have been able to anticipate customers' changing needs and would have had the opportunity to upgrade service levels before losing business. (The marketing director estimated that each major customer had cost some £150 000 over five years to win and retain.)

Systematic monitoring and review of strategy and market conditions on a regular basis could have averted the disaster.

In order to monitor the effectiveness of the strategic plan, there should be clear performance measures[1] in place. Typical small-company performance measures could include one or more of the following.

1   Financial measures

- Net profit margin (net profit before tax ÷ sales).
- Gross profit margin (gross profit ÷ sales).
- Net asset growth.
- Return on shareholders' funds (net profit before tax ÷ net assets).

2   Customer measures

- Percentage of sales revenue and profit contribution from selected markets/products.
- Percentage of sales revenue and profit contribution from top 5 or 10 customers.
- Customer retention ratio (number of customers at end of year [excluding new customers won during year] ÷ number of customers at start of year).
- Customer acquisition ratio (new customers won during year ÷ number of customers at start of year).

3   Internal processes

- Rate of innovation/new ideas development.
- Average defect/rejection rates (or number of customer complaints).
- Average response times to callouts.
- Productivity (total actual hours worked ÷ total capacity hours).

4   Learning and growth

- Employee satisfaction score (based on an employee survey).
- Employee retention ratio (number of employees at end of year [excluding new employees joined during year] ÷ number of employees at start of year).
- Average number of training days per employee.
- Proportion of employees with qualifications.

Use these measures selectively to set achievable goals and monitor them monthly through your management information system. Arrange monthly management meetings to review departmental plans. Quarterly review meetings of the strategic plan can be brief, unless of course major external change is imminent that could force you to set a new direction for the business.

If changes are required to either the strategic plan or operational plans, record decisions and changes systematically and follow up at the next meeting. Changes to strategy will almost certainly require alterations to all operational plans, so it is just as well that your key managers appreciate the flexibility of the planning process. Nothing should be cast in stone!

Note

1   Adapted from Kaplan, R. and Norton, D. (1996) *The Balanced Scorecard*, Harvard Business School Press, Cambridge, MA.

Further reading

1   Argenti, J. (1989) *Practical Corporate Planning*, Routledge, London.
2   Barrow, P. (2001) *The Best-laid Business Plans*, Virgin Books, London.
3   McDonald, M. (2002) *If You're so Brilliant, How Come Your Marketing Plans Aren't Working?* Kogan Page, London.

Hazards on the Path to Growth

CHAPTER 11

Key issues dealt with in this chapter are:

- Setting foot in new markets.
- Failure to let go.
- Finding a long-term role for the founder.
- Management succession: appointing a general manager.
- The family and the business.
- Undermining the management team.
- Owner-manager guilt.

Stay focused or venture into new markets?

The small, growing business faces a classic dilemma in its transition from small to medium-sized: which strategy offers the greatest potential for growth? Get it wrong and you're another failure statistic; get it right and you're a celebrated entrepreneur! Should expansion take place in existing areas of knowledge and skill, or should the business move into new areas – new markets and new products or services – and if the latter, in what order and at what speed?

For example, if you are selling to caterers in the south of England, should your next move be to caterers in other parts of the UK, or caterers in western Europe, or other non-catering market segments in the UK, western Europe or even the rest of the world? Or should you continue to focus on caterers in the south of England and investigate the options for introducing new products and services to them? The options are endless and it is not surprising that growing businesses make mistakes that could be avoided by identifying and evaluating their strategic options thoroughly.

A brief reprise of the product/market matrix and the core competence model will help to answer these difficult questions. They provide two useful frameworks for making difficult strategic decisions. Please refer to Chapter 2, Figures 2.2 and 2.3 and the accompanying explanations.

Taking the product/market matrix first, the main hazard you face is being over-optimistic about the prospects for sales growth and profit margins when adopting a *market development strategy*. The main difficulty is that new markets are defined as those where you have no prior experience of customer behaviour. So how can you understand them? Apart from 'gut feel', the only ways are through customer feedback (not particularly useful in this instance), market research (which can establish basic facts, but not covert factors) and piloting or test marketing in a controlled way, before taking the plunge and committing large-scale resources to prize open the market.

A more cautious approach should prevail over excessive optimism, for a number of reasons:

- Customer loyalty to existing suppliers – what will the marketing costs be of gaining their loyalty? Consider their motivation: what convincing reasons can you give them to break from existing suppliers? If none, downgrade your forecasts.
- Lack of customer education or knowledge – customers might not understand product benefits, particularly if you are launching a new generation of products, e.g. an invention or innovation.
- New markets might require new products or services, not necessarily the ones that have served you well in the past. The product preferences and buying behaviour of prospective customers in new markets can be uncovered to a certain extent, but you will always be left with some uncertainties. The difficulty is budgeting for additional unexpected product development costs and making a decision about their likely effect on prices and margins. By venturing into new markets with new products simultaneously, you are in effect pursuing a *diversification strategy* (Figure 2.2). This is many times more risky than either product development or market development on its own.
- New markets always require a different approach to marketing. Unless marketing is already professionally organized and is a core competence of your business, it is very risky venturing into new markets expecting substantial growth. A different approach is called for, one that emphasizes caution and recognizes that marketing is effectively weak when it comes to understanding customer behaviour in new marketplaces. Where previous sales growth has come about through applying a distinctive competence enthusiastically and diligently to a well-defined, narrow market segment, wider markets are typically more competitive and therefore always require a different marketing approach, driven by professional marketing people and larger-scale resources than the business has typically employed in its existing markets. It takes many years to build up such a capability from scratch and there are some tough recruitment decisions along the way. Growth by acquisition or merger is sometimes preferred as a means of gaining the appropriate capabilities quickly for accessing new markets. Nevertheless, they come with plenty of their own potential pitfalls and it is well known that few of the putative benefits of acquisition or merger ever materialize.
- Even if your forecasts of demand prove to be accurate and margins turn out as predicted, you aren't out of the woods yet, which brings us to another hazard. Weaknesses in operations – especially production and logistics – can

foul up the entire growth plan. Rapid growth calls for exceptional skills in organizational development (see Chapter 4) and before advancing into new areas, structure, people, processes and systems should be analysed to identify potential weak points.

It is important therefore to consider not only the profit and financing implications of venturing into new markets, but also the alignment of your existing core competences with proposed new areas of business (see Chapter 2, Figure 2.2). Some of these competences will need incremental improvement over time; others will need a radical overhaul, including the re-engineering of some processes. So before settling on a growth strategy, be sure to apply the core competence model to each strategic option, because it will help to:

- Identify parts of the business that need to be improved *before* you move into new markets or develop new products.
- Open up exceptional growth possibilities in markets that you have not seriously contemplated.

Finally, after a thorough reapplication of the 'strategic sieve' (see Chapter 2) to your chosen option, if you are convinced that real opportunities for growth are indeed ripe for plucking, take a further look at your present business – the source of your profits and your success to date. Are you convinced that you have the management resources to pursue growth opportunities *while keeping your existing customers happy and employees motivated*? What changes are you proposing to the organization to ensure that the needs of customers in existing as well as new markets can be met at *high and rising levels of service*? If you are satisfied that your organization can deliver growth in existing and new markets at planned profit margins, then you are probably in a good position to avoid the hazards associated with a change in strategy.

Failure to let go

People who set up and sustain the development of a business – entrepreneurs – are often exceptional. Founding a business that survives and grows and provides permanent employment for others requires vision, guts and energy as well as the application of a wide range of managerial capabilities. It is quite usual that every job in a small and medium-sized business has been done at some stage by the boss, because in the beginning he or she may have been the only person available to do it. So if we think in terms of organization, a business founder is likely to have at some stage embraced all the functions in the organization as well as occupied all the levels (Figure 11.1).

Business founders create their enterprises usually at considerable financial risk, and nurture them through the uncertainty of the early years when survival often is in doubt. Even businesses that achieve rapid market success are likely to struggle for financial stability for some years. Typically, everything a business founder has is tied up in the business, not just materially and financially; the business may be an all-consuming interest and family life becomes entangled with it.

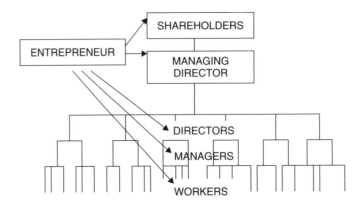

Figure 11.1: The entrepreneur's roles as the business grows.

The business founder identifies with the firm and the firm is an extension of him or her. It is not too fanciful to think of the business as the founder's child. There will have been a period when the founders have taken every decision personally.

Therefore it is not easy to relinquish control, even when the founder's ability to keep hold of everything comes under strain as the business continues to expand. Delegation is, of course, the textbook answer. Recruiting management staff to do the work is not initially a problem. But delegating, even at routine management levels, is often a major hurdle for founders, for it raises the issue of trust: Can I trust somebody else to deal with this matter as carefully as I would myself? At the back of the founder's mind is an awareness that nobody else can be expected to feel the same connection with the business as he or she does.

Matters are not helped when customers, suppliers and even employees themselves collude with such monomania. Customers who are accustomed to being served by the boss may fear that they are being sold short when an account handler is appointed to look after their needs. Suppliers originally brought in because of a personal connection way back may be less accommodating to a departmental manager. Employees expect to have their annual appraisal with the boss just as they have always done, which was fine when there were 10 employees but unrealistic with 50. However, what message will be sent out to those people who cease to have appraisals with the boss, if some are delegated to lesser mortals?

All of these issues can be dealt with successfully, given attention and planning. They have to be if the original founders are to reap the full reward of their investment in the company by eventually withdrawing or retiring from it profitably. If the company is not to die with its founders, it has to be established as an independent entity that can demonstrably be run successfully without their involvement or intervention.

In an attempt to reduce the risk in letting go and try to ensure that the people to whom they delegate management responsibility are trustworthy, solutions introduced by founders may fall into the following categories, not all of which will prove to be satisfactory:

- Business founders anxious about delegating power to others frequently try subterfuges to make the matter less scary. One such is to look for *clones*: If I must let somebody else run things and make decisions, could I find somebody who will think and react like I do? This leads to hiring people on the basis of a vague person specification and a tendency to rely on impressions and gut feel when assessing candidates. Heavy reliance is placed on recommendations from contacts and friends, which is perfectly satisfactory if the recommender fully understands the job specification and if the recommended person is measured against that specification and against other candidates. In practice, they seldom are.

- Or things are kept safe by keeping them in the *family*. Senior positions are reserved for family members, whether or not they are the best-qualified people available.
- Then there is the habit of appointing *loyal servants*. This essentially means that control is maintained by the boss, but true delegation does not take place. Loyal servants are selected for reliability in following the boss's instructions and not for their ability to take the initiative and help drive the business forwards.

If the founders are genuine about relinquishing control, two things have to happen for there to be a successful transfer of power to a CEO, general manager or senior management team:

1   The founders have to understand and communicate their role and the special knowledge, skills and qualities they bring to the business. They also need to know their own weaknesses, particularly in relation to the management needs of a more complex, growing business, rather than those of managing a new venture. It is this recognition most of all that will bring about a successful transfer of power from the founders to a new management team. This calls for an unusual quality not always found in entrepreneurs: the humility to accept weaknesses in key skills and knowledge.
2   The successors must be able to gain the trust of the founders. They will have to demonstrate their special knowledge, skills and qualities in relation to their future roles as directors, leaders and managers of the business. Above all, they should understand where and why the business makes its profits and what can be done to perpetuate the momentum for growth. They will have to take care of the important high ground of the business, but in addition they will have to demonstrate their capabilities to run a larger business and an understanding of what needs to be done to drive the business forward into its next phase of growth.

A future role for the founder

When the founders started the business, they probably never imagined that the time would come when they would have to contemplate changing their management style from controlling, closely in touch and hands on to a more remote, delegated style where other people take the major decisions. That is what is needed for successful growth as the business gradually becomes more complex and myriads of decisions are best left to people with all the relevant information. Then management by a central controlling figure becomes redundant.

To imagine what role the founders should adopt in the future, consider a simple model of their main roles in response to the needs of the business over the course of growth (Box 11.1).

Box 11.1 The founder's multiple roles

Role	Start-up stage	Early growth — simple organization	Sustained growth — complex organization
Worker	Most time spent on basic tasks	Some time spent on basic tasks, some on higher-order tasks	Entirely distanced from basic tasks
Manager	Occasional organizing and controlling others	Most time organizing and controlling others	Delegating to a management team; leadership role
Director	No explicit role	Some strategy setting	Setting strategy (critical); governance (important); working with a board (including non-execs)
Chairman	Nothing to chair!	Pulling together a nascent board of directors	Leading the top team; creating and realizing a vision
Shareholder	No value	Value starts to grow	Value significant

These roles wax and wane over time according to the stage of growth. Being hands on in the beginning sets the culture of the organization; being hands off in the later growth stage ensures that delegation can take its course. The founders should have the foresight to move through these roles ahead of each stage of development and to develop people to take their place in each former role as it is vacated.

As the business moves towards the right-hand side of Box 11.1, the founders need to relinquish some roles and assume new ones for growth to be successful. In creating their future roles, they need to recognize that:

- Each role calls for a specific focus of activity, e.g. the chairman's central function is to help the senior team pull together (a servant of the board).
- Taking on a higher-order role requires giving up most of a lower one (and relinquishing control of day-to-day operations).
- Each role calls for special knowledge, skills and qualities that the founders might not have in sufficient quantity and might not be able to learn in time (without hindering business growth). If they don't have them, they will need to find someone who does, which means drafting an outsider into a very senior position possibly for the first time – a daunting task itself calling for special knowledge and skills.

It should be evident that one of the special qualities of successful founders is to identify their own strengths and weaknesses at these different stages of growth and recognize the importance of bringing in outside help in key positions when they can't do the job themselves. So if there is a role for the founder in the future, it probably lies in being able to delegate effectively to people who have higher-order competences, giving up direct control while having confidence in the management team and finding a place where they can do the least damage. In some cases, this could be on the golf course or tennis court!

Appointing a successor to the founder CEO

A successful resolution to the problems of relinquishing control and finding a future role for the founders is bound to depend on the recruitment of a suitable successor to run the business. Many successful growth businesses have seen their financial performance plummet disastrously with the appointment of a new CEO or general manager when the founders decide to 'take a back seat'. Why is this so?

The founders may be intent on seeking someone who has the same outlook, attitudes, skills and knowledge as them. This narrow view of their recruitment needs centres misguidedly on their positions as owners and entrepreneurs, both of which have little bearing on the real management needs of the growing business. For one thing, the early years are characterized by a bias for action, a narrow strategic focus and attention mainly to tasks (getting a quality product or service to customers as rapidly as possible); in the growth stage, however, the CEO's principal focus of attention should be on building a management team, introducing systems, reviewing and analysing strategic options and looking after people and processes. The day-to-day tasks of looking after customers, operations and staff should be delegated to key managers. So the new CEO would need to be a hands-off manager: do the founders have the skills to identify such a person, when they have experience of managing in a distinctly hands-on way?

Can the founders trust the new general manager to take as much care of customers and staff as they have done? The direct intervention of the founders in the processes of customer acquisition and retention has typically been an important determinant of sales and margin growth and the new recruit might not have the same motivation as the founders, or perceive the same priorities. For example, the accent in the next phase of growth should be on introducing management information systems (so that the business does not have to rely on the founders as the sole source of vital customer, market, operations and financial information) and improving existing, as well as building new, organizational competences (to ensure that the founders' multidimensional roles are amply covered in the transition to a more professionally managed business). The founders may see these changing priorities as moving the business away from its core customer values and (wrongly) interpret the newcomer's priorities as inimical to their best interests.

An important consideration when appointing a general manager (as well as sales and marketing directors) is the opportunity afforded to add to the knowledge and skills bank in existing as well as planned new strategic areas. The founders (and some of their key managers) will have in-depth experience in existing product/market areas, but little or none in new markets where rapid growth is sought. Clearly, by recruiting someone with experience in these new areas, a major boost to growth could result at the same time as a reduction in risk. But the question remains: recruitment for what future strategy? If the founders have a business plan setting out future strategic direction, then recruitment can proceed with greater certainty. If not, expectations of the new recruit's ability to lead the business in new directions might need to be downgraded.

Where a successor is found inside the organization, the founder has to be careful to appoint a qualified candidate, not just the most loyal senior manager. (This applies to all appointments at a management level.) Unfortunately, the softest and (in the short term) least costly option is normally to find an internal candidate who can be trusted, whose dedication to the founder (and hence the business) is implicit and therefore who can be relied on to take care of the things that the founders value most. This habit breaks a major recruitment rule: do not match the business to available people; rather match people with the right skills, knowledge and qualities to the future needs of the business.

The answer to the succession problem is to adopt time-honoured best practice by planning for succession well in advance of the need and getting the recruitment process under way in good time. You will need to:

- Produce a long-term strategic business plan. The purpose is to establish target markets and organizational development needs, and in turn what type of senior management resources will be needed over the next three to five years.
- Identify the personal goals and preferred roles of the founders and a timetable for proposed changes to their involvement in the senior management team (and draw up a job specification for the founder CEO if one does not exist).
- Draw up a new job specification for the CEO elect (or general manager elect), focusing on overall purpose, main objectives and main tasks (see Chapter 4 for an outline of job and person specifications). Be sure to include responsibility for strategy formulation, governance, overall financial performance and leadership.
- Draw up a person specification, focusing on knowledge and experience in future product/market areas that complements that of the founders in existing product/market areas, and on the special knowledge, skills and qualities needed to work with the founders on the one hand, and an emergent management team on the other. The skills of recruiting and developing key managers should be high on the list of personal attributes. It is important that the CEO elect should have direct experience in the particular product/market areas of the growing business, mainly to give him or her credibility in the eyes of the founders. All too often when things go wrong, people are wont to draw the wrong conclusions and say: We could have told you so . . . he doesn't have experience of our type of business.
- Conduct the recruitment and selection process professionally (see Chapter 6). A high-quality candidate (the one you want to appoint) will discern from your recruitment and selection behaviour the seriousness of your intent, which will leave you with the enviable task of making a selection from the best possible list of candidates.

Family members on the payroll

The accusation of nepotism can apply to the appointment and promotion of family members in family firms of all types and sizes. While the business owners may feel that they have the right to provide opportunities for their kin, it is as well to be conscious of likely consequences, for the individual as well as the organization. Family appointees have to prove themselves in the eyes of other staff, which can place quite a burden on a young person or someone not fully competent in their role. And seeming to give preference to this person in prospects and promotion will undermine employee motivation and can lead to the loss of strong contributors who find their path blocked. If the business is to be run professionally, then family members must be, and be seen to be, subject to the same standards as other employees.

For a non-growth, 'lifestyle' business, the appointment of a family member to a key position regardless of their suitability may not be a calamity. A sedate pace of change will normally permit a review of performance followed by appropriate action before much damage is done, if either a) the family member is clearly out of their depth, or b) the new incumbent requires a longer period of adaptation and development than was previously thought.

However, for a rapidly growing business the problem of appointing ill-equipped family members to senior positions can be exacerbated by the rapid pace of change and the critical nature of quality, speed and relationships in maintaining sales and margin growth. There might not be time to turn the situation around before severe damage is done to customer or staff relations. The solution is to adopt proper recruitment and selection procedures even when appointing family members to the payroll, and to apply the same criteria for development and promotion to them as to their colleagues.

Failure to delegate effectively: Undermining management

Founders who undermine their management team by dominating relationships with key customers and suppliers and retaining close links with loyal staff – everybody asks for the boss and feels cheated if they don't get the boss – create bottlenecks in marketing, purchasing and other critical functions and prevent the development of key managers and of business.

As the business grows, the founder's desire to retain control over major decision-making areas results in their spreading themselves too thinly over an expanding hierarchy. There might be nominal delegation, e.g. people appointed as departmental heads but without effective empowerment. Constant interference by the boss in day-to-day operations undermines managers' status and authority: instructions are countermanded, unsolicited suggestions are made, unplanned improvements are implemented and people are taken away from their work to tackle pet projects. The result is a management team that is inclined to keep a low profile and more often than not to evade their duties. Cracks start to appear in the delegated decision-making process and the business suffers accordingly.

The imperative to build an effective, delegated management team and vest responsibilities in key managers accompanies successful business growth. Managers should be partly promoted from within and partly recruited for their specialist skills and experiences. Management development should embrace formal training courses to impart fundamental skills, supplemented by internal training, mentoring and coaching (people development should be high on the list of skills of the CEO). Time needs to be set aside for training and coaching in management skills.

What are the basic skills and knowledge that key managers in growing businesses should have?

- *Business development skills*: strategy, organizational diagnosis and design, marketing, financial analysis, business planning, budgeting, forecasting.
- *Skills of managing people at work*: self-management, interpersonal skills, motivation, team leading, briefing, goal setting, monitoring, feedback, performance appraisals, recruitment and selection, dealing with difficult situations.

Management training courses offering knowledge and skill development in all these areas are normally available from local colleges, universities and business schools and in the commercial training marketplace. Business Links in the UK, which are empowered by government to provide support services to growing businesses, can be a useful first port of call.[1]

Owner-manager guilt as a barrier to growth

It is not unusual for owner-managers to feel ambivalent about their business as a source of wealth, and to carry an awkward sense that owning its accumulated profits is somehow exploitive of employees. One owner had been in the habit of inviting employees to his (quite ordinary) house for an annual party. Under joint pressure from his wife and his financial adviser, he and his family traded up to a much grander property, whereupon he became seriously anxious about inviting staff to the new house for fear that they would see him as living off the fruits of their labours. Then there is the story of the owner who gave his wife a Mercedes sports car, which had to be garaged away from the place of work and taken out only at night, lest employees should see them in it and become resentful. In this case, the owner was reluctant to reveal profit and loss information even to managers, in case they got the wrong idea.

Running through this behaviour is an unexamined belief that employees will hold it against owners if they are seen to have made money from the business. This not only inhibits the personal freedom of the owner, but can also lead to secretive habits within the firm, with owners wasting time and energy deciding what financial information it is 'safe' to reveal to employees.

There are two hazards here for the business:

- A culture of secrecy sets up 'us versus them' assumptions among staff, lowering morale, reducing involvement and undermining people's willingness to take responsibility.
- The natural development of managers is prevented, and their ability to contribute sensibly to the development of strategy and understand priorities

seriously constrained, when they do not have access to a full and realistic business picture.

Secrecy is much more likely to create a barrier between owner and employees than is the disclosure of the real financial situation. In the absence of information people create their own interpretations, which are inevitably wide of the mark.

If we bring out into the open the unexamined belief that employees resent profits, it turns out to have little substance. Any benefits accruing to a founder from the firm's success need to be put into perspective with the risks taken to get it started and nurture its growth. The founder will probably have jeopardized personal financial stability and abandoned career prospects to start the business, and have put in huge amounts of time and effort for little reward over long periods. There is an entitlement to reward related to risk, as with any investment, and most people are willing to acknowledge this.

Disclosing business and financial information openly shows employees the real picture, explaining reasons for caution as well as for confidence. Financial performance measures are a crucial indicator of the health of the business – and disclosing them to employees gives the latter an opportunity to share in and celebrate the achievement that they represent.

Note

1   The central enquiry number for Business Links in the UK is 0845 6009006. Information is also available at www.businesslink.org.

Example of a Strategic Business Plan

Aaron Romano Recruitment Ltd.
Business Plan 2003–2005

Objectives

AR2 aims to become one of London's top 10 financial recruitment specialists, providing exemplary client service while actively building its reputation for quality, professionalism, trust and dedication to close working partnerships with candidates and companies alike.

The company's main objective is to produce a consistently rising annual net profit margin of from 6.7 per cent to 14 per cent over the next three years, in order to provide sufficient post-tax income to finance growth internally and to pay the shareholders' dividends.

Sales growth is expected to continue unabated with rising demand in both target market segments (specialist finance houses and financial services companies). The company's capacity weakness will restrict sales to £1.8m this year (best estimate). This year is to be regarded as a period of consolidation.

Box A1.1 AR2 sales forecast 2003–2005 (£m)

	2003	2004	2005
Sales	1.800	3.500	5.000
Growth %	10	94	43
Sales permanent	0.450	0.875	1.250
% Share	25	25	25
Sales temp	1.350	2.625	3.750
% Share	75	75	75
Gross margin	0.720	1.470	2.150
GPM %	40	42	43
Net margin	0.120	0.455	0.700
Net margin %	6.7	13	14

Marketing

To raise gross margins systematically from 40 per cent to 43 per cent over a three-year period by continuing to focus on the City's specialist financial (250) and investment (50) sectors, where demand exceeds supply of qualified operations, IT, accountancy and secretarial personnel. It is expected that commissions charged will rise from $17\frac{1}{2}$ per cent towards 20 per cent while simultaneously average salaries will rise ahead of inflation.

By 2005, to become a top 10 recruitment consultancy and a top 100 global recruitment consultancy.

Net worth

To raise net worth to £1m by 2005, in order to sell the company for £5m in 2006.

Structure

To have a delegated management structure with autonomous teams in place by 2005 so that the company is not totally reliant on AR/JB and can make the most of the entrepreneurial talents of its key managers.

Distinctive competence

- Ability to match clients' needs precisely.
- High standards of integrity and personal attention.
- Rapid response.

SWOT analysis (strengths, weaknesses, opportunities, threats)

Box A1.2 AR2 SWOT analysis summary

Item	Strengths	Weaknesses
Products and services	Right calibre of candidates Accurate pre-selection procedures Sensitivity to client time constraints Briefing of candidates	No scanning Candidate availability

Item	Strengths	Weaknesses
Marketing and sales	Time with candidates Narrow market focus Strong repeat business	Not keeping in touch with clients Inconsistent database usage Reactive temp desk Not member of FRES Lack of follow-up calls
Operations	Internal team communication Proximity to companies Real-time communication CV production	No urgency getting out CVs Lack of standards re job specs Insufficient capacity
Organization, management and people	Product and industry knowledge Job briefing skills AR as charismatic leader JB as organizational leader	Dependence on owners No database manager
Finance and controls	Profitable Positive cash flow Control of overheads	Inadequate management information system

Item	Opportunities	Threats
Social	Better-educated graduates Population growth in SE Influx of European graduates	Homeworking
Technological	Demand for IT staff	Reduction in non-IT staff because of technology advances
Economic	Growth in finance Emerging markets	Companies moving to more temp/contract working
Political	Change from state to private pensions	Attitude of government to pensions and investment industry
Markets	Growing demand for staff at all levels Growth of finance clients Growth in corporate investment in Lloyds	Nominated supplier agreements becoming more common Inconsistent candidate flow Competitors responding more rapidly
Clients	LGH relocation to London New business formed by Fred Holmes PM setting up new division in private banking	AB bad publicity

Strategy

Target markets – existing

The company will continue to target markets that have demonstrated their profitability in the past and are expected to show rising demand for staff at all levels from 2003 – 2005:

- City of London banks (*c* 250 main players).
- City of London investment managers (*c* 50 main players).

Target markets – new

After a period of consolidation in 2003, the company will investigate growth in the insurance investment sector for 2004 – 2005:

- Lloyds insurance market syndicates (<100 main players).

Products/services – existing

The company will continue to place permanent, contract and temporary staff in the following jobs:

- Operations managers (perm).
- Operations staff (perm + temp).

Products/services – new

Opportunities for introducing new positions will be exploited in 2004 as demand grows for permanent, contract and temporary staff in the following jobs:

- IT managers and staff (perm + contract + temp).
- Accountants/audit staff (perm + contract + temp).
- Secretarial staff (perm + contract + temp).
- Compliance managers and staff (perm).
- Syndicate analysts and executives (to be researched).

Non-recruitment services will be added to the portfolio in 2005 once new recruitment services have taken root:

- Salary surveys.
- Payroll service – SMA payroll.
- Careers services – appraisal, benchmarking, psychometric tests, CV preparation.
- Training – skills upgrading.
- Recruitment advertising – media buying, response handling, mailing.

Organization – Marketing

- Produce marketing plan for existing and new services.
- Consolidate account management approach.
  - Training for all consultants.

- Upgrade website.
  - Assess needs and competitor survey.
  - Commission redesign and Internet marketing plan.
  - Go live.
- Design and print new literature.
- Database development.
  - Agree procedures.
  - Train staff.
  - Recruit (see below).
- Join FRES.

Organization – operations

- Expand office space by 400 sq ft (adjacent).
- Expand office space to 5000 sq ft.
- Purchase workstations for new consultants.
- Expand IT system for website, e-mail, scanning.
  - Servers, scanner, software.
  - Internet site.

Organization – structure

- Change of structure into two operating divisions – finance banking and investors – with permanent and temp recruitment serving each market segment.
- Establish third operating division or separate company to sell non-recruitment services.
- Teams of consultants with admin support (ratio 2:1) set up within these divisions, to be replicated as demand and capacity dictate.
- Marketing function to be established, to include database operation, initially staffed by an experienced junior.

Organization – management

- JB to become operations director, responsible for smooth running of the office according to plan, including investors and management divisions (sales and operations), candidate recruitment, IT, personnel.
- Senior consultant to be recruited as manager/consultant for investors (permanent recruitment).
- Senior consultant to be recruited as manager/consultant for investment (permanent recruitment).
- Arrange management skills development for JB.

Organization – recruitment

- Eight permanent consultants.
- Three temps consultants.
- Two marketing assistants.
- Two admin assistants.

Organization – HR

- Introduce performance appraisals.
- Train all managers.
- Improve job descriptions.
- Introduce internal staff meetings.
- Introduce annual training plan.
- Evaluate Investors in People.

Finance/MIS

- Introduce budgets for use in monthly accounts.
- Improve management accounts – divisional information.

Box A1.3 AR2 schedule of actions 2003–2005

Action	By whom	Start date	Finish date	Budget (£)
2003				
Accounts – introduce budget vs actual reports	AR	1/2003	2/2003	0
Accounts – introduce divisional reporting	AR	1/2003	2/2003	0
Role – JB becomes ops director	JB	1/2003		0
Structure – 2 divisions (IB, IM)	AR	1/2003		0
Marketing – join FRES	JB	2/2003		200
Structure – teams of consultants with team leaders	JB	3/2003	4/2003	0
HR – introduce regular staff meetings	JB	4/2003		0
IT – review and agree database procedures	JB/HD	6/2003	8/2003	500
Recruit – 1 × senior consultant for IB	JB/AS	6/2003	9/2003	500
Recruit – 1 × senior consultant for IM	JB/AS	6/2003	9/2003	500
Training – JB management development/coaching	JB	6/2003	12/2003	2000
IT – improve e-mail + scanning	JB/HD	7/2003	9/2003	2500
Training – database procedures	RD	8/2003	10/2003	2000
HR – improve candidate job descriptions	JB	8/2003	10/2003	0
Marketing – print new literature	AR/FG	9/2003	12/2003	3000
Training – performance appraisals	AR	10/2003	10/2003	1200

Training – scanning	HD	11/2003	12/2003	1 200
Planning – review and write annual plan for 2004	AR/JB	11/2003	12/2003	0
HR – start performance appraisals	AR	12/2003	12/2003	0
Marketing – review and write annual plan for 2004	AR	12/2003	12/2003	0

2004

HR – introduce annual training plan	JB	1/2004	1/2004	0
Launch IT, accountancy/audit and secretarial service	AR	2/2004	6/2004	5 000
Premises – 400 sq ft new space needed	AR	3/2004	3/2004	500
Recruit – 1 × consultant (temps)	JB	3/2004	6/2004	500
Recruit – 1 × marketing assistant	JB	3/2004	6/2004	500
Recruit – 1 × senior consultant secretarial	JB	3/2004	6/2004	500
Marketing – research syndicate market	AR	4/2004	7/2004	1500
Structure – establish marketing department	AR	5/2004	5/2004	0
Training – account management	JB	6/2004	8/2004	1500
IT – redesign website	HD	6/2004	8/2004	2500
Marketing – produce web marketing plan	AR	7/2004	8/2004	0
Training – web management	HD	8/2004	8/2004	1500
HR – consider IIP	AR	9/2004	9/2004	0
Recruit – 1 × accountant	JB	9/2004	12/2004	500
Recruit – 1 × admin assistant	JB	9/2004	12/2004	500
Recruit – 1 × consultant (temps)	JB	9/2004	12/2004	500
Recruit – 1 × senior consultant accounts	JB	9/2004	12/2004	500
Recruit – 1 × senior consultant for IT	JB	9/2004	12/2004	500
Structure – establish accounts department	AR	10/2004	12/2004	0
Premises – expand to 5 k sq ft	AR	12/2004	3/2005	1500
Recruit – 1 × accounts assistant	JB	12/2004	3/2005	500
Recruit – 1 × admin assistant	JB	12/2004	3/2005	500
Recruit – 1 × middle office	JB	12/2004	3/2005	500
Planning – review and write annual plan for 2005	AR	11/2004	12/2004	0
Marketing – plan for 2005	AR	12/2004	12/2004	0

2005

Launch careers planning service	AR	1/2006	6/2006	10 000
Launch compliance recruitment service	AR	1/2006	6/2006	0
Launch payroll service	AR	1/2006	6/2006	0
Launch recruitment advertising service	AR	1/2006	6/2006	0
Launch salary surveys	AR	1/2006	6/2006	0
Launch training service	AR	1/2006	6/2006	0
Structure – new division to sell services	AR	4/2006	5/2006	0
Recruit – 1 × consultant	JB	6/2006	9/2006	500
Recruit – 1 × marketing junior	JB	6/2006	9/2006	500
Planning – review and write annual plan for 2006	AR	11/2005	12/2005	0
Marketing – plan for 2006	AR	12/2005	12/2005	0

Box A1.4 AR2 forecast profit and loss accounts 2003–2005 (£m)

	2003	2004	2005
Sales	1.800	3.500	5.000
Cost of sales	1.080	2.030	2.850
Gross profit	0.720	1.470	2.150
GPM %	40	42	43
Marketing/Selling	0.072	0.210	0.350
Marketing %	4	6	7
Establishment	0.036	0.050	0.150
Administration	0.475	0.655	0.909
Administration %	26	19	18
Finance	0.005	0.010	0.015
Depreciation	0.012	0.020	0.026
Net Profit	0.120	0.455	0.700
Net margin %	6.7	13	14
Taxation	0.030	0.110	0.175
Dividends	0.020	0.050	0.100
To reserves	0.070	0.295	0.425

Box A1.5 AR2 forecast balance sheets 2003–2005 (£m)

	2003	2004	2005
Fixed assets	0.035	0.080	0.150
Current assets			
– Debtors	0.300	0.500	0.700
– Cash	0.227	0.437	0.607
	0.527	0.937	1.307
Current liabilities			
– Trade creditors	0.125	0.175	0.075
– Taxation	0.030	0.110	0.175
– Dividends	0.020	0.050	0.100
– Overdraft	0	0	0
	0.175	0.335	0.350
Net Current Assets	0.352	0.602	0.957
Net assets	0.387	0.682	1.107
Financed by:			
Share capital	0.001	0.001	0.001
From P&L	0.070	0.295	0.425
Reserves (b/f)	0.316	0.386	0.681
Shareholders' funds	0.387	0.682	1.107

Abco Systems Ltd, Marketing Plan 2003–2004

Sue White, Sales and Marketing Director
John Steen, Marketing Executive

Part I: Marketing and sales review

1 Sales and contribution analysis 2002–2003

1.1   In the financial year 2002–2003 ABCO achieved sales of £3.1m, an 11 per cent increase on 2001/2002. The company made a net profit of £279k (9 per cent) with an average gross profit margin of 61 per cent.

1.2   Breakdown of sales and margins for 2002–2003:

Box A2.1 Breakdown of sales and margins for 2002–2003 (£m)

	Sales	%	Gross profit	%
By product group				
System A	1.4	46	0.8 (61%)	42
System B	1.0	31	0.7 (70%)	37
System C	0.7	23	0.4 (54%)	21
Total	3.1	100	1.9 (61%)	100
By market segment				
City banks	2.5	81	1.7 (68%)	89
SMEs	0.5	15	0.2 (40%)	10
Europe	0.1	4	0.04 (40%)	1
Total	3.1	100	1.9 (61%)	100

---

2 SWOT summary and conclusions (see attached SWOT)

2.1   Separate customer surveys and staff surveys were conducted to ascertain ABCO's strengths, weaknesses, opportunities and threats. The main findings were:

2.1.1 Distinctive competence: the main reason that customers come to us is our service levels (rapid response, professional approach) and product quality (technical skills).

2.1.2 Irregular deliveries are a long-standing source of complaint by customers – prospect of losing orders

2.1.3 17 per cent of customers admitted that ABCO was sole supplier, leaving a massive 83 per cent using the three main competitors – growth potential if we can back up quality with an excellent service.

2.1.4 77 per cent of customers rated our product quality 80 per cent or higher – regular staff training on quality issues will be maintained.

2.1.5 Helpdesk response was highly rated with 71 per cent of customers being more than satisfied with response.

2.1.6 Sales staff are running at 65 per cent effectiveness – too much time is spent taking unrelated telephone calls for other departments or staff, physically trying to locate colleagues so they can take calls, or taking messages and passing them on. Selling time is limited and additional duties should be a receptionist's responsibility.

2.1.7 Only 27 per cent of existing customers had at some time in the past tried our new products, 21 per cent bought these products regularly, leaving 52 per cent who had never sampled them. New products are a very sensitive issue: 64 per cent of customers surveyed could see no future whatsoever in this market (positioning).

2.1.8 Professional buyers are taking control of purchasing with emphasis on price and quality.

2.1.9 Staff views about training were strong – job descriptions for all staff, quarterly staff meetings, regular quality courses, internal training, team-building events and incentive schemes were mentioned.

2.1.10 Departments not communicating well.

2.2 Main strengths:
- Highest profit contribution from City banks.
- High level of professional conduct.
- Top quality product and service.
- Telesales knowledge and response times.
- Desire to learn among staff.

2.3 Main weaknesses:
- European profitability low.
- Deliveries irregular.
- Poor image with production managers.
- Poor inter-departmental communications.

2.4 Major opportunities for growth:
- City segment (highest contribution levels).
- New European legislation on workplace standards.

2.5 Major threats:
- Excessive competition in SME segment.
- Shortage of skilled professionals.
- Reduced budgets in banking (except euro specialists).

3   Competitor review

3.1 There are five competitors whose names come up more than twice in discussions with customers. Of these, three can be identified as ABCO's serious competitors:
- City Systems - strengths = well organized, strong balance sheet; weaknesses = expensive, bad press in August.
- Computer Networks - strengths = high-quality product range, strong sales team; weaknesses = high cost, located out of town.
- Digital Data - strengths = lowest price; weaknesses = inconsistent quality (three very dissatisfied customers).

3.2 We would be wise to avoid customers/prospects of City Systems (too expensive to take on) and Digital Data (too price sensitive) and should concentrate new business development on Computer Networks' customers and other new prospects with lesser competitors. Messages should centre on our quality and proximity.

3.3 ABCO's distinctiveness is its product range and quality. Actions should be taken to develop these distinctive factors.

Part II: Marketing and sales plan

4   Targets for 2003–2004

Our aim is to grow sales by 15 per cent to £3.6 m with a gross margin of 63 per cent.

5   Marketing and sales strategy 2003–2004

Box A2.2 Target markets and product mix (£m)

Segment	System	Sales 2003–2004	Sales share %	Gross profit £m/%
City banks and finance houses	A, B, C	2.88	80	1.90 /66
SMEs	B	0.36	10	0.17 /47
Europe	A, B	0.36	10	0.20 /55
TOTAL		3.60	100	2.27 /63

6   Marketing and sales actions

6.1 Improve lists of target customers to check new additions and telemarket aggressively.

6.2 Segments 2 and 3 to be reviewed to raise margins.

6.3 Reposition in UK market as financial sector specialist.

6.4 Products A and C to receive PR/publicity and new marketing ideas to raise awareness and interest.

6.5 Target buyers as well as production managers.

6.6 Promotional marketing to target high-margin segments with clear positioning of ABCO. Consider:

- Website redesign.
- Quarterly seminar programme.
- New brochure.
- Corporate hospitality.
- Ads in key trade magazines and at Tube stations.
- Concurrent editorial in same magazines.
- Mailshots to decision makers.

6.7 Organizational improvements:

- Introduce sales briefings for non-sales staff.
- Introduce regular team meetings for sales staff.
- Customer care and telesales training.
- Investigate NVQs for sales staff.
- Sales staff/sales manager to write job descriptions.

7 Marketing and sales budget 2003–2004

7.1 Total sales and marketing budget is £0.40m (11 per cent of sales).

7.2 The annual budget is broken into monthly actions and budgets in the attached spreadsheets.

Box A2.3 ABCO Systems marketing and sales budget

	2003–2004 (£k)	2002–2003 (£k)	Notes
Marketing expenses			
Advertising	30	0	Repositioning campaign to be agreed – agencies' quotes received
Seminars	24	0	New marketing events @ £3k/month for 8 months
PR and publicity	10	0	Achieve press publicity in UK and European journals
Telephone marketing	30	86	Telemarketing activities to reduce drastically to targeted lists
Postage (mailing)	20	0	Marketing budget to absorb marketing postage
Print (mailing)	30	102	Printing activities to reduce to annual brochure and inserts
Market research services	16	0	Running satisfaction survey – quotes received + new market research in Europe
Marketing salaries	60	54	No changes and no salary increase (ref performance-related pay)
Total marketing	220	242	
% of expenditure	55	50	

	2003–2004 (£k)	2002–2003 (£k)	Notes
Selling expenses			
Travel and subsistence	30	76	Reduce overseas travel
Motor running expenses	50	62	Reduce unnecessary travel
Hospitality	5	0	Allocate realistic budget
Sales support	5	0	Purchase various aids
Sales salaries	90	100	Change salaries from commission to % of gross profit
Total selling	180	238	
% of expenditure	45	50	
Grand total	£400	480	Total budget set by forecasts in strategic plan
% of sales revenue	11	15	

8 Marketing SWOT analysis

Box A2.4 Marketing SWOT analysis

Item	Strengths	Weaknesses
Targeting	City banks most profitable	Not focused enough, European profitability low
Segmentation		Imprecise data on segments
Distinctiveness	Very clear: rapid response and personal relationships	
Positioning	Clear: professional, good value, quick, willing to listen	Not clear vs two main competitors
Market research	Recent survey produced excellent data (average 92% satisfaction)	
Customer feedback		No new product feedback
Products	High quality (technical)	
Services	Customer service excellent (95%)	
Product differentiation	Excellent generally	Except against two competitors
New product development		Not good track record
R&D		None
Pricing	Responsive	
Costing procedures	Excellent (by job)	
Channels of distribution	N/A	
Logistics (stock, warehousing, transport)		Irregular delivery
Selling	Highly effective telesales	

Item	Strengths	Weaknesses
Relationship management Account management		Not up to scratch (survey) Teams not working efficiently
Promotional marketing Marketing communications	Good and focused Generally good	Copy too wordy – distinctive competence not communicated
Internet marketing		Website and brochure, out of date!
Marketing organization: structure, people, processes	Clear internal structure, good meetings, training, learning, qualified staff (graduates)	Message taking erratic, production uncertain about marketing role, no employment contracts and job specs
Marketing management		Management of sales, marketing data and website not up to scratch
Budgetary control of marketing	Good	
Marketing information systems		Profitability and segmentation data not always available, data not available to other departments

	Opportunities	Threats
Existing customers	European banking expanding fast	Possible merger of UBS/SBC, reduced budgets
Existing markets	Corporate segment growing and new IT needs emerging	Intense competition
New markets	Larger corporates employing professional buyers for IT	
Economic factors		Rising interest rates, rising GBP, shortage of skilled IT professionals
Political factors	New laws on workplace standards	
Technology	Need to upgrade ever present	

9 Marketing schedule 2003–2004 (first quarter)

Box A2.5 Marketing schedule

Action	Priority	Responsibility	Resource	Start	Finish	Budget £	Notes
April 2003							
Product A review	2	MM	ME	4/03	6/03	0	Check enhancements
Clean and enhance lists, to include product managers	1	ME	list brokers	4/03	5/03	2 000	Check YP
Brief market researchers for major study	1	MM	ME, AGB	4/03	9/03	10 000	Invite three agencies to pitch
Review segments 2, 3	2	Sales director, MM	Sales team	4/03	6/03	0	
Produce PR mini-plan for products A, C	3	MM	ME, Hill & Knowlton	4/03	8/03	5 000	Invite three agencies to pitch
TOTAL APRIL						15 000	

Box A2.5 (continued)

Action	Priority	Responsibility	Resource	Start	Finish	Budget £	Notes
May 2003							
Devise and launch seminar programme	3	ME	Key managers	5/03	6/03	2 000	Check competitors
Review brochure and redesign	2	ME	Designers	5/03	9/03	10 000	Add in 'distinctive competence'
Investigate box at Twickenham + Lords	3	ME	Nil	5/03	12/03	5 000	Check spec with MD
Place ads in key trade magazines	1	MM, Sales director	Ad agency	5/03	7/03	20 000	Tie in with promotional campaign
TOTAL MAY						37 000	
June 2003							
Seek editorial for 2004	3	MM	Nil	6/03	03/04	500	Hospitality budget
Review corporate gifts and propose new ones	3	ME	Designers	6/03	01/04	2500	New ideas needed!
TOTAL JUNE						3 000	

Priority ranking: 1 = high urgent, high important; 2 = high important, low urgent; 3 = high urgent, low important; 4 = low urgent, low important

10   Sales forecasts and marketing/sales budget 2003–2004

Box A2.6 Sales forecasts and marketing/sales budget

ABCO Systems sales forecast 2003–2004

Customer	Product/ project	2003/04 Poten-tial £	Factor (Method)	2003/04 Fore-cast £	Apr	May	Jun	Jul	Aug	Sep	Oct	Nov	Dec	Jan	Feb	Mar	Total
HSBC	IT review of systems	750 000	1 (CBP)	750 000	0	120 000	120 000	100 000	100 000	50 000	30 000	70 000	40 000	40 000	40 000	40 000	750 000
Grindleys	Back-office project	685 000	0.9 (CBP)	616 500	85 000	65 000	60 000	70 000	70 000	70 000	80 000	20 000	37 000	30 000	20 000	9 500	616 500
London Bank	Back-office project	460 000	1 (CBP)	460 000	0	0	0	0	0	50 000	50 000	50 000	60 000	100 000	100 000	50 000	460 000
Citibank	Derivatives support	321 000	0.8 (CBP)	256 800	0	20 000	20 000	50 000	50 000	20 000	20 000	20 000	20 200	23 000	13 600	0	256 800
Floyds Bank	Derivatives support	290 000	0.75 (CBP)	217 500	20 000	20 000	20 000	20 000	20 000	20 000	40 000	10 900	20 000	20 000	6 600	0	217 500
Other banks (4)	Various	450 000	0.75 (E)	337 500	30 000	30 000	0	0	45 000	45 000	45 000	60 000	40 000	40 000	2 500	0	337 500
New banks (3)	Various	400 000	0.6 (T)	240 000	0	0	25 000	25 000	25 000	25 000	25 000	25 000	25 000	25 000	25 000	15 000	240 000
Total banks		3 356 000		2 878 300	135 000	255 000	245 000	265 000	310 000	280 000	290 000	255 900	242 200	278 000	207 700	114 500	2 878 300
SMEs (7)	Various	480 000	0.75 (T)	360 000	30 000	30 000	30 000	30 000	30 000	30 000	30 000	30 000	30 000	30 000	30 000	30 000	360 000
Euro (3) banks	Various	720 000	0.5 (T)	360 000	0	60 000	60 000	60 000	60 000	60 000	20 000	10 000	10 000	10 000	10 000	0	360 000
Grand total		4 556 000		3 598 300	165 000	345 000	335 000	355 000	400 000	370 000	340 000	295 900	282 200	318 000	247 700	144 500	3 598 300
Gross Profit																	
Banks				1 899 678	89 100	168 300	161 700	174 900	204 600	184 800	191 400	168 894	159 852	183 480	137 082	75 570	1 899 678
SMEs				169 200	14 100	14 100	14 100	14 100	14 100	14 100	14 100	14 100	14 100	14 100	14 100	14 100	169 200
European banks				198 000	–	–	33 000	33 000	33 000	33 000	11 000	5 500	5 500	5 500	5 500	–	198 000
Average				2 266 878	103 200	215 400	208 800	222 000	251 700	231 900	216 500	188 494	179 452	203 080	156 682	89 670	2 266 878

Legend: Forecasting methods CBP = Customer business plan; T = Target (no reliable information); E = Extrapolation (using previous year's sales and customer/market trends

Box A2.6 (continued)

ABCO Systems marketing/sales budget 2003–2004

	2003/04	% of sales	2002/03	% of sales
Sales				
Banks	2 878 300	80.0	2 496 456	80.5
SMEs	360 000	10.0	502 700	16.2
Europe	360 000	10.0	101 233	3.3
Total	3 598 300	100.0	3 100 389	100.0
Gross profit	2 266 878	63.0	1 891 237	61.0
Marketing expenses				
Advertising	30 000	0.8	13 256	0.4
Seminars	24 000	0.7	2300	0.1
PR and publicity	10 000	0.3	–	0.0
Telephone marketing	30 000	0.8	75 980	2.5
Postage (mailing)	20 000	0.6	32 090	1.0
Print (mailing)	30 000	0.8	65 087	2.1
Market research services	16 000	0.4	–	0.0
Marketing salaries	60 000	1.7	54 000	1.7
	220 000	6.1	242 713	7.8
% of expenditure		55.0		50.6
Selling expenses				
Travel and subsistence	30 000	0.8	75 877	2.4
Motor running expenses	50 000	1.4	59 870	1.9
Hospitality	5 000	0.1	2390	0.1
Sales support	5 000	0.1	–	0.0
Sales salaries	90 000	2.5	99 145	3.2
	180 000	5.0	237 282	7.7
% of expenditure		45.0		49.4
Grand total	400 000	11.1	479 995	15.5
Contribution	1 866 878	51.9	1 411 242	45.5

Box A2.6 (continued)

ABCO Systems marketing/sales budget 2003–2004

	Apr	May	Jun	Jul	Aug	Sep	Oct	Nov	Dec	Jan	Feb	Mar	Total
Sales													
Banks and financial services	135 000	255 000	245 000	265 000	310 000	280 000	290 000	255 900	242 200	278 000	207 700	114 500	2 878 300
SMEs	30 000	30 000	30 000	30 000	30 000	30 000	30 000	30 000	30 000	30 000	30 000	30 000	360 000
Europe	–	60 000	60 000	60 000	60 000	60 000	20 000	10 000	10 000	10 000	10 000	–	360 000
Total	165 000	345 000	335 000	355 000	400 000	370 000	340 000	295 900	282 200	318 000	247 700	144 500	3 598 300
Cost of sales	61 800	129 600	126 200	133 000	148 300	138 100	123 500	107 406	102 748	114 920	91 018	54 830	1 331 422
Gross profit													
Banks and financial services	89 100	168 300	161 700	174 900	204 600	184 800	191 400	168 894	159 852	183 480	137 082	75 570	1 899 678
SMEs	14 100	14 100	14 100	14 100	14 100	14 100	14 100	14 100	14 100	14 100	14 100	14 100	169 200
Europe	–	33 000	33 000	33 000	33 000	33 000	11 000	5 500	5 500	5 500	5 500	–	198 000
Total	103 200	215 400	208 800	222 000	251 700	231 900	216 500	188 494	179 452	203 080	156 682	89 670	2 266 878
Gross profit margin (%)	63	62	62	63	63	63	64	64	64	64	63	62	63
Marketing expenses													
Advertising	2 500	2 500	2 500	2 500	2 500	2 500	2 500	2 500	2 500	2 500	2 500	2 500	30 000
Seminars	2 000	2 000	2 000	2 000	–	2 000	4 000	2 000	2 000	2 000	2 000	2 000	24 000
PR and publicity	833	833	833	833	833	833	833	833	833	833	833	833	10 000

Box A2.6 (continued)

ABCO Systems marketing/sales budget 2003–2004

	Apr	May	Jun	Jul	Aug	Sep	Oct	Nov	Dec	Jan	Feb	Mar	Total
Telephone marketing	2 500	2 500	2 500	2 500	—	5 000	2 500	2 500	—	5 000	2 500	2 500	30 000
Postage (mailing)	2 000	2 000	2 000	2 000	—	2 000	2 000	2 000	—	2 000	2 000	2 000	20 000
Print (mailing)	2 500	2 500	2 500	2 500	—	5 000	2 500	2 500	—	5 000	2 500	2 500	30 000
Market research	—	2 000	8 000	—	—	—	—	—	—	4 000	2 000	—	16 000
Marketing salaries	5 000	5 000	5 000	5 000	5 000	5 000	5 000	5 000	5 000	5 000	5 000	5 000	60 000
Total	17 333	19 333	25 333	17 333	8 333	22 333	19 333	17 333	10 333	26 333	19 333	17 333	220 000
Selling expenses													
Travel and subsistence	2 500	2 500	2 500	2 500	500	3 500	3 500	2 500	2 500	2 500	2 500	2 500	30 000
Motor expenses	4 167	4 167	4 167	4 167	1 000	4 167	5 200	4 267	2 000	5 200	5 500	6 000	50 000
Hospitality	100	1 800	100	100	100	100	1 800	100	500	100	100	100	5 000
Sales support	417	417	417	417	417	417	417	417	417	417	417	417	5 000
Sales salaries	7 500	7 500	7 500	7 500	7 500	7 500	7 500	7 500	7 500	7 500	7 500	7 500	90 000
Total	14 683	16 383	14 683	14 683	9 517	15 683	18 417	14 784	12 917	15 717	16 017	16 517	180 000
Grand total	32 017	35 717	40 017	32 017	17 850	38 017	37 750	32 117	23 250	42 050	35 350	33 850	400 000
Contribution	71 183	179 683	168 783	189 983	233 850	193 883	178 750	156 377	156 202	161 030	121 332	55 820	1 866 878
Contribution %	43	52	50	54	58	52	53	53	55	51	49	39	52

Sales and marketing manager

Name: Fred Watson

Job context

Title: Sales and Marketing Manager
Department: Sales
Reports to: Managing Director
Based at: City Office

Central purpose of the job

To achieve sales and marketing objectives and sales and gross profit margin targets by managing effectively and efficiently.

Main job objectives

1 To contribute effectively to company and departmental plans and budgets.
2 To plan, organize and control company sales and marketing activities to achieve target sales and profit margin levels.
3 To set individual account executives challenging but achievable sales targets for existing and new customers within agreed budgets.
4 To manage, recruit, deploy, motivate, train and develop staff.
5 To maintain and enhance personal effectiveness through training and development.

Tasks	Performance Standards
1 Provide analysis of sales, gross margin and marketing data.	Comprehensiveness, relevance, accuracy.

2	Produce marketing and sales plan with forecasts and budget and agree with directors.	Realism, detail, relevance, cost-effectiveness.
3	Set account management guidelines and brief team.	Agreed procedures and guidelines, customer retention rates, new business development performance.
4	Allocate resources, set targets for existing and new customers and brief team.	Clarity, efficiency, motivation levels.
5	Meet weekly to monitor team progress vs targets and budgets.	Agreed performance levels against target, relevance of feedback to plan.
6	Organize promotional marketing activities.	Effectiveness and efficiency, outcomes against targets.
7	Undertake account management duties, including sales and caring for own customers.	Higher-level feedback, outcomes against targets, existing customer retention rate, new business rate.
8	Monitor and give feedback to staff.	Job satisfaction, morale, motivation, staff turnover, positive feedback.
9	Write job and person specs, recruit, induct and support new staff.	Accuracy/relevance of specs, positive feedback from new staff, team morale.
10	Undertake annual performance appraisals and reviews.	Positive feedback, improved job performance, adhere to procedures.
11	Agree training and development plans.	Improved job performance, higher customer feedback.
12	Design and implement market research.	Relevance, accuracy and cost-effectiveness.
13	Meet with team and contribute to company activities.	Higher team and company morale, quality of personal contributions.
14	Attend performance appraisals with directors.	Positive feedback, achievement of objectives.
15	Produce and implement personal training and development plan.	Relevance, realism, cost-effectiveness of training/development.

Company standards of performance and behaviour

1 Honesty, integrity and professionalism in all business dealings.
2 Commitment to the aims of the company and those of the departments in which we work.
3 Attention to detail as well as to the big picture.
4 Professional conduct in all customer contact, with an appropriate balance between the needs of the customer and those of the company.

Responsibilities and relationships

Staff reporting to job: 8.
Budget responsibility: Sales and marketing budget.
Other resources responsible for: Sales cars, computers.

Key internal relationships

Directors, sales and marketing team, other staff.

External relationships

Customers, suppliers, designers, press.

Terms of employment

Annual appraisal and salary review with Managing Director.
Other terms as Employee Handbook.

Costing and Pricing Example

Dorset Electronics, a small manufacturer of electronic components, has been asked to quote for two jobs. Job A entails producing 5000 components for a large piece of electronic equipment. Estimates of sales and production resources and costs are as follows:

Box A4.1 Sales and production estimates

Production time	840 man hours + 360 machine hours
Engineers' annual productive hours	1 320 hours pa (@44 weeks, 75 per cent productivity)
Engineers' hourly rate	£17.23 (@ £22 750 pa incl. NIC)
Materials costs and wastage	£12 750
Subcontracted costs	£18 620
Machine usage	1 000 hours pa
Machine depreciation	£25 000 pa (£25/ hour)
Machine finance costs	Interest £12 500 pa
Machine maintenance costs	£8250 pa
Selling time	6 days (out of 230 working days)
Salesman's salary	£35 340 pa (incl. NIC, car lease)
Sales conversion rate	3:1 (leads:closes)
Travel and subsistence costs	£10 000 (500 miles per lead @ 40p/mile + £35/ day subsistence)

Job B (5500 components) is similar to A, but requires a small amount of additional work amounting to 50 hours of engineering time, 30 machine hours and £2 200 of specialist subcontracted work. The order was negotiated over the telephone (about a half day altogether), it being a 'rush job'.

Dorset's business plan contains a P&L forecast as follows:

Box A4.2 P & L forecast

	£	%
Sales	1 890 000	100.0
Production costs	1 152 000	61.0
Gross profit	738 000	39.0
Selling and distribution costs		
Direct sales/travel	95 000	5.0
Contribution	643 000	34.0
Indirect selling costs	66 000	3.5
Establishment costs	104 000	5.5
Administration costs	350 000	18.5
Finance and depreciation costs (excluding machinery costs)	28 000	1.5
Net profit	95 000	5.0

Costing and pricing steps are:

Step 1

Calculate variable and direct machinery costs per job:

Box A4.3 Variable and direct machinery costs per job

Details	Job A (£000)		Job B (£000)	
Materials	12.75		12.75	
Subcontractors	18.62		20.82	
Engineers' time	14.47	45.84	15.33	48.90
Direct machinery overhead				
Machinery depreciation	9.00		9.75	
Machinery finance	4.50		4.88	
Maintenance	2.97	16.47	3.22	17.85
Total variable and direct machinery costs		62.31		66.75

Step 2

Calculate variable and direct machinery costs per unit:

Box A4.4 Variable and direct machinery costs per unit

Details	Job A (£000)	Job B (£000)
Total variable and direct machinery costs	62.31	66.75
No. of units produced	5000	5500
Unit variable cost	£1.25	£1.21

Step 3

Calculate direct overheads per job:

Box A4.5 Direct overheads per job

Details	Job A (£000)		Job B (£000)	
Selling costs				
Salary	2.77		0.08	
Travel and subsistence	1.23	4.00	0.00	0.08

Step 4

Calculate indirect overheads per job and per unit:

- Additional information required to calculate overhead recovery rate:

No. of engineers	12
Total productive hours pa	15 840 (12 × 1 320)
Formula for overhead recovery rate	Total overheads ÷ total productive hours
Overhead recovery rate for Dorset Electronics	£34.60 per hour

Box A4.6 Indirect overheads per job and per unit

Details	Job A (£000)	Job B (£000)
Estimated production hours	840	890
Overhead recovery rate	£34.60	£34.60
Overhead recovery	29.06	30.79
No. of units produced	5000	5500
Unit overhead cost	£0.58	£0.56

Step 5

Calculate total cost per job and per unit:

Box A4.7 Total cost per job and per unit

Details	Job A (£000)		Job B (£000)	
Materials	12.75		12.75	
Subcontractors	18.62		20.82	
Engineers' time	14.47	45.84	15.33	48.90
Direct factory overhead				
Machinery depreciation	9.00		9.75	
Machinery finance	4.50		4.88	
Maintenance	2.97	16.47	3.22	17.85
Total variable and direct machinery costs		62.31		66.75
Direct selling costs				
Salary	2.77		0.08	
Travel	1.23	4.00	0.00	0.08
Total variable and direct overheads		66.31		66.83
Overhead recovery		29.06		30.79
Total costs		95.37		97.62
No. of units produced		5000		5500
Unit total cost		£1.91		£1.77

Step 6

Consider pricing options:

Box A4.8 Pricing options

Details	Job A (£000)	Job B (£000)
Total costs	95.37	97.62
Price (@ 5 per cent net margin)	100.39	102.76
No. of units produced	5000	5500
Unit price	£2.01	£1.87

The prices calculated for Jobs A and B are cost plus a 5 per cent net profit margin. It is up to the sales manager to decide what prices to charge, i.e. whether they can be adjusted up or down to take into account competition, previous prices paid, the importance of winning the business and customer retention targets.

An alternative costing method using contribution is as follows:

> Steps 1–3 as above
> Step 4 – to calculate prices, apply the inverse
> (66 per cent) of the required contribution rate
> (34 per cent) to total and direct overhead costs,
> as follows:

Box A4.9 Price calculations using contribution rate

Details	Job A (£000)	Job B (£000)
Total variable and direct overheads	66.31	66.83
Price @ contribution rate of 34 per cent	£100.47	£101.26

This produces a slightly different set of prices because of variations in overhead recovery.

Index